ENVIRONMENTAL POLICY
UNDER REAGAN'S
EXECUTIVE ORDER

URBAN AND REGIONAL POLICY
AND DEVELOPMENT STUDIES
Michael A. Stegman, Series Editor

Environmental Policy under Reagan's Executive Order

THE ROLE OF BENEFIT-COST ANALYSIS

Edited by V. Kerry Smith

THE UNIVERSITY OF NORTH CAROLINA PRESS

CHAPEL HILL AND LONDON

Library of Congress Cataloging in Publication Data

Main entry under title:
Environmental policy under Reagan's Executive order.

Bibliography: p.
1. Environmental policy—United States—Cost effectiveness—Addresses, essays,
lectures. 2. United States—Politics and government—1981–   —Addresses, essays,
lectures. I. Smith, V. Kerry (Vincent Kerry), 1945–
HC110.E5E49878   1984   363.7'056'0973   83-23397
ISBN 0-8078-1600-0

CONTENTS

PREFACE

WHEN the Reagan administration came into power, it had a strong popular mandate to change the role of government in the private affairs of households and firms. Regulatory reform was a prominent component of its platform. Within weeks after assuming the presidency, Ronald Reagan issued Executive Order No. 12291 requiring a benefit-cost analysis for all new major regulations. Although this order can be considered to be the culmination of the efforts of several administrations' attempts to control the regulatory burden that government has imposed on the private sector, it marks the first time that a formal benefit-cost requirement has been considered an integral part of the evaluative process for regulations. The order's general requirements given in Section 2 specify:

In promulgating new regulations, reviewing existing regulations, and developing legislative proposals concerning regulation, all agencies, to the extent permitted by law, shall adhere to the following requirements:

(a) Administrative decisions shall be based on adequate information concerning the need for and consequences of proposed government action;

(b) Regulatory action shall not be undertaken unless the potential benefits to society for the regulation outweigh the potential costs to society;

(c) Regulatory objectives shall be chosen to maximize the net benefits to society;

(d) Among alternative approaches to any given regulatory objective, the alternative involving the least net cost to society shall be chosen; and

(e) Agencies shall set regulatory priorities with the aim of maximizing the aggregate net benefits to society, taking into account the condition of the particular industries affected by regulations, the condition of the national economy, and other regulatory actions contemplated for the future.

The purpose of this volume is to take stock of the effects of Executive Order 12291 on environmental policy making. After more than two years of experience with the order, it is possible to investigate how it has affected the character of environmental regulations and policy in general. In the process, we also realize a second objective.

Executive Order 12291 establishes a set of goals and calls for the use of benefit-cost analysis as if this analysis consisted of completely accepted procedures that could be used together with research results on both the benefits of realizing specified changes in environmental quality and the costs of achieving these changes. Neither of these maintained assumptions is accurate. Consequently, it is possible to use our appraisal of how the Environmental Protection Agency responded to the order to identify the limitations of conventional benefit-cost analysis and to begin the process of defining the research needed if a benefit-cost requirement is to be maintained as an integral part of the design and implementation of environmental regulations.

Research for this volume was initiated with a Conference on Executive Order 12291 and Environmental Policy Making at the University of North Carolina at Chapel Hill. Preliminary drafts of several of the papers published in this volume were presented at that conference. Others were initiated after the conference. Support for the conference and my research activities was provided by the Alfred P. Sloan Foundation through a grant to the University of North Carolina at Chapel Hill. I am especially grateful to the foundation and its president, Albert Rees, for their support and patience in seeing this work through to completion.

This effort was truly collaborative. All of the authors agreed to strict deadlines and met them. It has been a genuine pleasure to work with all of them. A number of individuals also contributed to this research activity both through participation in the conference and in commenting on the papers. Special thanks should be given to John Akin, Allen Basala, William Desvousges, Wesley Magat, David Moreau, and James Seagraves. Thanks are also due Maynard Hufschmidt and an anonymous reader for their thoughtful reviews of an earlier draft of this manuscript.

Mary Pettis helped to organize the conference, handling both the logistical details of the meeting and the administrative aspects of my research associated with the project. Sue Piontek has helped me to pull the work together in this final product and assured its timely completion. Whitney Eckler assured that deadlines would be met by providing long hours in proofing the manuscript. Special acknowledgment is also due Gwen Duffey and all the staff of the University of North Carolina Press for their excellent and constructive handling of the manuscript. I am sincerely grateful for the help of all those mentioned and those I may have inadvertently omitted.

Finally, but certainly not last in my appreciation, are my wife, Pauline, and children, Tim and Shelley, whose support and patience are essential to all that I do.

V. Kerry Smith
Nashville, Tennessee

December 1983

LIST OF ACRONYMS

AISI	American Iron and Steel Institute
BAT	Best Available Technology Economically Achievable
BOB	U.S. Bureau of the Budget
BPT	Best Practicable Control Technology Currently Available
CAA	Clean Air Act
CBO	Congressional Budget Office
CEQ	Council on Environmental Quality
CERCLA	Comprehensive Environmental, Response, Compensation and Liability Act
COWPS	Council on Wage and Price Stability
CPO	Central Planning Office
DOD	U.S. Department of Defense
DOL	U.S. Department of Labor
DOT	U.S. Department of Transportation
EIS	Environmental Impact Statement
EPA	U.S. Environmental Protection Agency
FEPCA	Federal Environmental Pesticide Control Act
FEV	Forced Expiratory Volume
FIFRA	Federal Insecticide, Fungicide, and Rodenticide Act
FWPCA	Federal Water Pollution Control Act Amendments
GAO	Government Accounting Office
HEW	U.S. Department of Health, Education and Welfare
IIS	Inflation Impact Statements
LAER	Lowest Achievable Emission Rate
NAAQS	National Ambient Air Quality Standard
NEPA	National Environmental Policy Act
NPDES	National Pollutant Discharge Elimination System

NRDC	National Resources Defense Council
NSPS	New Source Performance Standards
OECD	Organization for Economic Cooperation and Development
OIRA	Office of Information and Regulatory Affairs
OMB	Office of Management and Budget
OPPE	Office of Policy, Planning and Evaluation
OSHA	Occupational Safety and Health Act
OTEC	Ocean Thermal Energy Conservation Plants
PPB	Planning, Programming, Budgeting System
PSD	Prevention of Significant Deterioration
QOL	Quality of Life Reviews
RARG	Regulatory Analysis Review Group
RCRA	Resource Conservation and Recovery Act
RIA	Regulatory Impact Analysis
SIP	State Implementation Plans
TSCA	Toxic Substances Control Act
TSP	Total Suspended Particulates
UNIDO	United Nations Industrial Development Organization
WRRC	Water Resources Research Council

ENVIRONMENTAL POLICY
UNDER REAGAN'S
EXECUTIVE ORDER

1

ENVIRONMENTAL POLICY MAKING UNDER EXECUTIVE ORDER 12291: AN INTRODUCTION

 FEDERAL regulation of the production and marketing of goods and services as well as of other activities that have implications for human health has taken place in the United States, in varying degrees, for more than fifty years. Indeed, it was the use of health criteria, according to Senator Edmund Muskie, that was instrumental in promoting the Clean Air Act Amendments of 1970—the first of the major environmental regulations.

Today, interest in environmental quality may well be even more broadly based than in the 1970s. Clearly, it is still motivated by concern for maintenance of clean air and water as one means of preventing detrimental health impacts. But there has also been an increasing recognition of the importance of aesthetics in the public's desire for continued efforts to maintain and enhance environmental quality. Nonetheless, this interest has not precluded environmental regulations from the scrutiny that has accompanied increasing public awareness of the costs of social regulations, in general, and the performance of government, in particular.

Each year legislative initiatives, judicial decisions, and agency activities lead to thousands of new regulatory constraints on the actions of firms and individuals. For example, in 1980, 7,192 final regulations were published in the *Federal Register* from February to December. In addition, the proposed new regulations published in this period amounted to another 4,979.[1]

*Centennial Professor of Economics, Vanderbilt University. This research was supported by the Sloan Foundation. Thanks are due Allen Basala, Maynard Hufschmidt, and an anonymous reviewer for most helpful comments on an earlier draft.

Although many of these individual actions would be considered relatively minor, there appears to have been increasing acceptance of the conclusion (based largely on informal analysis) that taken as a whole these regulations do impose a "drag" on the U.S. economy by diverting resources from privately productive tasks to regulatory compliance and thereby slowing productivity growth.[2]

In addition, the interest of the three past presidents in controlling the generation of new regulations has led to attempts to distinguish the major regulations from all new rules.[3] The definition of what constitutes a major regulation has evolved over the past ten years. Today, it is interpreted as any regulation that satisfies one or more of the following criteria: be likely to have an annual effect on the economy of $100 million or more; lead to significant increases in prices; lead to reductions in employment; or have major impacts on industries, regions, or state and local levels of government.[4] For 1981 and 1982 the number of major regulations has constituted between 2 and 3 percent of the regulations reviewed by the Office of Management and Budget (OMB). Understanding the implications of all regulations (especially the ones with important impacts), reviewing their performance, and developing methods for improving them both at the individual level and in the aggregate, has become a major preoccupation of social scientists. Regulatory analysis and evaluation is a "big business" in social science research. Of course, this interest is a reflection of the importance of regulations to economic activities and to the social interaction between firms and households generally.

The objective of this volume is to consider the latest in a series of initiatives from the executive branch of government to control the process of generating new federal regulations. On 17 February 1981, shortly after entering office, President Reagan signed Executive Order 12291. This order required that all new major regulations be subjected to a benefit-cost analysis before they could be acted upon. The order also specifically states that economic efficiency should be the basis for evaluating new major regulations or revisions to them. Indeed, it proposes that alternatives to regulatory initiatives be considered and that the criteria for selecting a regulation be consistent with maximizing the aggregate net benefits associated with the results of regulatory activity.

Although this executive order is in many respects the culmination of the activities of several preceding presidents to control the regulatory burden imposed on the economy, it is nonetheless a significant departure from past policies. It is the first order explicitly to call for benefit-cost analysis in the evaluation of regulations. Past administrations—in particular that of Jimmy

Carter, through its Regulatory Analysis and Review Group (RARG) and through the mandate of EO 12044—also evaluated the impacts of new regulations. Indeed, the RARG, headed by the chairman of the Council of Economic Advisers, often used benefit-cost analyses in these evaluations. Nonetheless, the analysis was not mandated by Carter's order. Indeed, at the time Executive Order 12044 was introduced, President Carter explained that an important motivation for the order was to eliminate the "bureaucratic gobbledy-gook," which he suggested had come to characterize many federal regulations. A return to "plain English" was cited as a major component of the order in his memorandum explaining the action to the relevant department and agency heads. Thus, although concern was expressed over the regulatory burden, no mechanism was provided for putting "teeth" into those aspects of the order associated with regulatory control. Equally important, those evaluating the experience with RARG suggest that it had limited impact on the regulatory process and may well have been more of an administrative review than a program for screening regulations.

Although EO 12291 has implications for all federal regulations, our focus in this book is directed specifically at its impacts on the prospects for and process of environmental regulation. How does the executive order relate to the pattern of environmental policy as it has evolved over the past decade and a half? What will EO 12291 do to the current process of environmental regulation? How can it, or will it, fit into the administrative sequence associated with defining specific regulatory standards under the legislation governing the activities of the Environmental Protection Agency (EPA) in air, water, solid waste, and toxic and hazardous substances? Can OMB, the watchdog agency for implementing EO 12291, be effective in evaluating EPA's proposed regulations? Will the level of environmental regulation be reduced? Can we expect environmental quality to suffer as a result? These are all important and difficult questions.

In principle, EO 12291 clearly provides for a change in the way federal regulations are ultimately defined. It does not, however, change the fundamental nature of the regulatory process within EPA. Rather, it is attempting to change, for cases in which statute does not explicitly preclude the benefit-cost criterion, the "yardsticks" used to evaluate certain types of regulations. Critics of existing environmental regulations suggest that a change in our measuring rods is not enough. They argue that environmental policies have evolved into a confusing and ineffective muddle. The current policies are incapable of realizing the goals that provided their initial motivation, and incremental changes in the rulemaking process are unlikely to change this picture significantly. Consequently, one might reasonably ask whether alterations such as those proposed under EO 12291 are really worthwhile.

Finally, the order assumes that it is possible to prepare benefit-cost analyses for fairly detailed environmental regulations. It assumes a general acceptance of methods for benefit and cost estimation, a level of technical information, and a clear understanding of the effectiveness of each proposed regulation. In most cases, none of these components exists in ideal terms. Often substantial judgment is required to piece together even a small fraction of the information that would ideally be desired for a complete benefit-cost analysis. Indeed, this issue lies at the heart of many of the areas of controversy with EPA's regulatory activities—the state of available information and scientific understanding of the problems involved may be inadequate. Thus there may be ample scope for reasonable people to disagree over the impacts of specific levels of pollution. Nonetheless, sensible policies must be defined; there are often significant potential harmful effects without intervention but little basis for judging the complete nature of these impacts with our existing information.

William Ruckelshaus's 22 June 1983 speech before the National Academy of Sciences clearly recognized these issues in the context of risk assessment. They hold with equal force in the use of benefit-cost analysis for specific regulatory analyses. Ruckelshaus observed:

> EPA's laws often assume, indeed demand, a certainty of protection greater than science can provide at the current state of knowledge. The laws do no more than reflect what the public believes and what it often hears from people with scientific credentials on the 6 o'clock news. The public thinks we know what *all* the bad pollutants are, *precisely* what adverse health or environmental effects they cause, how to measure them *exactly* and control them *absolutely*. Of course, the public and sometimes the law are wrong, but not all wrong.

He continued, noting that ten years ago (at the time Ruckelshaus left EPA after serving as its first administrator):

> I believed it would become apparent to all that we could virtually eliminate the risks we call pollution if we wanted to spend enough money. When it also became apparent that enough money for all the pollutants was a lot of money, I further believed we would begin to examine the risks very carefully and structure a system which forced us to balance our desire to eliminate pollution against the cost of its control. This would entail some adjustment of laws, but really not all that much,

and it would happen by about 1976. I was wrong. . . . We must now deal with a class of pollutants for which a safe level is difficult, if not impossible to establish. . . . The scientific consensus has it that any exposure, however small, to a genetically active substance embodies some risk of an effect. . . . We must now assume that life takes place in a minefield of risks from hundreds, perhaps thousands, of substances. *No more can we tell the public: you are home free with an adequate margin of safety.*[5]

The largest share of the benefits estimated for environmental policies designed to control air pollutants is associated with the reduction in the risks of these health effects. For example, A. Myrick Freeman's appraisal of the benefits associated with the air quality improvements from 1970 to 1978 (which he assumed to be a 20 percent reduction in stationary source pollutants) suggested that health effects accounted for 78 percent of the aggregate benefits.[6] Of course, it should be acknowledged that visibility effects and acidic deposition provide examples that could easily change the relative importance of health effects in any tabulation of the aggregate benefits associated with air quality improvements.

Even aside from the difficulties associated with appraising health risks, there is significant uncertainty regarding the estimates of the benefits associated with environmental quality improvements in a number of other areas. We will return to some of these below. What is really at issue is whether significant mistakes would arise from a policy that optimistically assumed the available research along with EPA's staff input would be sufficient to develop a credible benefit-cost analysis within a time horizon that is compatible with the regulatory time schedules.

Each of these issues deserves detailed treatment that is not possible within a single volume. Here we can only begin the process of considering their implications. By doing so, however, it is possible to identify a compelling set of issues associated with the role of policy, politics, and analysis in regulatory design and evaluation. Before proceeding to the detailed consideration of the implications of EO 12291 for environmental policy making presented by the authors in this volume, this essay will provide some background for and perspective on the chapters that follow and highlight some of the issues that tie them together.

We begin this process by considering why it is we regulate in the first place. What are the motivations and practical realities of the definition and implementation of regulations? I will briefly describe the initiatives designed to control regulations that preceded EO 12291. This discussion is brief because the volume begins with Richard Andrews's detailed discussion of the Reagan administration's environmental policy and EO 12291's role in it in relation to the evolution of environmental policy over the past decade and a half. With this background on the motivation for regulation and the process of attempting to control it, we can then consider what, under ideal conditions, provides the conceptual framework for benefit-cost analysis. Following this discussion, we return to some of the practical realities associated with performing benefit-cost analyses in a policy setting. No benefit-cost analysis is capable of living up to the idealized views of how it should be implemented. Consequently, in evaluating its prognosis for improving the process of environmental policy making, we must consider the practical form it takes in applications to the evaluation of regulations designed to improve environmental quality.

Of course, if Executive Order 12291 is to be effectively implemented, it implies that there must exist a role for how benefit-cost analysis will "fit in" to the rulemaking process for defining regulations associated with air and water quality criteria. By following this structure, we can set the stage for how each of the chapters that follow contributes to our understanding of the implementation, performance, problems, and likely effects of Executive Order 12291 for environmental policy making. Consequently, the conclusion to this introduction is both a road map to the chapters and a discussion of whether EO 12291 is likely to make a difference.

THE JUSTIFICATION FOR AND FORMAT OF REGULATION

Most economists would suggest that the primary motivation for public intervention into private activities arises from a market failure. That is, there are (1) types of goods and services that cannot be provided through the privately motivated actions of firms and households acting through markets; and (2) other cases in which markets are involved in providing particular goods or services but are incapable of assuring efficient resource allocation decisions. As a rule, these problems arise from the inability to develop a well-defined set of property rights for the resources used in producing or providing these goods and services. Under ideal conditions markets assure an efficient allocation of resources. When there is market failure (whether partial or complete), the theoretical description of the public sector's role is usually suggested as one of taking actions that move the resource allocation to the efficient allocation that markets cannot provide.[7] Of course, it is important to distinguish this justification for regulatory activity that arises from a normative economic model of the role of government in influencing the allocation of resources from that which would provide an explanation of regulatory activity. It would be naive to postulate that regulatory activity arises exclusively from a desire to correct inefficiencies in resource allocation perceived by the Congress. A large portion of congressional activities can be explained by treating legislative actions as attempts to redistribute the gains and losses associated with economic and political activities. Thus distributional objectives can be an important influence on the form of regulatory actions. Indeed, the objectives of efficiency and distribution are the elements in nearly every explanation for regulatory activity.

The use of the term "distributional objectives" rather than "equity" to describe how regulations affect the sharing of benefits and costs is deliberate. Equity can easily give the impression that the rules seek to "improve" the distribution of benefits or costs—to create a "more fair" assignment. This need not be the case, and, indeed, it is seldom an accurate characterization of distributional effects of regulations. The 1977 Clean Air Act Amendments vividly illustrate this point. A number of authors have sought to explain various aspects of the 1977 amendments as reflecting the political objectives of particular interest groups.[8] In other words, these groups sought to redistribute the gains and losses resulting from existing environmental policies. The original National Ambient Air Quality Standards (NAAQS) and the New Source Performance Standards (NSPS) (specifically those associated with stationary sources emitting sulfur dioxide) had large distributional side effects that most of these authors have argued were not fully appreciated when the legislation was enacted. NAAQS provided a comparative advantage to the Sunbelt South and West over the Midwest and Northeast in economic growth, and NSPS fostered a substantial advantage for low-sulfur western coal over the coals of the East and Midwest. Thus the implementation of these regulatory programs from the original legislation offered at least a twofold economic advantage to the West.

Peter Navarro argued that these effects led to a coalition of environmentalists with eastern and midwestern coal and industrial interests that found its results in four major provisions of the 1977 amendments: (1) revisions to NSPS requiring the use of scrubbers to remove sulfur regardless of the sulfur content of the coal used; (2) a specific limit on the use of low-sulfur coal in existing stationary sources of air pollution; (3) the introduction of policies to limit the increases in emissions of air pollutants (and the corresponding deterioration in air quality) in areas that were in compliance with the National Ambient Air Quality Standards—the so-called prevention of significant deterioration (PSD) policy; and (4) two provisions added to protect visibility in the West,[9] which would have the effect of limiting growth in this region.

Taken together these changes substantially reduce the economic benefits experienced by the Sunbelt through growth and industrial relocation and expansion because of this region's favorable position under the original provisions of the Clean Air Act. In some cases, they also serve other objectives, such as maintenance of the visibility conditions at unique natural environments—our national parks and wilderness areas in the West—and thus one can understand why environmental groups supported them. Nonetheless, the form the measures took (especially those limiting the use of low-sulfur coal) have had and will lead to significant losses in economic efficiency. It is not clear that under any equity criterion these losses could be justified. Paul R. Portney's recent calculations, for example, suggest that the jobs in coal mining saved as a result of two of the coal-related provisions of the amendments cost as much as $750,000 a year for each job.[10]

Does all of this mean that distributional motivations for regulations are the root cause of the problems with environmental regulations? Although most economists would contend that efficiency provides the only legitimate basis for regulation (they argue that policies designed to redistribute income and wealth can be used as instruments to achieve "fair" distributions of each independent of regulation), they would probably not pin the sole responsibility on distributional motives. Indeed, Richard Zeckhauser has argued that policy makers' concern over the distribution of benefits and costs is legitimate. In a democratic society, the distribution of gains and losses arising from a policy affects whether that policy will be adopted. He observed:

> The political process recoils from the "let the chips fall where they may" nature of traditional efficiency maximization. In particular, it attempts conscientiously to redistribute resources so that cost impositions are reduced, even if this can only be achieved at the expense of substantially greater reduction in benefits.
>
> This pattern of choice is in sharp contrast with the dictates of benefit-cost analysis which focuses exclusively on efficiency and considers not at all the distribution of chips.[11]

Zeckhauser developed his basic theme using ten major pieces of environmental legislation proposed from 1970 through the first half of 1977. He found that the seven bills (of these ten) that passed during this period all either incorporated mechanisms for distributing the costs they imposed or "clouded" the identity of those groups who would lose. Three primary approaches were used to enhance the chances for consensus: (1) linking the proposals imposing costs with other legislation that provided benefits to the constituencies that were slated to be harmed; (2) phasing the implementation of the programs so that the effects were delayed, often for a number of years; and (3) purposely introducing uncertainty that makes it difficult for the organized interest groups to determine whether their constituents will be more likely to incur costs than benefits.

Zeckhauser's analysis of the role of distributional considerations to the policy-making process is important for several reasons. It directly identifies a practical reality of regulation. Regardless of the economic merits (that is, the efficiency gains) of a particular regulatory action, if the proposal will convey benefits to some groups and costs to others, we must consider whether the measure will be undertaken. For regulatory actions arising from the legislative process this determination is especially important. To realize the net benefits, even if they are smaller as a result of these strategic considerations, the legislation must be passed.

One might argue that most regulations remove or amend a property right. Often the right has been implicit, but it nonetheless has value to the individuals or firms whose actions are affected. From an efficiency perspective, these changes are judged desirable when the gains from them outweigh the costs. This does not, of course, imply that the same individuals will experience both gains and losses. Indeed, when we think of regulations in this way, it is clear that it is very likely that someone must lose.

These changes do not occur simply because they represent potential improvements in aggregate well-being, and this is Zeckhauser's point. The design of a program of regulatory initiatives is at least as much a result of what program will be likely to pass as it is an efficiency criterion. Consequently, the structure of the regulations will not often adhere to what economists might desire on purely efficiency grounds. On theoretical grounds, therefore, we can recognize that the most compelling economic argument for regulation arises as a result of market failure. Nonetheless, it must also be acknowledged that, as a practical matter, regulatory programs derived from legislation must be the result of political consensus. Economic merit measured as the aggregate net benefits realized by a society does not in and of itself assure that consensus—especially when compensation of the losers involved is not an explicit component of the program. As a result, distributional effects must be a part of the considerations that arise in the evaluation of the format of and justification for any specific regulatory program.

Of course, these issues are most clear when we treat regulations as arising from legislative actions. But legislative action is only one of the ways in which regulations can develop. The specific details of most regulatory programs are left to the discretion of the executive departments and agencies of the federal government with some regulatory mandate from the independent regulatory agencies such as EPA. In each case, the department or agency bases its actions on legislative authority. Indeed, from Zeckhauser's arguments, it is reasonable to assume that regulatory legislation would delegate substantial responsibility and discretion to the agency, allowing the specific features of each regulation to be defined by its staff, as one of the means of realizing the purposeful uncertainty about the impacts of the original statute.

Consequently, there is another policy maker to contend with in addition to the legislator designing statutes in a world where compromise may be essential to the acceptance of any regulatory proposal. The agency policy maker is just as important a component of the process leading to the ultimate character of each regulation. Thus it is reasonable to ask what motivates the policy maker's behavior.

Clearly, agency policy makers must be accountable to Congress and the courts. Congress, through the budgetary process and through new legislation, can control their activities.[12] The courts provide the basis for judging whether an agency's administrative procedures and rulemaking process represent the intent of its governing legislation. The heads of executive departments and agencies are directly accountable to the president. Presidential efforts to manage and control the proliferation of regulations have extended to the independent regulatory agencies as well, and EO 12291 is an example of the forms such control can take.

To understand more fully the potential motivations for the agency policy maker we must consider specific examples. The first of these involves the standard-setting process for the NAAQS for criteria air pollutants. Figure 1.1 is taken from a recent article on EPA's standard-setting process for the criteria pollutants by Joseph Padgett and Harvey Richmond (the current director of the Strategies and Air Standards Division at EPA and one of his staff members; this group is responsible for the definition of primary standards). The Clean Air Act and court cases have served to define the seven criteria pollutants. The law also requires the EPA administrator to propose and, after public review, to promulgate these standards to protect public health with an adequate margin of safety. It is also generally acknowledged that the legislative history of the act implied that the primary standard should be designed to protect the most sensitive groups for each criteria pollutant. The determination of this most sensitive group, the margin of safety, and the form of the standard are all subject to discretion as a part of the rulemaking process. Each of these issues can have important implications for the severity of the standard.

To understand how these decisions exert an influence on the impacts of regulation, we must describe how ambient standards affect the emission of specific pollutants. In principle, an ambient standard prescribes the level judged to protect human health for the concentration for a specific pollutant. The definition of such a standard does not in itself involve the specification of how it will be attained. The process of deciding how emissions are to be limited to meet the standard is left to the states with their state implementation plans (SIPs). These plans must be submitted to and approved by EPA. If a state's air quality does not meet the national standard, specific requirements are imposed on the emissions of pollutants within that state. It is designated a nonattainment area. We need not pursue the details of these policies to appreciate that the form of the standard has direct implications for emissions control policies.[13] The selection of pollution measures, definition of a violation (according to a specific exceedance rate), and specification of the time period for evaluating performance under the standard are all part of the process of defining a standard, and all affect its severity in practice. These decisions as well as a number of other dimensions of the standard are at the discretion of the administrator of the Environmental Protection Agency.

A similar set of issues arises for the case of water quality regulation. Here the enabling legislation set a broad goal—to improve water quality throughout the United States so as to permit fishing and swimming. A two-level set of technology standards was defined in the Federal Water Pollution Control Amendments of 1972 to meet these goals—the adoption of the Best Practicable Control Technology Currently Available (BPT) by 1 July 1977 —and then more stringent technology standards—Best Available Technology Economically Achievable (BAT) by July 1983. Clearly, someone has to define what these standards mean in practice for each industry. What is the best practical technology? It has been interpreted as requiring an evaluation of the costs of specific control equipment relative to the emissions reductions realized with some recognition of the ability of the industry involved to absorb these cost increases. If this description sounds vague, there is a reason—the process itself is vague. Similar issues arise in the specification of the BAT standards. Thus we again see that substantial discretion is left to the administrator. This discretion affects the severity of the standard. But this description is still too superficial to describe fully the

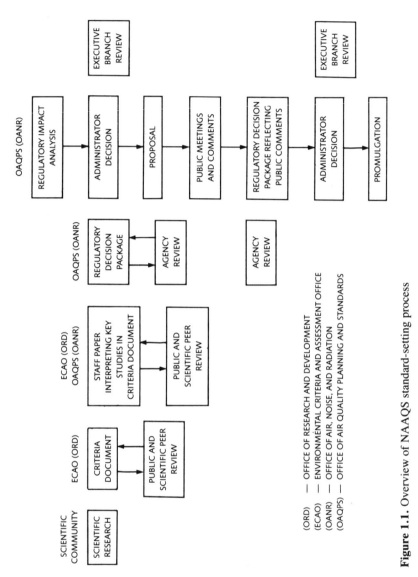

Figure 1.1. Overview of NAAQS standard-setting process

Source: Padgett and Richmond, "The Process of Establishing and Revising National Ambient Air Quality Standards," p. 14.

specification of one standard. EPA staff must subcategorize, for each industry, the production activities and specify for each subcategory a standard; identify the specific pollutants that are to be controlled through each standard; and ultimately define the stringency of the standard.[14] For example, in the case of the BAT standards for the iron and steel industry, there were twelve subcategories: coking, sintering, ironmaking, cold-forming, steelmaking, vacuum degassing, continuous casting, hot-forming, salt bath, acid pickling, alkaline cleaning, and hot coating. Although these categories correspond to distinct production activities within iron and steel manufacturing, it is reasonable to ask why this classification was chosen.[15] One might have proceeded in either of two directions—more detail identifying more specifically the production activities, or less detail combining activities according to the logical tasks accomplished (for example, the production of molten iron requires coking, sintering, and blast furnace activities; finishing requires another set of activities including some combination of slab rolling, hot rolling, acid pickling, and cold rolling). This definition will affect the severity of the standards. Indeed, interest in EPA's "bubble" policy, which permits plants to trade off requirements between subcategories within a plant, is a reflection that adjustment in these standards can lead to cost savings in meeting a specific set of emission requirements.

These same general points could also be applied to other aspects of EPA's regulations, whether through the New Source Performance Standards or the controls for toxic and hazardous wastes.

Given acceptance that technical aspects associated with the definition of specific regulations at the discretion of the administrator are also important to the impact of regulations, we must understand what motivates these decisions. As Figure 1.1 illustrates, the process is by no means clear-cut. A similar judgment could be reached in the case of water quality regulations.[16] Based on the available descriptions of the process, a complex array of forces defines the ultimate form of any standard—the state of scientific information, judgments of analysts as to what is feasible, judgments of other analysts as to the effects of alternative standards, industry and public reactions to initially proposed standards, and the attitude of the administrator in responding to the information developed in support of the standard and how it has been received. It is unlikely that a simple behavioral model could capture the realities of this process. Nonetheless, it is probably fair to suggest that these processes are more likely, all else equal, to distort the ultimate outcome away from the efficient choice than toward it.

Thus although market failure and the need for government intervention to promote an efficient allocation of resources are the principal economic rationales for regulation, they are by no means the sole (or even the primary) influences on the ultimate format of regulatory programs. It is reasonable to assume that the legislative process may well depart from strict efficiency goals. A primary motivation for these departures, I have argued, folllowing Zeckhauser, is the consensus-building that is required to assure passage of the legislation in the first place.[17] As a rule, amendments to a regulation, designed to respond to instances of inefficiency, affect the distribution of benefits and costs among those affected by the regulation. They may do so directly or may disguise, cloud, or even defer the decisions necessary to judge their incidence.

These factors, together with the inherent complexity of the processes leading to observed levels of environmental quality, imply that agency discretion will also play a significant role in definition of environmental regulations and may further contribute to the movement away from an efficient regulatory policy. Consequently, it seems reasonable to expect that in some circumstances regulations will be so dramatically shifted from their resource allocation objectives that they can no longer be justified. That is, the compromises required to pass regulatory legislation and/or the discretionary actions of the agency charged with implementation may be so substantial as to eliminate the basis for the regulations. How do we detect these cases? How much compromise and pragmatic adjustment can we afford? Viewed in light of these questions, especially given the decentralized nature of these decision processes, EO 12291 can be interpreted as a response that permits an accounting to be made of the consequences of these adjustments to what might otherwise be "ideal" regulations. By enforcing an efficiency criterion in evaluating specific regulations, even if it is crude and incomplete, one might argue that the order can serve to limit the costs that have been implicitly added to regulations through legislative compromise and agency discretion.

BENEFIT-COST ANALYSIS: THE IDEAL

Benefit-cost analysis has been interpreted to imply a wide variety of methods for organizing information that is relevant to a particular issue and decision. Some authors have used the term "benefit-cost analysis" to refer to informal attempts to describe and enumerate the advantages and disadvantages of the possible actions under consideration. Most general descriptions and all economic discussions of benefit-cost analysis, however, imply a specific empirical appraisal of the aggregate benefits and the aggregate costs (in constant dollar values) of the action under consideration. Benefit-cost analysis has its roots in welfare economics and was intended to provide a pragmatic method for implementing this theory. In its purest form, benefit-cost analysis maintains that decisions are made using an efficiency criterion to allocate resources to their highest valued uses. These values are derived based on consumer sovereignty. That is, individuals are assumed to be their own best judges of the value of the goods or services they receive (or lose) as a result of the action being evaluated. Because these values are expressed in dollars, the effects of an action, whether positive or negative, can also be treated in dollar values.

As a rule, the analysis maintains that the action under consideration affects a small component of the resource-allocation decisions of all relevant economic agents (households and firms). It implicitly views the public sector as identifying an area in which there is a departure from efficiency and acting to improve the resource allocation without disturbing activities taking place in other sectors or among other economic agents. This is, of course, an extreme simplification, but it is probably one that could be regarded as plausible for the early applications of benefit-cost analysis in the water resources field. Today, it is somewhat less tenable. Indeed, the specific cases in which EO 12291 requires benefit-cost analyses to be conducted are, by definition, not likely to satisfy all of these assumptions.

The theoretical rationale for using a comparison of the aggregate net benefits (the difference between aggregate benefits and aggregate costs) to judge the desirability of certain actions is generally regarded as following from the conditions for a Pareto efficient allocation of resources. These conditions are based on examining all possible incremental reallocations of resources among activities or individuals and continuing to accept such changes so long as they improve the well-being of at least one individual without harming another. When it is no longer possible to realize this objective through reallocations, the resource allocation is termed Pareto efficient. Resources are thereby allocated to their highest valued uses for the given distribution of income and wealth. It is important to acknowledge, however, that this criterion is based on marginal analysis. That is, it relies on marginal comparisons of the consequences of moving an increment of resources from one assignment to another.

A benefit-cost analysis does not focus on marginal benefits and marginal costs. Usually the action under consideration involves a substantial change in resource usage for the affected economic agents and not an infinitesimal increment.[18] Consequently, to understand the role of benefit-cost comparisons as an efficiency standard, we must consider the transition from marginal conditions to aggregate net benefits.

To begin, the term "aggregate" can be misleading. It refers to aggregate across all the individuals affected by the action. For each person we must measure the benefit (or cost) experienced as a result of the action. The action under consideration changes some component of that person's goods and services. It may, for example, improve the levels of air or water quality at locations of direct interest to the individual. The benefit (or cost) referred to in benefit-cost analysis is not associated with the new level of environmental quality but rather with the change from the old to the new level. This distinction is important because a finding of positive aggregate net benefits for an action simply implies that the action represents an improvement over the existing resource allocation. If the existing allocation were efficient, improvement would not be possible; no reallocation of resources will improve the well-being of an individual more than it reduces that of another when the initial allocation is efficient.[19]

Thus a finding of positive aggregate net benefits for an action does not assure that the action will lead to *the* efficient allocation of resources. Rather, it merely confirms the inefficiency of the status quo. Of course, in so doing it moves society in the direction of improving the resource allocation. Figure 1.2 illustrates this distinction. Assume $B(A)$ defines the total benefits associated with providing society with a specified level of an environmental service, such as air quality, designated by the symbol A. Also let $C(A)$ define the full costs of maintaining A units of the environmental services. The Pareto conditions for an efficient resource allocation can be described in this diagram as selecting a value for A which maximizes the total net benefits. In this case, total net benefits refers to the full value generated over cost by providing A at a level greater than zero. The ideal will correspond to A^*, where the marginal benefits from increments to A $(dB(A^*)/dA)$ are exactly equal to the marginal costs of providing them $(dC(A^*)/dA)$. As the figure illustrates, the vertical distance between $B(A)$ and $C(A)$ is greatest at this point. Thus this position is the ideal allocation. In practice, both $B(A)$ and $C(A)$ are exceptionally difficult to measure. Consequently, benefit-cost analyses evaluate how the levels of the benefit and cost functions change with predefined actions. Consider, for example, A_1 as the status quo point. We seek to evaluate an action that will increase A by ΔA, such that $A_2 = A_1 + \Delta A$. Benefit-cost analysis computes the additions to total benefits and total costs as a result of ΔA—GH and EF respectively in Figure 1.2. A net benefits calculation in benefit-cost analysis is simply the process of considering the size of GH in comparison to EF. Whenever the difference is positive, we can demonstrate that the changes under evaluation are consistent with movements toward A^* (the efficient level of the environmental service) regardless of whether they begin from above or below A^*.

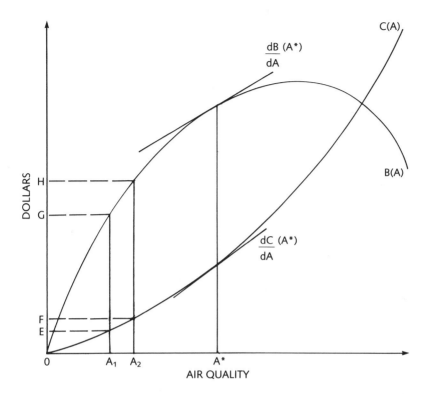

Figure 1.2. A comparison of benefit-cost analysis versus net benefit maximization

With this general background we can now turn to some of the more important aspects of the implementation of the analysis. First, what do we mean by benefits and how do we measure them? The answers are direct for the simplest cases but become more involved for specific environmental applications. Benefit-cost analysis accepts consumers' values as the basis for benefits. Thus to measure benefits we accept the individual's willingness to pay for the good or service provided by the proposed action as the ideal benefit measure. When the goods involved exchange on ideal markets and there are no externalities associated with their production or consumption, we can (conditional on the existing income distribution) accept the market prices as the individual's willingness to pay for the last unit consumed. Hence for small changes in the levels of the good provided, the price can serve to value the increment in estimating benefits. Unfortunately, this is the exception rather than the rule in applying benefit-cost analysis to environmental regulations. It is the absence of markets which motivates the intervention to begin with. Hence a substantial focus of benefit-cost analyses in these cases has been directed toward measuring these values.

The process of deriving estimates for these values has been described as analogous to detective work.[20] That is, we must appraise whether the actions of individuals (or firms) in their other resource-allocation decisions provide clues about their respective valuations of environmental services. As with any form of detective work, there are numerous ways to find, or indeed elicit, these clues. Figure 1.3 describes the nature of these approaches based on their recognition of the actions of individuals and firms as well as the assumptions necessary to apply these clues successfully to the valuation problem.

Obviously, considerable attention could be devoted to explaining each of the methods, including their strengths and weaknesses.[21] Basically the distinctions between the methods lie in their assumptions of how individuals can adjust to changes in environmental quality and in whether we observe those adjustments. At one extreme we might assume that the effects of reduction in environmental quality are technically determined and that we need only measure these relationships to estimate the physical impacts of changes in environmental quality. This perspective characterizes the damage function approach.

Alternatively we can assume that individuals are aware of changes in environmental quality and have ways to adjust their behavior—either to choose a desired level of environmental amenities or to react to a change. To the extent that this behavior is observable and involves changes in these individuals' resource allocations, it is often possible to use the economic

	Types of Linkage Between Water Quality Change and Observed Effects		Types of Assumptions Required	Measurement Approaches
No Role for Behavioral Responses of Economic Agents	Physical Linkages		Responses are determined by engineering or "technological" relationships	Damage Function
Behavioral Responses of Economic Agents Are Essential	Behavioral Linkages	Indirect Links	Restrictions on the nature of individual preferences OR observed technical associations in the delivery of goods or services	Hedonic Property Value Travel Cost
		Direct Links	Institutional	Contingent Valuation (including Contingent Ranking)

Figure 1.3. A taxonomic framework for benefit estimation methods

Source: Desvousges, Smith, and McGivney, *A Comparison of Alternative Approaches for Estimating Recreation and Related Benefits of Water Quality Improvements*, based on description in Smith and Krutilla, "Toward Reformulating the Role of Natural Resources in Economic Models."

theory together with specific assumptions and information on those behavioral actions to measure individual willingness to pay.

In the absence of this information, or even with it, some economists believe direct questioning of individuals, eliciting their valuation of hypothetical experiences, provides the most viable method for measuring individual willingness to pay. In these cases the analyst can exercise control over the conditions under which an individual reports his (or her) valuation of an environmental resource. That is, the manner in which the valuation questions are asked controls the conditions each respondent is assumed to experience. Of course, this judgment is not uniformly held by all economists. Analysts favoring the use of actual behavior criticize the survey approach because, they argue, it relies on individuals' responses to hypothetical situations.[22] What is important for our purposes is that each of the methods requires specific sets of assumptions that are different. Although each method recognizes the "realities" of households' and firms' reactions to air and water pollution, each attaches differing degrees of emphasis to how these responses are best modeled.

This chapter is not intended as an exhaustive review of these approaches.[23] They have been described in general terms so as to point out the level of refinement in these methods which is routinely assumed by EO 12291's dictum to perform benefit-cost analyses for all major regulations. For example, to conduct a benefit analysis for the NAAQS associated with criteria pollutants using damage functions, one must be able to distinguish the individual effects of each pollutant on human health and to value these effects. This process can become especially controversial when the effects involve mortality risks.[24] The assumptions are also significant with the use of one of the behavioral methods for benefit estimation. In these cases, we must assume that individuals can perceive and respond to different levels of each individual pollutant. We will return to more specific consideration of some of these questions and the research agenda they imply in the next section.

To complete this description of benefit-cost analysis under ideal conditions, two further components of the analysis need to be addressed—the measurement of costs and the treatment of benefits and costs that accrue over time.[25]

In principle, costs are to be measured by the opportunity costs of the resources involved in the allocation decision. This process can be difficult. Nonetheless, it is probably fair to suggest that most economists regard it as relatively easier than the estimation of benefits. Lest this seem too simple, two important distinctions should be drawn between cost analyses undertaken for a water resource project or other public investment and the cost analysis of a regulation. For the former, the public sector is generally involved in the "production" of the service flow through the investment itself. It is undertaking tangible activities—building a dam, channeling a stream, improving a recreational facility, and so on. By contrast, in the case of a regulation, the public sector is restricting in some way the activities of the private sector. Thus the costs that must be estimated are those incurred by the private sector in complying with the restriction. Acquiring this cost information may be difficult and controversial. Firms may have significant incentives to overstate their costs of compliance.

The second distinction is that in water resource projects, often (but not always) investments are viewed as desirable by individuals living in the areas where the activities are slated to take place. Thus the distributional issues involve selecting sites for the development and thereby allocating the benefits among individuals with the costs borne in a less clear-cut fashion by all taxpayers.

For most environmental regulations the distribution of benefits and costs is quite different. The benefits are often diffuse and the costs concentrated on a small number of economic agents. That is, the majority of the costs of implementing such regulations are associated with the compliance activities of the firms that are required to control their residual emissions to meet the regulation. As a rule, these regulations tend to fall on specific sectors (and the regions where the firms are located). Consequently, the issues involved are more likely to be distributional, associated with the allocation of the costs of these regulations and not the benefits.

Although this general description is probably the most appropriate overall characterization of these regulations, it should be acknowledged that in some cases the process of defining regulatory standards has not been independent of the distribution of benefits. The clearest example of this linkage arises with the primary standards for criteria pollutants. These standards are defined based on protecting the health of a sensitive group. Thus the definition of that group is important in setting the standard. For example, with the carbon monoxide standard EPA selected the sensitive population as individuals with angina pectoris. There is some evidence that had the sensitive group been designated as hemolytic anemics, the standard would have been more stringent. If we assume that only the sensitive group is experiencing benefits from the standard, we would expect the distribution of benefits to be even more concentrated than costs. Whether this assumption is plausible depends on the pollutant and the concentration level. In some cases, our best estimates may indicate that the benefits received by the overall population are small. Hence in these cases one might find extreme "implicit" valuations of the health effects of these sensitive groups.[26] Under these circumstances, both the costs and the benefits would be concentrated with small (and different) groups of economic agents.

The benefits and costs stemming from improved environmental quality will be realized over time. As a consequence, these contributions must be made commensurate. This has generally implied the acceptance of a present value measure of aggregate net benefits. Future benefits and costs are discounted to measure their current dollar "equivalents."

There are two aspects of this process that should be distinguished because they affect the interpretation given to arguments concerning the appropriate rate to be used in these calculations. The first aspect concerns the assumptions to be made about the preferences of individuals and technologies of firms experiencing the regulations and their results in the future. This is an empirical question. As a rule, benefit-cost analysis has generally maintained that preferences do not change over time. Thus future generations' preferences are assumed to be the same as those of the current generation. Of course, as a practical matter, the relevant time horizon for environmental regulations often does not extend beyond one generation.[27] This assumption does not, however, imply that real willingness to pay might not systematically increase over time. That is, if we can anticipate real income growth and the existence of high income elasticities of demand, there are good reasons to postulate increasing willingness to pay.[28]

Similarly, the technologies associated with complying with regulations are assumed to correspond to what is known (or what is specified as practical) today. Cost estimates are then based on these assumptions. To the extent that there are good reasons to expect cost-saving technological changes, these can be incorporated as systematic reductions in the real costs of meeting the regulation.

In both cases, however, the decisions are essentially empirical judgments and should be contrasted with what is, in part, an ethical judgment—how to treat future generations' benefits. This issue arises in the selection of a discount rate. Most environmental economists would advocate the use of a social rate of discount criterion (as opposed to the private opportunity cost of capital) in selecting a discount rate.[29] In principle, the value for this rate would depend upon the characteristics of the services provided by the regulation. Nonetheless, rates ranging from 2 to 6 percent generally form the consensus estimates for the social rate of discount. OMB has required the use of a 10 percent real rate of discount for benefit-cost analyses prepared under EO 12291. Consequently, there may well be a substantial bias away from regulations associated with problems having long time horizons.

Moving from principle to practice in any discipline is never easy, and this is certainly true for the application of benefit-cost analysis. Special problems are posed, however, by attempts to apply these methods to environmental regulations. They are important because they affect the likelihood of EO 12291's success in improving the efficiency of environmental regulations. Consequently, we will turn in the next section to the realities of applying benefit-cost analysis in evaluating environmental regulations.

BENEFIT-COST ANALYSIS: THE REALITIES

A general description of any methodology, regardless of whether it is intended to provide economic, engineering, or natural science information, cannot account for all of the specific details that can arise with each application. And this is certainly true in the use of benefit-cost analysis applied to the evaluation of environmental regulations. In this case, however, these details serve to identify areas in which fundamental advances in research methods are necessary. That is, without extensions in our current understanding of the methods available for benefit and cost estimation, the benefit-cost analyses conducted under EO 12291 will necessarily require substantial professional judgments in areas in which there is no professional consensus on the appropriate way (or ways) to deal with specific issues. Because it is difficult to describe these issues in general terms, the requirements of current and past air and water quality regulations will be used to illustrate some of the problems that can be encountered.

We consider first the methodological issues posed by the specific form of air quality and water quality standards for benefit and for cost estimation. Following this discussion, the section concludes by briefly reviewing the "off-the-shelf" research results that can be used to meet the needs posed by conducting a benefit-cost analysis for each regulatory action and the research agenda implied by the deficiencies in these results.

Measuring the Benefits for a Standard

Consider the task of measuring the benefits associated with alternative specifications for the primary standards (that is, NAAQS) for a criteria pollutant. Because the Clean Air Act requires that the primary standards for the criteria pollutants cannot consider costs, the most we can expect from EO 12291 is that current procedures for defining standards will consider the benefits of each and that a benefit-cost analysis will be performed after the selection of a final standard. This practice seems to have been followed in developing the Regulatory Impact Analysis (RIA) for the new particulate standard.

A standard generally includes decisions on at least six issues: the pollutant indicator, the form of the standard (generally statistical format for air quality standards), the averaging time for the standard, the exceedance rate to define a violation, the method of determining an exceedance (whether based on a daily maximum or on all hours), and the actual concentration level specifying the standard.[30] As a rule, the methods used in the benefit analyses that have been conducted for air quality standards have considered only the first two of these characteristics of the standard in measuring benefits. The others, though potentially important to the benefits from an air quality standard, cannot be reflected with existing data and methodologies.

Theoretically, specific decisions on each of these variables are made based on the best measures for identifying the health effects of the relevant pollutant and on assurance that the observations derived from EPA's monitoring system accurately reflect the degree of protection intended by the standard. The standard, however, is not necessarily specified in terms that are amenable to a benefits analysis. For example, the recently proposed changes to the particulate matter standard have been expressed as particles of ten microns or less (PM10) because recent health science research suggests that particles of these sizes are primarily responsible for the important health effects.[31] Unfortunately, all measures of particulate matter are defined by total suspended particulates (TSP). There is very limited information on the distribution of particle sizes within a given TSP reading under current conditions and none under a standard expressed in PM10. Consequently, nearly all empirical estimates based on actual health records or laboratory experiments are not measured by using the indicator variable providing the basis for the standard. Therefore, the results from these studies must be adapted to conform to this indicator measure, and we can expect inaccuracies in the estimates. Although these errors may be significant, this is not the primary point of this example. The example illustrates that standards are generally defined in terms that bear little or no compatibility with the requirements for a consistent benefits analysis.

The problems do not end here. Once a standard is defined, a benefits analysis must evaluate the increment to air quality and presumably households' well-being as a result. This requirement implies the definition of a baseline or a state of air quality without regulation. This definition introduces a number of important issues and has been the source of some controversy within EPA.

The baseline will reflect conditions in the absence of the specific regulation being evaluated. But what about other regulations? That is, under the Clean Air Act Amendments there are several regulations that can affect ambient concentrations of air pollutants. Equally important, often the process of controlling one pollutant will lead to the control of other pollutants at the same time. Thus to define the baseline for evaluating the NAAQS standard for a particulate standard we must consider the status of any New Source Performance Standards that affect particulate matter. In addition, we might also need to consider pollutants that would lead to the joint control of particulates. (Actually, these issues affect the estimation of costs as well, and we return to them below.) These effects arise exclusively from the assumptions made with respect to the regulatory environment. The baseline is also affected by the assumptions made concerning economic activity in the absence of the standard and the degree to which voluntary action would lead to improved environmental quality.

The baseline is, of course, one part of the increment. To calculate an increment we must also define the endpoint, and this need not be the standard. Some areas may not comply with the standard. To determine the endpoint, the analysis must, in effect, "second-guess" what will be the nature and effectiveness of each state's SIP.

Equally vexing problems arise in measuring the benefits for water quality improvements. The available research methods relate primarily to recreation benefits.[32] Thus these have generally been all that could be considered. Unfortunately, there is a fundamental difficulty in evaluating water quality standards. Two sets of transformations must be considered. Water quality standards are defined in technological terms and imply for subcategories of the production activities of each industry specific emission rates of each type of pollutant. These emissions must be related to a change in water quality and then to some feature of the use of water quality that affects human activity. Both steps involve significant difficulties. The second is especially important for benefit estimation. Water quality must be related to the activity or activities undertaken by households that involve water bodies. For example, in measuring recreation benefits, we must determine how different water quality levels enhance particular recreational activities in order to gauge what is likely to be an individual's willingness to pay for water quality improvements.

As in the case of standards for air pollutants, a baseline and implementation set of estimates for water quality must be defined. The analyst must second-guess the other influences to the water quality along a particular river or lake in order to distinguish the effects associated with the specific regulation. In the case of the RIA for the iron and steel industry, for example, this assumption was important to the derivation of benefit estimates for the BAT standards, as W. Norton Grubb, Dale Whittington, and Michael Humphries note in Chapter 5.

Of course, these technical difficulties arise for benefits analysis with other standards in other areas as well, and further examples of difficulties in setting standards could be enumerated. These examples are sufficient, however, to summarize the generic nature of the problems with the three issues. (1) The form and exact definition of the proposed standard are generally defined independent of the benefit-cost analysis. Comparisons of the net benefits associated with each alternative must therefore be limited to the alternatives that have been defined. Thus it is not possible to consider general efficiency trade-offs in the form of the standard. (2) The interconnected nature of different regulations, both across pollutants and across regulations, affects the feasibility and consistency that can be expected for the individual benefit estimates "attached" to each regulation. (3) The measurement of the benefits associated with improved environmental quality often requires that these improvements be "translated" into terms that permit the identification of tangible effects on households. These transformations are not well known but can have a significant impact on the benefits estimates derived for any standard.

Measuring the Costs of a Standard

Cost estimation for environmental regulations involves second-guessing the actions of firms in response to the standard. For the case of NAAQS, the process is even more complex because the analyst must postulate a set of state implementation plans as well as control technologies undertaken by firms in response to the emission controls implied by these plans. The presence of other regulations can have a most important influence on these cost estimates. For example, the current estimates of the costs of compliance with the revised NAAQS standard for particulate matter generally assume full compliance with NSPS and replacement rates for capital equipment that implicitly maintain that the regulation does not affect the investment process. That is, capital equipment is assumed to have an exogenous life. The cost model maintains that it is replaced on a fixed schedule independent of economic incentives. Under some circumstances this assumption may be a reasonable approximation (though there is accumulating evidence following the argument of Martin S. Feldstein and Michael Rothschild that replacement investment is endogenous[33]). In this case, however, the NSPS regulations directly affect the incentives to replace capital by requiring stringent controls for new capital and not affecting existing equipment. Consequently, it seems unreasonable to ignore these incentives. Moreover, the incremental costs of meeting the standard and the form of the implied SIPs would be quite different if these assumptions were relaxed. As a rule, these issues are not considered as part of the benefit-cost analysis conducted for a single standard.

With water quality standards, the subcategories of industries for each standard are defined without complete recognition of the potential impacts of alternative definitions for the cost of compliance. Otherwise, there would be no scope for, or interest in, a bubble policy for the BPT and BAT standards. The judgments as to the specific technologies designated as BPT and BAT seem arbitrary. In the iron and steel case, for example, most of the BPT standards by subcategories were judged BAT. One might ask why.

Despite the presence of the alternative technologies considered, only the final proposal was subjected to a benefit-cost analysis. The emission-control levels for the various pollutants often varied up and down over the progressively more stringent options considered—with some emissions decreasing and others increasing. Therefore, the final selection had to assume some relationship between emission rates and water quality. Yet this relationship was not defined. These issues simply touch the surface of the problems associated with cost analyses. Engineering approaches are uniformly used. Often, conventional economic principles are not followed. Thus despite the common belief that this area is the easier of the two components of the analysis, detailed analyses of the procedures used to date suggest that this judgment may have been made simply because few economists have studied the practices carefully.

Availability and Adequacy of Information

It is probably fair to suggest that if one asks any scientist whether the available information in his or her field is sufficient to guide a public policy decision the answer will involve a call for more research to assure a more credible policy decision. Thus in judging what we know about the benefits and costs of improvements in any aspect of environmental quality, it is important to use an appropriate standard. The information will never be complete. We would not want it to be because the acquisition of information itself requires resources that may, at some point, serve more productive alternative ends. Nonetheless, even with this pragmatic perspective for evaluating the state of our "off-the-shelf" stock of knowledge on the benefits and costs of environmental quality improvements, it is clear that the information is not up to the tasks demanded by EO 12291.

On the benefits side of the ledger we have estimates from three general areas (following the schematic framework given in Figure 1.3)—damage functions, indirect market models, and contingent valuation surveys. Each has its own individualized problems. Moreover, when each is used to develop comparable benefits estimates for a given environmental improvement, the range can be large.[34]

To document these judgments fully would require an extensive review, but a few general comments can illustrate the difficulties with each method. The two most important applications of damage functions have been to the analysis of the effects of air pollution on human health and agricultural production. In both cases, the findings have been controversial. For the human health effects, Shelby Gerking and William D. Schulze have described the shortcomings of macroepidemiological studies.[35] They are sensitive to the specification of the model and to measures of health effects and air quality used. Indeed, it is generally not possible to distinguish the individual effects of separate pollutants on health. The available empirical models are based largely on mortality rate information. The results with morbidity are even more limited and face genuine difficulties with the measurement of the health effect itself. The typical measures available are the number of work days lost or the number of days in which activities were restricted. Both are influenced by economic factors as well as by potential pollutants. For example, an individual's willingness to lose a day of work and experience the associated costs will depend on his occupation and working conditions. Little direct attention has been given to these considerations.

The results derived from controlled laboratory experiments are limited for other reasons. The controlled conditions cannot resemble real-world exposures either in duration or circumstances. As a rule, changes in physiological conditions are measured in such ways as by forced expiratory volume (FEV). These measures are not readily converted to tangible health effects.

Finally, the health effects must be valued, and this opens the door to a very controversial area, both with respect to the implications of the valuation itself and to the range of estimates available, based on labor market studies of individuals' willingness to accept increased job risks.[36] Indeed, a recent comparison of the implicit marginal valuations of risk based on occupational risks versus the valuation of air quality risks within a common hedonic wage model indicated substantial differences in their respective marginal valuations of risk reductions—with as much as twenty times larger values implied by the valuation of air quality.[37]

These examples involve general issues associated with the use of damage functions in estimating the effects of air pollutants in general on health. More specific problems arise in attempts to distinguish the effects of individual pollutants and to assign health effects to specific changes in them. Similar technical issues can be raised concerning our knowledge of the effects of specific pollutants on crop yields. Thus, laying aside the errors this approach would encounter by failing to take account of the prospects for adjustment in response to increased (or decreased) ambient concentrations of one or more pollutants, they should be regarded as uncertain.

The track record for indirect market and survey methods is not much better. There are several important differences between these methods and the damage function approach. Both the indirect market and the survey methods incorporate adjustment and generally include in their estimates all motivations for valuing an environmental improvement. But each encounters other substantive problems in responding to the specific needs of a benefit-cost analysis for an environmental regulation.

Consider, for example, the indirect market approaches. These generally involve analysis of housing prices or wage rates. With the property value models, we maintain that individuals reveal (under ideal conditions) their willingness to pay for improvements in air quality through their locational choices. Of course, they are making these decisions in response to the air quality as they perceive it and for whatever reasons they feel are important. Both of these qualifications are important. Perceptions may not correspond to our technical measures of ambient air quality (or water quality for sites near water bodies). In addition, analysis of each standard, especially for air quality, requires that we develop benefits from reductions in each individual pollutant and frequently that we separate the motivations for these values. This issue is easily illustrated with the NAAQS standards, which are to be based on health criteria alone.

Property value (and wage) studies have also not been able to separate the effects of individual pollutants.[38] Moreover, the pollutant measures used and cities covered are incomplete. Finally, the studies provide point estimates of the willingness to pay for one pollutant and not its demand function.[39]

The last source of information on benefits is from surveys—asking individuals about their willingness to pay for specific aspects of environmental improvement. Although initially economists took a negative attitude toward the use of surveys, current evidence suggests that they can be used to provide plausible order-of-magnitude estimates when the survey respondents are familiar with the service being valued and the survey is carefully structured. Both of these qualifications are important, as the literature in this area clearly documents.[40] Nonetheless, surveys are not free of problems. The ability to control the circumstances within which an individual is asked valuation questions is a mixed blessing. Although the analyst can describe specifically the aspect of environmental quality to be valued, there is increasing evidence that these values will be sensitive to the state of other components of environmental quality. If these other components are not specified, we must assume that individuals will respond based on what they think they will be. Moreover, it is reasonable to expect that preconceptions will vary from one individual to the next.

Finally, as a practical matter, there have not been a large number of these surveys. The applicability of their findings is also limited because their overall design was not the result of a coordinated research plan. As a consequence, the coverage is limited with respect to geographic area, pollutant, and motivation for valuation (for example, health effects versus materials damage).

On the cost side of the ledger our information is even more limited. We do not have enough information to gauge the plausibility of cost estimates. What is available is largely from engineering studies prepared by or for EPA as part of the standard-setting process. Data availability has limited the number of econometric studies of the costs of control. Early results for electric power and paper should probably be regarded as demonstrating the feasibility of this form of analysis, rather than as providing a basis of policy estimates.[41] Moreover, the character of many standards (as a requirement that a specific control technology or its equivalent be used, for example) precludes the use of these studies for cost estimates.

The available research on engineering-economic cost estimates appears to be limited. As a rule, these studies are tedious. What is available derives largely from the early work of Resources for the Future's industry studies program.[42] Based on this work and extensions using the models developed as part of the research, it would appear that the cost estimates for controlling emissions of atmospheric and waterborne pollutants in iron and steel plants can be sensitive to model structure.[43]

Do all of these qualifications call for a "counsel of paralysis"? That is, are the problems with our current information so great that we cannot realistically proceed? This conclusion does not follow from these qualifications and concerns. Rather, the difficulties imply that two changes in the way we approach benefit-cost analyses are warranted.

First, greater attention must be given to quantifying the degree of uncertainty in the benefit-cost estimates provided as part of the evaluation of regulations. In other words, these evaluations must explicitly recognize the uncertainty that arises from the judgments used to adapt the information that is available to the problems at hand. This has not been done well.

Second, our agenda for future research must consider the consequences of the pragmatic judgments that are made as part of conducting benefit-cost analyses. Some examples would include the following: (a) Benefits transfer—what are the consequences of alternative methods for transferring benefits estimates derived from a survey for a specific area or property value study for a single city to another area or set of cities? (b) Benefits decomposition—is it feasible to identify the components of benefits estimates derived from the indirect market models and associate them with specific motivations such as health effects, aesthetics, materials damage, and so on? (c) Benefits aggregation—how do the various contributions to environmental quality, both from individual air pollutants and from the availability of other environmental amenities affect an individual's valuation of any one component? (d) Cost estimation—what is the scope for the practical use of economic analysis in what are now largely engineering cost estimates?

The list could be expanded indefinitely. What is needed is a mechanism to assure that the issues that arise in conducting benefit-cost analysis as part of EO 12291 help to influence the research agenda on the theory and practice of these methods for environmental problems. The simple prospect of having the RIA documents in the public domain is not sufficient to assure that this will take place.

EXECUTIVE ORDER 12291: A GUIDE TO THE VOLUME AND PROGNOSIS

The prospect for improving the environmental regulations clearly continues to attract research interest. It is therefore reasonable to introduce this volume by answering a question. How is this volume different from studies undertaken in the past? The difference is straightforward. This volume makes the first comprehensive evaluation of the implications of EO 12291 for environmental regulations. In so doing we consider OMB's and EPA's respective roles in responding to the order and in designing and performing analyses that are responsive both to legislative mandates and to the requirements for an "efficiency test" for the proposed regulations.

The volume also considers the performance to date of EPA in meeting these requirements in comparison with other departments and agencies of the federal government. These tasks necessarily provide a rich research agenda. Two aspects of this agenda—the development of benefit estimates for regulations from existing research or from new studies, and the consistency between risk assessment and benefit-cost analyses—deserve special attention. Thus one chapter is devoted to each. Finally, we close with the bottom line—will EO 12291 make a difference to the level of environmental quality and/or for the efficiency with which the public sector delivers it? Our last two chapters provide different perspectives on the prospects for the order's success.

The volume begins with Andrews's thoughtful review of the evolution of environmental policy, placing the Reagan administration's approach for controlling regulations within the context of our past history. Andrews provides essential background for our interpretation of EO 12291 as an important component of the administration's environmental policy. At the same time, he highlights some of the limitations in relying on benefit-cost analysis and the efficiency standard as the sole arbiter of potentially conflicting objectives.

This background prepares us for the chapters by Arthur G. Fraas and Ann Fisher. Fraas provides OMB's perspective on how EO 12291 will function. After a brief description of the order's requirements and our experience with it over the past two years, he discusses what OMB's oversight role can be and how environmental policies pose special problems for implementing EO 12291. This insider's view of what OMB can accomplish is especially important because the available evaluations of OMB's performance in implementing EO 12291 have not been favorable. For example, the General Accounting Office's (GAO) report on OMB's performance under the order to the Senate Committee on Governmental Affairs observed that "the record of OMB oversight under E.O. 12291 can be considered mixed. Delays in rulemaking have generally been kept to a minimum, at least for most rules. However, shortcomings with regulatory analyses carried out under E.O. 12044 are still prevalent in analyses conducted under 12291. The actual effect of OMB on most rules is modest, largely because of the great number of rules that they review. Finally, we have reason to believe that OMB's review has serious disclosure and consistency problems."[44] This report also criticized OMB for failing to provide a broader role in overseeing the regulatory analysis process (a point also made in Chapter 5). In 1981, for example, OMB waived the Regulatory Impact Analysis requirement for twenty-one of the forty-three major rules it reviewed. Only ten of these twenty-one had factors present that were consistent with the five reasons OMB has cited for waiving the RIA requirement.[45]

Executive Order 12291 conferred on OMB a variety of powers including the authority to prescribe procedures for agencies to follow in conducting their RIAs; designate any rule or set of rules as major and thereby require the preparation of an RIA; waive requirements of the executive order so a rule can be issued expeditiously when necessary; designate existing rules for review and establish schedules for these reviews; and extend the review period for final rules and their RIAs beyond the thirty days provided for in the executive order.[46] At the same time, the review task facing OMB is large. In 1981 it reviewed 2,679 new rules. Often the process of review involved informal interaction between OMB and the relevant agency staff. It is clear that the resources available for these reviews are not commensurate with the full requirements of the order. Consequently, we must ask how OMB has planned to cope with the problem and what strategy it feels will be most effective in conducting regulatory oversight. Fraas provides this perspective with particular focus on OMB's role in the RIAs associated with environmental regulations.

This view of what is feasible for the office charged with implementing the order contrasts with those of the agency trying to respond to the order. Fisher provides this perspective. How do we translate the theoretical requirements for an ideal benefit-cost analysis into pragmatic guidance to meet the needs of the regulatory process? Inevitably there must be compromise between what is theoretically desirable and what is practically feasible. Nonetheless, her judgment is that the analysis and the information available for decision making will be improved as a result of the order.

Does this appraisal square with the record? Grubb, Whittington, and Humphries have reviewed some thirty-seven Regulatory Impact Analyses to answer that question. They report the first evaluation of the quality and character of the analyses conducted to meet EO 12291's requirements. By evaluating all RIAs prepared during 1981, these authors provide a basis for judging EPA's track record. Although EPA's analyses have been among the best, the authors clearly do not give it a glowing endorsement. Indeed, considering the three RIAs prepared by EPA by October 1982, it is hard to conclude that the information in these RIAs would be likely to improve decision making. Not only do the analyses contain some important errors but they seemed to fail to appreciate the rationale for benefit-cost analyses. If the analyses are to be effective discriminators between good and bad regulations on the basis of efficiency, they must consider the objectives of the regulation, how the particular regulatory form meets these objectives, and the net contributions to individuals' well-being that are likely to result.

Are these outcomes EPA's fault? The authors have used their review of these RIAs to consider this issue. They ask questions relevant to all agencies affected by the executive order—what information would a comprehensive program of regulatory evaluation require and how should it be organized? The answers place important responsibilities with OMB and are more critical than the GAO assessment.

As I have noted throughout this introduction, the benefit-cost mandate of EO 12291 raises significant research issues. Two of these are dealt with by A. Myrick Freeman and Carlisle Ford Runge in Part III of the volume. Freeman addresses the tactics of benefit estimation in response to the order's requirements. When does it make sense to use the available studies and models—transferring and adapting them to the problems at hand in the evaluation of a specific regulation—and when are new studies warranted? By using examples, Freeman describes the direct and relevant issues involved in making these decisions and thereby provides a conceptual framework for deploying EPA's scarce research resources.

Runge considers a more specific but equally important problem in responding to EO 12291 for air quality regulations associated with the primary standards. Originally, EPA interpreted the Clean Air Act to imply that the primary standards were to be based on health risks without regard to either the benefits or the costs of control. This places the policies implied by a risk assessment at odds with those associated with a benefit-cost criterion. Indeed, Thomas C. Schelling noted the central importance of this problem to environmental policies on air quality, observing,

> The most critical difference between focusing on a measure of damage and focusing on emissions or concentrations [of air pollutants] is likely to lie in the attention given to population density or total exposed population. *It is hard to find any methodological or philosophical issue in environmental protection that is more divisive or more important than whether exposure ought to be minimized in the aggregate or equalized among individuals in different localities and situations.* This issue can be avoided, or at least evaded, if costs can be neglected and all exposures of any significance are deemed unacceptable. But when costs cannot be neglected as insubstantial, or when at no feasible cost can all significant exposure be eliminated, this inherently distributive question has to be faced.[47]

Because the Clean Air Act Amendments require risk assessments for an important class of environmental regulations, the role of EO 12291 in influencing these policies depends on the relationship between these two methodologies. Runge provides a conceptual basis for considering both and relates it to the implications of these conflicting criteria for environmental policy.

The volume closes with two disparate prognoses. Robert W. Crandall reviews the state of regulations affecting air pollution and concludes that the Reagan administration's program with EO 12291 will at best "have a marginal impact on a program that needs more radical surgery." By contrast, Paul R. Portney is less demanding of the review process and notes that the "margins" we are talking about may well be large. Indeed, he observes that "if regulatory analysis and oversight result in no more than a 0.1 to a 1.0 percent annual cost saving when compared to total incremental compliance costs, it will pay for itself. In fact, it seems possible that $25 million [one-tenth to 1 percent of highest and lowest estimates of compliance costs for major regulations] could easily be saved by the careful analysis of a single important regulation."

Regulatory analysis will add both time and cost to the definition and promulgation of new regulations. It is not a substitute for improving the overall structure of environmental policy. But in a practical world, in which ideal regulations are not the relevant standard, it looks to this observer like a good buy, despite the limited information we have and the flaws in our methods.

NOTES

1. The sum of these two figures would overstate the number of regulations because a regulation is counted at least twice over time—once when it is proposed and a second time when it is finally promulgated.
2. See Haveman and Christiansen, "Environmental Regulations and Productivity Growth"; and Gollop and Roberts, "Environmental Regulations and Productivity Growth."
3. This practice can be traced at least as far back as Executive Order 11821 issued by President Ford on 27 November 1974, formally initiating the Inflation Impact Statement Program.
4. This is a summary of the definition taken from Executive Order 12291. See the Appendix to this volume for the text of the order and specific definitions.
5. Ruckelshaus, "Science, Risk, and Public Policy," pp. 4–7; emphasis added.
6. Freeman, *Air and Water Pollution Control*.
7. John V. Krutilla has offered the best general statement on the implicit assumptions and rationale for benefit-cost analysis, by observing: "While intervention is required to correct divergencies between private and social product and cost, both the initial conditions and the associated side effects of intervention are of relevance in assessing the welfare implications of supermarket allocations of resources. . . . Assuming that the gross benefit achieved [from intervention] exceeds the associated opportunity costs, if, in addition: (a) opportunity costs are borne by beneficiaries in such ways [sic] as to retain the initial income distribution, (b) the initial income distribution is in some sense 'best,' and (c) the marginal social rates of transformation between any two commodities are everywhere equal to their corresponding rates of substitution except for the area(s) justifying the intervention in question, then welfare can be improved by such intervention and, to the extent that the objective is pursued to the point where the social marginal rates of transformation between commodities in this area and other sectors are likewise equal to the rates of substitution for corresponding paired commodities, welfare is maximized" ("Welfare Implications of Benefit Cost Analysis," p. 227).
8. Navarro, "Clean Air Act Amendment"; Pashigian, "Environmental Regulation"; Pashigian, "How Large and Small Plants Fare under Environmental Regulation."

9. The first required a visibility impact review in permit applications for source construction or expansion that might affect visibility in Class I areas (national parks and wilderness areas, designated to have no impairment in air quality). The second requires visibility regulations on existing sources that might affect Class I areas. Thus in principle the provisions affect visibility conditions in the East as well. It is fair to suggest, however, that the primary focus to date has been on western visibility.

10. See Navarro, "Clean Air Act Amendment"; and Portney, "How *Not* to Create a Job," for discussion and estimates.

11. Zeckhauser, "Preferred Policies When There Is a Concern for Probability of Adoption," p. 218; see also Zeckhauser and Shepard, "Principles for Saving and Valuing Lives."

12. The recent Supreme Court decision eliminating specific congressional veto authority precludes this approach to control. It is reasonable to expect that other mechanisms will be developed by Congress in response to this decision.

13. See Freeman, "Air and Water Pollution Policy"; Harrington and Krupnick, "Stationary Source Pollution Policy and Choices for Reform"; and Chapter 8 in this volume.

14. See Krupnick, Magat, and Harrington, "Understanding Regulatory Decision-Making," for an empirical analysis of the decision making in setting standards under the Clean Water Act.

15. See Russell and Vaughan, *Steel Production*, for a detailed discussion of the technology in relation to the major emission-generating activities.

16. See Ferland, "Benefit-Cost Analysis in Environmental Decision-Making."

17. This point, of course, has played an important role in the public choice literature. For a general overview see Mueller, *Public Choice*, and for literature more specific to environmental issues, Russell, ed., *Collective Decision Making*.

18. This comment does not contradict my earlier statement of assumptions. There are two judgments of the size of the project being evaluated. One is relative to the aggregate economy in which it is undertaken. In the application of benefit-cost analyses for projects within developed economies conventional practice maintains that the resource reallocations have small, localized effects on the economy as a whole. This does not preclude the project from having a large effect on a small subset of the economic agents that make up that economy.

19. See Bradford, "Benefit-Cost Analysis and Demand Curves for Public Goods." Of course, in practice we readily accept a Kaldor-Hicks criterion by evaluating investment or regulatory decisions in terms of the aggregate net benefits regardless of who receives the costs or benefits.

20. National Academy of Sciences, *Decisionmaking for Regulating Chemicals in the Environment*.

21. See Freeman, *The Benefits of Environmental Improvement*, for a review of the benefit estimation methods; and Brookshire, Thayer, Schulze, and d'Arge, "Valuing Public Goods"; and Desvousges, Smith, and McGivney, *A Comparison of Alternative Approaches for Estimating Recreation and Related Benefits of Water Quality Improvements*, for comparative evaluations of their performance.

22. Feenberg and Mills have provided one of the clearest statements of the reasons

for these doubts. They observed: "The second reason for economists' skepticism about such surveys is that people have no incentive to consider questions carefully. Figuring out what an improvement in water quality of a nearby lake would be worth to you is extremely complex. If it were announced that the lake had been partially cleaned up, you might try it a couple of times, compare it with other lakes, ask friends, and read accounts of the results in the press and elsewhere. Gradually, you would decide the most appropriate modification of your recreational behavior. You are motivated to do these things because the quality of your recreational experience depends on it. *But you have no such incentive if you are asked a hypothetical question*" (*Measuring the Benefits of Water Pollution Abatement*, p. 60; emphasis added).

23. See Schulze, d'Arge, and Brookshire, "Valuing Environmental Commodities," and Desvousges, Smith, and McGivney, *Alternative Approaches*, Chapter 2, for discussions of the theoretical relationship between these methods.

24. For a discussion of the performance of the mortality/air pollution models see Gerking and Schulze, "What Do We Know about Benefits of Reduced Mortality from Air Pollution Control?" and Freeman, "The Health Implications of Residuals Discharges." In addition, Violette and Chestnut, "Valuing Reductions in Risks," have provided a detailed overview of the problems associated with the available methods for measuring individuals' valuation of risks on the job.

25. This is not intended to be a complete list of the theoretical issues that are important to the practice of benefit-cost analysis. One of the most important omitted areas is in the treatment of uncertainty. See Lind, "A Primer on the Major Issues Relating to the Discount Rate for Evaluating National Energy Policy," for a discussion of the implications of uncertainty for the selection of a discount rate and Smith, "Benefit Cost Analysis and Risk Assessment," for discussion of the treatment of uncertainty in benefit-cost analysis in comparison to risk assessment.

26. Crandall and Portney, "The Environmental Protection Agency in the Reagan Administration," have made this point. They observed that based on estimates of the Regulatory Analysis and Review Group (under the Carter administration), a stringent carbon monoxide standard (9 parts per million versus 12 parts per million) implied a valuation of $6,000 to $250,000 per sick day of those suffering from angina pectoris. Of course, such estimates maintain that this group is the only one realizing benefits from the standard.

27. There are, of course, exceptions to this judgment. Examples of the most important current environmental policy issues that extend the time frame for long-term environmental risks to an intergenerational context would include the problems associated with CO_2 accumulation and climate change, acidic deposition, and the disposal of nuclear and hazardous waste.

28. See, for example, Fisher, Krutilla, and Cicchetti, "The Economics of Environmental Protection," for the introduction of this approach, and Krutilla and Fisher, *The Economics of Natural Environments*, for a detailed discussion of its implications.

29. See Lind, "Primer on the Discount Rate," for a complete discussion of the implications of alternative critera for selecting a discount rate.

30. See Richmond, "Criteria for Specifying Alternative Primary Standards."

31. This problem can be further complicated by the fact that not all health effects can be associated with the same indicator variable. Chronic health effects may require different measures than acute effects.
32. See, for example, Freeman, *Air and Water Pollution Control*.
33. Feldstein and Rothschild, "Towards an Economic Theory of Replacement Investment."
34. Freeman, *Air and Water Pollution Control*, discusses these issues for air and water quality estimates.
35. Gerking and Schulze, "What Do We Know about Benefits of Reduced Mortality from Air Pollution Control?"
36. See Blomquist, "The Value of Human Life"; Viscusi, "Labor Market Valuations of Life and Limb"; and Violette and Chestnut, "Valuing Reductions in Risks."
37. Smith and Gilbert, "The Valuation of Environmental Risks Using Hedonic Wage Models."
38. See Palmquist, "Estimating the Demand for Air Quality from Property Value Studies"; and Smith, "The Role of Site and Job Characteristics in Hedonic Wage Models."
39. See Brown and Rosen, "On the Estimation of Structural Hedonic Price Models"; and Fisher and Smith, "Economic Evaluation of Energy's Environmental Costs with Special Reference to Air Pollution."
40. Schulze, d'Arge, and Brookshire, "Valuing Environmental Commodities"; Mitchell and Carson, "An Experiment in Determining Willingness to Pay for National Water Quality Improvements"; and Desvousges, Smith, and McGivney, *Alternative Approaches*.
41. Gollop and Roberts, "Environmental Regulations and Productivity Growth"; Tran and Smith, "The Role of Air and Water Residuals for Steam Electric Power Generation"; Meidema, "Factor Demand and Particulate Emission Control Regulations"; Fuller, "Steam Electric Generation under Residual Emission Constraints"; and Pittman, "Issues in Pollution Control."
42. Bower, "Studies of Residuals Management in Industry."
43. See Smith and Vaughan, "The Implications of Model Complexity for Environmental Management," and "Strategic Details and Process Analysis Models for Environmental Management."
44. U.S. General Accounting Office, "Improved Quality, Adequate Resources and Consistent Oversight Needed if Regulatory Analysis Is to Help Control Costs of Regulation," pp. 54–55.
45. The five factors which OMB has stated could lead to waiving the RIA requirements were emergency regulations; regulations subject to statutory deadlines; nondiscretionary regulations related to spending programs; regulations for which sufficient analysis had already been conducted; and regulations for which OMB finds it appropriate to delay preparation of an RIA until a later stage in the proceeding (ibid., p. 42, n. 7).
46. Ibid., pp. 46–47.
47. Schelling, *Incentive Arrangements for Environmental Protection*, pp. xiv–xv; emphasis added.

Part I

THE BACKGROUND FOR
AND IMPLEMENTATION OF
EXECUTIVE ORDER 12291

2

RICHARD N. L. ANDREWS*

ECONOMICS AND ENVIRONMENTAL DECISIONS, PAST AND PRESENT

 EXECUTIVE Order 12291 represented at face value a major symbolic commitment to economic efficiency as the goal and benefit-cost analysis as a primary means of evaluating federal regulations. Other chapters in this volume address in detail the questions of how the order has been interpreted and implemented and whether this apparent symbolic commitment has in fact been realized. This chapter addresses a prior issue: what was the significance of the executive order itself? What was new about it, if anything? How did it emerge from the prior histories both of economic analysis and of what has come to be called social regulation—the regulation of health, safety, and environmental quality? And what implications does it hold for the future development of those domains?

My thesis is that the executive order represents a new and significant twist in three interwoven threads of historical development, all of which were well under way before the Reagan presidency: first, the development of benefit-cost analysis as a methodology for evaluating public projects and programs; second, the integration of economic analysis into many federal regulatory decision processes, often by statute and specifically in most environmental regulatory decisions; and third, the use of economic impact claims as arguments for greater executive or legislative control over regulatory agencies, arguments used increasingly by the regulatory reform and antiregulatory movements that gathered momentum beginning in the mid-1970s. All these threads incorporated economic analysis, but each in prac-

*Professor of Environmental Sciences and Engineering and Director, Institute for Environmental Studies, University of North Carolina at Chapel Hill.

tice reflected competing views of the public interest among such goals and objectives as economic efficiency, health/safety/environmental quality per se, business autonomy from government constraints, and the reasoned analysis of government action proposals.

The executive order also represents an explicit instrument of presidential policy in the Reagan administration, deliberately invoked by the president to assist in achieving the primary objectives of his overall domestic policy. This policy was to reduce drastically the overall influence of the federal government in domestic affairs, with a primary emphasis on reducing its regulatory role, both by reversing the historical trend toward additional regulation and by reassessing existing regulations. It must therefore be understood both in long- and short-term historical contexts as the product of earlier developments but also as the tool of a particular president's policy purposes.

First, I will describe the evolution of the economic analysis of federal environmental policies in terms of each of the three historical threads identified above, summarize their status at the end of 1980, and highlight the complementaries and conflicts among them. Finally, I will identify the primary stated policies of the Reagan administration toward these and related domains and the role of the executive order as an expression and instrument of those policies and compare these policies and instruments to the prior uses of economic analysis in environmental policy that were previously described.

ECONOMICS AND ENVIRONMENTAL DECISIONS

The primary purpose of this chapter is to evaluate Executive Order 12291 in particular and more generally the use of benefit-cost analysis in the environmental regulatory process. To appreciate the role of this executive order, however, and the significance of the particular requirements it imposes for benefit-cost analysis—such as its emphasis on an efficiency test and on the oversight authority of the president's Office of Management and Budget— one must consider it in the light of other uses of benefit-cost analysis both in public investment decisions and in previous applications to regulatory decisions.

The involvement of the federal government in major environmental decisions is not new, nor is the application of economic principles and methods to such decisions. As early as the 1780s and continuously for a century, Congresses debated the prices and other terms on which public lands would be disposed into private ownership, weighing both the economic benefits and the distribution of gains and losses in decisions that would profoundly affect both the physical and social environment of the future nation. Since at least the 1820s, Congresses and presidents have debated the merits of supporting local and regional environmental investments with federal funds—canals, roads, railroads, dams and levees, fish hatcheries, headwater lands for watershed protection, and many others—and in each case, economic arguments have been as prominent as arguments of political equity and substantive environmental preferences. Similar evidence can be found for a vast array of decisions in which the federal government throughout its history has involved itself in shaping environmental conditions. Clearly, many would dispute the quality of these analyses as well as the substantive merits of the decisions. But the point is that the federal government has made major environmental decisions throughout its history and that economic criteria as well as criteria of substantive environmental purposes have been applied to the decisions that have been made.

Four aspects of these decisions, however, are relatively new and are the subject here: the use of formalized economic objectives and procedures for analysis of government decision proposals; the requirement that administrative agencies (rather than the Congress) develop and use these analyses; the application of this requirement to regulatory decisions rather than merely to public investment options; and the use of such requirements as a weapon for oversight and control of regulatory decisions by the president and potentially by the Congress and courts. Even these relatively new elements, however, all predate the Reagan administration in some respects.

Public Investments and Benefit-Cost Analysis

WATER PROJECTS. The use of formal benefit-cost analysis by federal administrative agencies usually is dated to the 1936 Flood Control Act, which mandated that for projects built under its authority, federal investments might be made only if "the benefits, to whomsoever they accrue, exceed the costs."[1] This provision at face value was not operational, but it stimulated a succession of at least nine interagency committees and commissions between 1937 and 1970 to attempt to give it useful meaning.[2]

In principle, "benefits" and "costs" have no absolute meaning: they are simply categories for accounting and evaluating the effects of proposed actions in relation to the actions' intended objectives. If the objective is to increase overall national income, benefits and costs should be measured in economic efficiency; if the objective is to improve the plight of the poor, or to preserve wild areas, or to protect human health or some other objective, benefit-cost analysis can still in principle be used but would measure different benefits and costs. If the real objective is to achieve some mixture of objectives, benefits and costs of each of them must be measured and criteria assigned for weighting or constraining each objective relative to the others.

In practice, however, the interagency committees and especially the Bureau of the Budget (BOB, now OMB) gradually settled upon two key principles that have fundamentally shaped the use of benefit-cost analysis. The first was that national economic efficiency would be used as the sole objective to be maximized in benefit-cost analysis, and the second (consistent with the first) was that only benefits to that objective would be considered in evaluating the merits of water resource projects and programs—not community well-being, not environmental quality, not the alleviation of regional poverty or other purposes, but simply contributions to aggregate national income. Beginning in the early 1950s BOB promulgated a series of intentionally narrow criteria documents[3] to force all water projects to meet high standards of economic efficiency irrespective of their other merits. Although later guidelines spoke in general terms about broader categories of benefits,[4] in practice only demonstrable economic benefits and costs based on market values were included in the analyses.[5] BOB gave preference to projects that had high ratios of these benefits to costs irrespective of any other merits (and for that matter, irrespective of environmental costs as well, a practice that helps to explain why the water agencies were leading initial targets of legal attack after the National Environmental Policy Act [NEPA] was passed in 1969 and became law in 1970).[6]

The initial reasons for these choices stemmed in part from the influence of the new welfare economics, which focused on economic efficiency, and in part from the fact that most of the Depression-era water projects were primarily intended to achieve improvements in national income; efficiency analysis was a legitimate constraint requiring that a class of public works investments purported to provide economic benefits be justified on those grounds. Some professional economists felt (and still feel) that such projects should be built for efficiency reasons alone, leaving other objectives to be achieved in other and more direct ways; and some economists simply preferred to work out the methodological problems of efficiency analysis before tackling the more difficult analysis of other objectives.[7]

The persistence of efficiency as a sole objective, however, especially in the policies of the Bureau of the Budget, stemmed less from initial statutory or intellectual sources than from institutional politics. Water projects intrinsically involve redistributive expenditures—however much they benefit the nation as a whole, which bears their costs, they provide concentrated benefits to particular congressional districts—and therefore have always invited pork-barrel spending, which may differ from presidential priorities in individual cases and violate the budget in the aggregate. Although other projects have the same problems (defense contracts, highways, and sewage treatment plants, for instance), the language of the 1936 Flood Control Act gave BOB a weapon with which it could attempt to discipline this pattern in at least one major and expensive category of investments. Not until 1973, amid the enormous political pressure of the "environmental era," was a revised criteria document issued (by the U.S. Water Resource Council rather than OMB, at Congress's insistence) that established environmental quality as an objective coequal with economic efficiency; and even then, at OMB's insistence, regional development and social well-being were included only as "accounts" for analysis rather than as project objectives.[8] Under the Reagan administration these "principles and standards" have been demoted to the more vague status of "guidelines," and economic efficiency is once again the only official criterion for choice unless a cabinet official grants an exception to this rule.[9]

PROGRAM BUDGETING. In the 1960s, the use of formal economic analytical requirements was extended to a wide range of public investments in addition to water projects. In this case the efficiency objective was not the dominant control mechanism, but once again analytical procedures intended to provide objective methods of economic analysis were instituted for the additional purpose of increasing central oversight and control over agency decisions, and in this case, too, the perception of that second purpose strongly influenced the result.

In the early 1960s, Secretary of Defense Robert McNamara instituted in his department the Planning, Programming, Budgeting system (PPB), an analytical process that centered on major secretarial policy decisions and combined information on explicit military security objectives with projections of the economic costs and effectiveness of alternative means of achieving them. Among the core premises of the system were that such decisions should be made on explicit criteria rather than by compromise; that needs must be related to costs; that top administrators should consider alternatives rather than a single staff recommendation; and that analysis should be open and explicit.[10] The purposes of the system, in short, were to promote better analysis of the costs and effectiveness of defense investments but, more important, to permit more informed decision making by the head of the agency. It was set up by a secretary who clearly believed in analytical decision making, and reports of its value emphasize that factor as essential to what success it had.[11] Its record as an analytical system was mixed, producing some good analyses as well as many poor ones; but it clearly and deliberately served, by putting these analyses in the hands of the secretary, to increase his control over services within his department.

After some five years of the use in the Department of Defense (DOD), the PPB system was extended by presidential order in 1965 to all civil agencies, and the Bureau of the Budget was assigned to lead and monitor this process. In principle, BOB was simply supposed to provide managerial assistance in spreading this new system for departmental decision making. In practice, however, BOB and the president had mandated the system, and BOB was also the chief demander and user of many of the agencies' PPB outputs. For these reasons, as well as the difficulty of implementing a major new decision process throughout government, PPB came to be viewed as a Budget Bureau paperwork routine to force the president's will on departmental programs and budgets.[12] PPB as a system of formal analytical requirements lasted until 1971, when it was officially abandoned and replaced by the more vague slogan "management by objective" (MBO), although some agencies adopted some of its techniques on their own.

PPB was an important demonstration of the value of explicit policy analysis in government decision making and of the feasibility and effectiveness of such analyses in the hands of agency heads who believed in government by explicit objectives, criteria, and analysis of alternative means. Intellectually, it reopened the door to the broader potential of benefit-cost analysis that had been held shut in the water sector by BOB's narrow focus on the efficiency objective, and it nurtured both a literature and a professional community of policy analysts whose effects are still growing.[13] As a mandatory analytical system, however, PPB failed and was abandoned, chiefly because its forced linkage to the oversight and control goals of the president and Budget Bureau conflicted with the analytical priorities that would best serve the agencies' own missions.[14]

BENEFIT-COST ANALYSIS IN PRACTICE. The application of benefit-cost analysis to public investment proposals produced large literatures of both applied analyses and commentary, as well as gradual but uneven (and still highly incomplete) refinement of methods. Despite these efforts, fundamental methods and assumptions remained open to dispute: for instance, what economic effects count as benefits and as costs, which of these are properly attributable to the proposed project, how can they be measured or estimated, what range of alternatives should be considered, how should we value (or how much discount) future benefits and costs, and how should we deal with uncertainty and bias? Despite its attractiveness in principle, therefore, benefit-cost analysis in practice developed as a highly imperfect and manipulable procedure for justifying political decisions and as an instrument for influencing those decisions. On the one hand, it produced information that reduced the legitimacy of the most egregiously inefficient or ineffective proposals; but at the same time it was itself influenced by pressures to justify the vast majority of proposals, lest it threaten too deeply the political consensus among advocates of public investments in Congress, in the agencies, and among the interests that benefit from them. Despite its merits in principle, therefore—and despite substantial growth and refinements in the scholarly literature by economists such as John V. Krutilla, at Resources for the Future—its practice attracted antagonism and distrust, not only from those whose projects were rejected by it but also from those who saw it as justifying—by biased analysis—proposals that should be rejected.[15]

NEPA AND ADMINISTRATIVE REFORM. The narrowness with which benefit-cost analysis was applied through the 1950s and 1960s (especially in the water sector but also in others such as highways and nuclear energy) triggered a groundswell of political opposition, first from regional interests and congressmen whose projects it might block—for instance, many of the large western reclamation projects that relied upon heavy federal subsidies—but later and for different reasons, from ad hoc citizen environmental action groups because of the failure of benefit-cost analysis (BCA) as practiced to count the environmental costs of actions that were purported to be economically efficient or cost-effective. Benefits measurement was expanding rapidly because of the natural incentive for agencies to develop surrogate measures to justify their projects;[16] but the cost side included only the investment costs of capital, operation, and maintenance, not the full social and environmental adverse effects of disrupting existing ecosystems and communities. The very narrowness of BCA criteria that made it an effective weapon against the worst pork-barrel subsidy proposals also made it seem the insensitive villain that ignored environmental and social values displaced by development projects. This result was not inevitable—all the projects suggested for discontinuance on President Carter's celebrated "hit list" in 1977, for instance, were considered poor investments by both economic and environmental criteria—but in the late 1960s the narrow application of BCA and the agencies that practiced it became principal targets of the rising environmental movement.

Two results important to the subject of this chapter came of this political pressure. The first was the Water Resources Council's "Principles and Standards," which explicitly legitimized environmental quality as an objective coequal with economic efficiency. The second and more general was the enactment of the National Environmental Policy Act of 1969 and especially its provision requiring environmental impact statements (EISs) for all major federal actions.[17] These statements were a new form of analytical requirement, binding on all agencies of the federal government and on regulatory decisions as well as public investment and management actions. Like benefit-cost analysis, the EIS was intended to use analytical requirements to control the behavior of administrative agencies. Its authors believed that if the agencies were forced to document in advance all expected consequences of their proposals (rather than only the economic or other mission-oriented justifications) and compare them to alternatives— borrowing the conceptual logic of PPB and practicing "true" benefit-cost analysis in its broadest meaning—then reasonable officials would be led by the force of logic to choose the best options.[18] As safeguards, the law also required that the analyses be circulated for comment to all other affected federal and state agencies and made available to the public with those comments in advance of the proposed decision. An executive agency was created to oversee implementation of the law (the Council on Environmental Quality [CEQ]), though without the budgetary powers of BOB or any equivalent veto authority over agency proposals.

NEPA was a profoundly important vehicle, not just of environmental policy but of decision analysis and administrative procedural reform. It forced explicit analysis of many nonmonetary costs and benefits of government actions and methodological efforts to forecast impacts of alternative proposals before classifying them as benefits or costs. Moreover, it required this analysis for regulatory and management decisions as well as public investments; and although many environmental regulatory actions were exempted (for political rather than intellectually defensible reasons), early court decisions affirmed that all environmental impacts must be reasonably balanced along with economic and other objectives in federal regulatory decisions.[19] One significant but little noted implication of these court decisions was that federal regulatory decisions were increasingly seen simply as one more class of discretionary government actions, analogous to public investments, rather than judgments of rights subject to limited and explicit public criteria.

NEPA was, in short, fully consistent with the intellectual spirit of bene-fit-cost analysis as an approach to the evaluation of government decisions, even as it challenged the narrow practices of BCA and other justification processes that were commonly used at the time.

NEPA's greatest significance in practice, however, was that unlike con-ventional monetary BCA and cost-effectiveness analysis, it served as an instrument of popular rather than executive control over agency decisions. The driving force for its implementation was its public disclosure require-ment and associated threat of litigation, which forced agencies to seek early input from and negotiations with all potentially affected parties.[20] Whereas Secretary McNamara intended PPB to substitute objective criteria for ad hoc compromises, the EIS process forced comprehensive coordina-tion and compromise among all affected interests rather than optimization of defined missions by each agency. The result was a major shift in admin-istrative decision processes toward increasing responsiveness to the poten-tial victims of government decisions—equalizing their access to adminis-trative processes that were already heavily influenced by potential beneficiaries[21]—but it also epitomized the problem foreseen by Arthur Maass in which multiple-purpose planning (emphasizing the products of decisions) was overdeveloped as a poor substitute for multiple-objective planning (emphasizing the social justifications for decisions).[22]

SUMMARY. In both water project analysis and PPB, its principal homes in the U.S. government before 1970, benefit-cost analysis developed pre-dominantly in the context of public investment project analysis, and that development was fostered in each case primarily by executive oversight agencies as a means not only of better analysis for its own sake but of presidential and secretarial control over agency decision processes and their bureaucratic and congressional advocates. An important side effect of this history was that the application of benefit-cost analysis to public deci-sions developed in narrower and more rigid patterns—oriented to the paperwork requirements and political control objectives of oversight agen-cies—than required by law, warranted by economic theory, or appropriate to most government decisions.

The environmental analysis requirements of NEPA emerged in part as a challenge to this narrow pattern, as well as to the older justification prac-tices of the federal "mission" agencies themselves. Philosophically consis-tent with benefit-cost analysis, these requirements both greatly expanded the scope of the analytical process and applied it to regulatory decisions as well as public investments, making the EIS an important and direct ancestor of the Regulatory Impact Analysis requirement of Executive Order 12291. In practice, however, it differed from previous BCA requirements in serving ad hoc public accountability rather than executive management control.

In light of this history, today's requirements for regulatory decision analysis must be evaluated not only with respect to their nominal objectives of analytical explicitness and reasoned choice but also with respect to other purposes and uses in practice, including their possible bias toward economic efficiency over other legitimate objectives and their use to achieve the different and possibly conflicting objectives of presidential power and control.

The Revolution in Social Regulation

A second historical context for economic analysis of environmental decisions is the language of environmental and related regulatory statutes. Before 1970 the federal government had only a few relatively narrowly defined regulatory roles related to health, safety, and environmental quality: it directly regulated aspects of foods, drugs, cosmetics, pesticides, and radiation, and it provided a few incentives—widely viewed as ineffective—to encourage state regulation of air and water quality. In the main its regulatory activities were directed to pricing by natural monopolies and other explicitly economic practices (for instance, in transportation, communications, hydropower, trade practices, and securities transactions), and what environmental policies it had were set through public investment programs (such as those discussed above) and public land management activities.

Beginning in 1970, the federal government entered a decade of dramatic expansion of regulatory authorities to protect health, safety, and environmental quality, involving more than a dozen major new regulatory statutes and a large number of regulations of particular substances and processes pursuant to those laws. Table 2.1 summarizes the most important of these laws.[23] A few of them were relatively straightforward expansions of existing mandates, such as the Federal Environmental Pesticide Control Act of 1972 (FEPCA), which toughened the existing federal insecticide, fungicide, and rodenticide acts. Most, however, included new and dramatic changes in both the scope and the means of federal regulatory control. The Clean Air Act Amendments of 1970 (CAA), for instance, established national ambient air quality standards for the first time, based on health criteria, and set deliberately "technology-forcing" statutory timetables for meeting them; it also created a federal approval process to regulate state implementation of these standards and a permit process for all new sources of air pollution. The Federal Water Pollution Control Act Amendments of 1972 (FWPCAA) similarly required federal permits for all new water pollution sources and again used technology-based standards—"best practicable" and "best available" technologies—as norms to force uniform pollution reduction by all firms in each industry. The Toxic Substances Control Act (TSCA) required premanufacturing notification to EPA for all new chemical substances and potentially substantial increases in toxicity testing for some of them. The Occupational Safety and Health Act (OSHA) authorized government to require potentially costly controls over a vast range of workplace health hazards. Other laws, such as the Resource Conservation and Recovery Act (RCRA) regulating hazardous waste management, regulated not only other activities but also—perhaps most significantly—other facets of many of the same activities, especially in basic materials processing industries such as chemicals, petroleum, iron and steel, pulp and paper, textiles, and metal finishing.

It is important that economic concepts and arguments were heavily used from the start in the deliberations that led to most of these laws and regulations. The first annual report of the U.S. Council on Environmental Quality, for instance, identified misplaced economic incentives as a primary cause of most environmental problems: pollution reflected the economic "externality" of using air and water as unpriced factors of production for waste disposal, ignoring the costs thereby imposed upon others, and pollution also had real economic effects such as increased medical and cleaning bills, reduced agricultural yields, and lost opportunities for recreation businesses.[24] The arguments leading to these laws included frequent references to the interpretation of environmental problems—advocated by at least one group of economists for over a decade but newly popularized to a more general audience—as economic efficiency problems, that is, as market failures caused by externalities involving the unpriced common-property resources of air and water.[25] Many other arguments were also used, of course—that government problems were caused by overpopulation, blind introduction of damaging technologies, ignorance and shortsightedness, or simply individual or corporate greed—but the conceptual model of economic efficiency became a dominant interpretive paradigm from the start for much of the debate over environmental regulations and continued so throughout the "environmental decade" of the 1970s. The economic costs of pollution and of pollution abatement were discussed explicitly and at length in every one of the first twelve CEQ annual reports and were the subject of entire chapters in seven of them.[26] Persistent themes

Table 2.1. Major New Federal Laws Regulating Health, Safety, and
Environmental Quality, 1970–1980*

Name	Year
National Environmental Policy Act	1970
Clean Air Act Amendments	1970, 1974, 1977
Occupational Safety and Health Act	1970
Federal Water Pollution Control Act Amendments	1972, 1977
Marine Protection Research and Sanctuaries Act (ocean dumping)	1972, 1974
Federal Environmental Pesticide Control Act	1972, 1975
Consumer Product Safety Act	1972, 1976
Noise Control Act	1972, 1978
Safe Drinking Water Act	1974, 1977
Hazardous Materials Transportation Act	1975
Toxic Substances Control Act	1976
Resource Conservation and Recovery Act	1976
Surface Mine Conservation and Reclamation Act	1980
Comprehensive Environmental Response, Compensation and Liability Act	1980

*Not including several additional major laws, primarily regulatory activities in public lands:
the Endangered Species Act (1973, 1978), Resources Planning Act (1974), National Forest
Management Act (1976), and Federal Lands Policy and Management Act (1976) and others
less regulatory in their approach such as the Coastal Zone Management Act (1972).

in these chapters, which included annual quantitative estimates of the
incremental costs of pollution abatement expenditures necessitated by federal regulation, were that even the minimum estimable cost impacts of
pollution were severe; that the cost impacts of abatement were measurable
but not severe, being less than 2.5 percent of GNP and less than historic
wage increases and in any case less than the estimated economic benefits of
pollution abatement; and that the adverse effects of abatement costs on
inflation, productivity, and plant closings were at most 0.5 percent, far less
than the exaggerated claims being made by industry in the press. It is fair to
say that many of these estimates on all sides were little more than guess-
work, but their presence in the reports at all indicates the importance of
potential economic effects in the minds of those who framed and executed
the environmental statutes.

Despite this climate of economic reasoning, the laws varied widely in
the extent to which they incorporated economic objectives and analytical
requirements into their provisions.[27] Nearly all of them required some sort
of "balancing" by the regulatory agency of health/safety/environmental
quality objectives to be achieved against the costs of achieving them.[28] The

very diversity of laws with which each agency must comply also necessitated balancing as a practical response to sometimes inconsistent mandates. The degree of discretion given to the agencies, however, depended upon the specific laws enacted by the Congress and varied widely from statute to statute.

In some regulatory statutes, for instance (such as the Federal Insecticide, Fungicide, and Rodenticide Act [FIFRA] and the Toxic Substances Control Act [TSCA]), consideration of economic effects and requirements to balance regulatory benefits against costs was explicit from the start, either as discretionary authority to guide administrative judgment or as a requirement. In others, however (such as OSHA), economics was included only as a feasibility constraint: whole industries should not be regulated out of business, but short of that result all workers must be provided safe and healthful work environments. A similar approach is manifested in the "best practicable technology" approach of the air and water quality statutes. In still other laws, statutory standards were established as absolute constraints irrespective of costs; the most familiar example is the 1962 Delaney Amendment to the Food, Drug and Cosmetics Act, which prohibited the use of any animal carcinogen in any quantity as a food additive. The Clean Air Act precludes consideration of economic costs in establishing national ambient air standards and a few other circumstances, though it permits them to be considered in most other decisions.[29] They also enter in through subtle technical decisions, such as how a standard and its related monitoring requirements will actually be defined, as, for example, a twenty-four-hour, daily high, or annual average.

A central issue in the use of regulatory analysis requirements such as under Executive Order 12291, therefore, is the extent to which the Congress intended, in each statute conferring regulatory authority, to delegate discretion to the agency to balance health, safety, and environmental quality norms against economic or other costs. A subsidiary issue is whether it intended such balancing to reflect economic efficiency, in the correct meaning of that term as a societywide increase of benefits over costs, or to reflect some cruder political weighing of expected benefits to statutory mission against costs to the regulated parties. In cases for which Congress authorized discretionary balancing, Regulatory Impact Analysis in principle provides an instrument for documenting the criteria and reasoning used to strike that balance and thus for justifying such decisions to the public as well as to the president, the Congress, and the courts. In cases when the Congress set particular objectives, standards, criteria, or priorities by statute, however, the use of such analyses has in practice raised questions as to whether the agencies (and the president) were exceeding their authority by reweighing a balance already established by legislation.

Because of these statutory mandates, EPA and some other federal regulatory agencies conducted benefit-cost "balancing" analyses of one sort or another for some years before any of the several presidential orders that mandated them for executive oversight purposes. EPA, for instance, began sponsoring studies of the economic effects of pollution and of its remedies immediately upon its creation in 1970 (*The Economics of Clean Air, The Economics of Clean Water*); by 1972 it had produced studies of the economic effects of pollution abatement compliance on a series of at least fourteen especially affected industries including automobiles, electric generators, petroleum, pulp and paper, and metals.[30] Through the 1970s it continued to sponsor studies of the macroeconomic and microeconomic effects of its regulations; and at least one retrospective study in the late 1970s showed that although both EPA and industry studies tended to overestimate compliance costs, EPA's estimates were considerably closer to the actual outcomes.[31] By June 1979 EPA had produced or sponsored some 427 economic analyses, most of them focusing on particular industries or plant closings with an emphasis on the cost of regulation.[32]

The actual substance of this balancing, however—the methods and procedures, assumptions, and data used, the explicitness of the analytical process, and the quality as well as the content of the result—varied widely from one agency and even one analysis to another. Under mandates from diverse statutes reflecting different objectives and degrees of discretion, and lacking any consistent statutory procedures or assumptions, each agency developed its own procedures for striking the balances called for by its statutes, with little coordination among them either on substantive priorities or on methodology. Even in EPA, moreover, economic analysis was primarily a flank-protection strategy against potential business attacks; relatively little was done on benefits analysis by EPA until the late 1970s, and at no time did economists hold central policy-making roles in the agency.

This unevenness of practice, coupled with the rapid and open-ended growth of federal regulation itself, triggered counterpressures from the business community not only against particular regulations but for "regulatory reform"; for stronger oversight and control of federal "social" regulation as a whole; and on the part of some, for regulatory "relief."

Regulatory Reform

The scholarly literature on government regulation for many years has included a strong regulatory reform theme, embracing from economics the principles that regulation tends to create barriers to entry and thus distort market processes and from political science the thesis that regulatory agencies tend to be co-opted by the regulated industries into providing special privileges for them (such as barriers to newcomers' entry). This literature, however, was devoted to federal economic regulation, government supervision of such sectors as transportation and communications pricing, public utilities, and securities and trade practices; little attention was devoted to health, safety, and environmental regulation, probably because before 1970 there was so little of it. By the 1970s these various writings were approaching a rough consensus that many economic regulations favored the regulated industries at the expense of consumers and of the public interest in general and that such regulations should therefore be reformed or eliminated. Even as federal social regulation was entering its period of expansive growth, therefore, the idea of regulatory reform was gathering momentum toward the reduction of other forms of federal regulation; and although the principles and issues involved were different, the distinction was often ignored.

The health, safety, and environmental regulatory laws enacted in the 1970s staked out a new domain of federal regulatory authority that was probably without precedent in its breadth except for wartime economic controls. These laws were supported both by bipartisan popular consensus and by arguments from the mainstream economic literature of externalities and other market failures.[33] Little formal analysis, however, was devoted by the statute writers to the relative costs and effectiveness of alternative means of regulation. The welfare economics literature of around 1970 addressed only the efficiency justification for government intervention to correct market failures; it did not point out corresponding "government failures" whose costs might equal or exceed those of the market failures.[34]

Moreover, the political consensus favoring regulatory expansion arose in part from a widespread perception that business was simply avoiding compliance with existing state laws, voluntary measures, and other approaches short of enforceable federal mandates.[35] Accordingly, the major environmental laws of the early 1970s—especially the Clean Air Act Amendments of 1970, Occupational Safety and Health Act, and Federal Water Pollution Control Act Amendments of 1972—deliberately emphasized minimum federal standards as the criterion and uniform technological controls as the means of achieving national health and environmental quality objectives. Although some balancing was required, this balancing in most cases represented not economic efficiency per se but goal maximization subject to a feasibility constraint. It also represented "speculative augmentation,"[36] the deliberate use of technology-forcing standards and deadlines to spur innovation in abatement beyond currently feasible technology—by how much could not be known at the time.

Not only federal social regulation as a whole, therefore, but technology-based standards in particular represented a major new departure for U.S. policy making. Such standards necessitated that complex technical value judgments about each industrial process be made by a federal agency, in effect attempting to duplicate each industry's expertise in order to second-guess it. Because they resulted in uniform technology requirements, more-over, they also inevitably caused new inefficiencies by ignoring variations among both individual plants and their environmental settings; in effect, they reduced enforcement costs but raised compliance costs. Interestingly, technology-based standards have been England's approach to air pollution control for more than a century, with moderate success.[37] As a major change in U.S. policies, however, they came under immediate and continuing attack by both businesses and academic economists, who urged that they be recast to work more flexibly through market incentives. The results of this regulatory reform movement included both specific changes in several regulatory approaches (particularly by EPA) and a general increase in the analysis of alternative means of regulation and their economic effects.

ECONOMIC VIEWS OF REGULATION. Economists from the start generally approved of the apparent ends but disapproved of the means of federal environmental regulation. Its purpose in their view was to remedy market imperfections that patently existed and thus to improve the efficiency of the economy. To do so, however, its means should first be subjected to benefit-cost analysis, as for any public investment, to be sure that efficiency would be improved,[38] and regulations should be designed to create incentives for "optimal" pollution reduction to the efficient point rather than rapid reduction across the board and not reducing it more than justified by the expected benefits. A barrage of economic opinion articles in the early 1970s therefore urged that technology-based standards be replaced by effluent charges or taxes per unit of discharge, generally ignoring or discounting the (probably equal) political and administrative difficulties of the latter.[39] As the difficulties with this approach were raised, similar studies urged instead the creation of "marketable rights" to pollute air or water up to a given standard, ignoring the implications of thus vesting private rights to degrade the public's air or water.[40] Critics of occupational safety and health regulations similarly urged the use of information requirements (such as hazard labeling) and voluntary personal protection devices (such as dust masks) rather than requiring expensive new technological systems in the workplace.[41]

In the annual reports of the Council on Environmental Quality one can also see a clear shift of emphasis over the decade concerning economics and the environment. The 1970 report stressed the role of misplaced economic incentives in causing pollution and advocated strict and clear enforcement of standards; economic incentives (such as effluent and emissions charges) should be demonstrated and evaluated but should be used in conjunction with enforceable standards rather than as a substitute for them.[42] The 1971 report stated flatly that "property rights do not extend to the right of individuals and firms to pollute air and water," that no one has a license to befoul the amenities and property rights of others, that such befouling amounts to a taking of public property, and that the responsibility for cleanup lies with the discharger; but just five pages later, it articulated a benefit-cost balancing approach to regulation of such activities. It reiterated, however, the centrality of standards and enforcement, with economic incentives as supplementary measures.[43]

By 1973, however, the Ford administration's first report discussed not only pollution damage and abatement costs but also "avoidance costs" and "transaction costs" (the costs of research, planning, monitoring, and enforcement to achieve abatement). Although it noted the problem that these various costs are borne by different parties, it nevertheless asserted that the goal of policy was simply to minimize the total of the four types of costs— a pure efficiency concept.[44] The 1975 report added the observation that existing federal laws had the principal effect of reducing damage and avoidance costs by increasing abatement and transaction costs, not necessarily reducing the sum of all four.[45]

In 1976 a further shift of emphasis occurred, with the assertion that the costs of abatement "might be very high if national standards and rapid timetables were rigorously enforced for all emitters," especially in some individual industries and communities; it recommended ameliorating this problem by flexibility in setting and enforcing abatement regulations to consider the special characteristics of individual emitters.[46] This statement apparently grew out of the rising concern that some regulations, if uniformly imposed, would cause some great expenditures for little benefit, and it was thus intended to underscore again the efficiency objective. But the same flexibility that was intended to increase efficiency opened a major avenue for special pleading by particular polluters who would inevitably identify their own business positions with the overall efficiency of the economy.

Finally, the 1979 report explicitly adopted the ideas of the regulatory reform economists that all environmental regulations should reflect a balancing of rewards against economic dislocations; that enforcement of uniform standards even in theory denies opportunities for cost savings; and that because it is uneconomical to require identical cutbacks from all polluters, instead the largest cutbacks should be required from those who can achieve them most cheaply.[47] Economic incentives such as effluent charges or marketable permits were now suggested as possible substitutes for standards; the frame of reference was now trade-offs among goals rather than justice among individuals, the balancing of costs and benefits rather than the clarification of rights and duties.

In short, the official literature of the 1970s documents a gradual but clear shift, in the name of regulatory reform, from initial concepts of efficiency as forcing polluters to internalize their costs so as to protect public air and water resources, to a system that vested private rights in the existing standards and allowed flexible enforcement and private trading in order to avoid disrupting normal business growth and change while incrementally approaching those standards. The price of reducing administrative costs and political pressures was administrative acceptance of the idea of "licenses to pollute" that had been so vigorously opposed when the statutes were debated.[48] Even these measures purported to improve efficiency held dangers for analysis, however, for although some regulations did require expensive remedies for arguably small benefits, some of the pressures for reform were not strictly favoring efficiency for its own sake but seeking individual relief from onerous deadlines. The balancing process thus risked becoming less an effort to achieve socioeconomic efficiency as a whole and more simply a crude political balancing of often unquantifiable benefits against the claims of costs and unfairness and ensuing pleas for flexibility by the regulated firms.

REGULATORY REFORM IN EPA. From the early 1970s on, EPA in particular experimented with economic incentives as instruments of regulatory policy; but the responses to these initiatives generally reinforced their use to ease the bite of the laws rather than to achieve their full purposes. Effluent charge proposals were repeatedly introduced into Congress but never enacted, and when EPA sought to reduce urban automotive air pollution by parking surcharges, the Congress blocked it.[49] On the other hand, EPA's promotion of more lenient economic incentives in application of the laws, such as "offsets," "bubbles," and controlled trading of emission rights under the Clean Air Act, was welcomed and partially ratified by the 1977 amendments to the Clean Air Act.[50]

These latter regulatory reforms arose in part from principle but also from the reality of confrontation, as abatement deadlines approached, between statutory demands for environmental cleanup and political demands for business expansion in areas that did not meet the statutory standards, especially, for instance, in southern California and old industrial cities. The "bubble" allowed each firm to trade off abatement investments between low-cost and high-cost pollution sources at the same site, in effect allowing the firm to meet a performance standard rather than a technology standard. The offsets policy allowed "trading" of emissions among different sites and firms so long as the firm that increased pollution obtained—presumably for a price—equal or greater offsetting reductions in pollution from an existing firm in the same area.[51] The effect was to avoid a freeze on new economic activity in the area (and thus a confrontation that might lead to weakening the law itself) and to reduce pollution at least somewhat, but far more incrementally than had the law been enforced outright.

The Carter administration made regulatory reform a major initiative, emphasizing the use of innovative regulatory techniques as alternatives to traditional command-and-control regulation. These techniques included marketable rights, economic incentives through fees or subsidies, and performance rather than technology standards as well as others.[52] In January 1979 EPA revised its emission offsets policy to allow not only offset trading per se but also "banking" of offsets—receiving "credit" for "excess" pollution reduction below a standard, which could later be used for the firm's own expansion or sold to other firms.[53] The effect was further to confirm the establishment of private, marketable rights to pollute up to the standards then in existence. EPA also developed proposals such as fleet-averaging of emissions compliance for mobile sources (the "mobile bubble"), noncompliance penalties to tax away the profitability of noncompliance, and voluntary labeling rather than direct regulation of noisy products.[54] Most of these proposals, although labeled regulatory reforms, also had the effect of regulatory relaxation in that they allowed businesses to comply flexibly with those requirements that could be satisfied most cheaply.

Along with these specific techniques of regulation, the Carter administration intensified the application of benefit-cost analysis to them and to their alternatives within EPA. Unlike PPB and the EIS, these applications of BCA were introduced not primarily as an instrument of executive or public oversight but by the agency itself to demonstrate the effectiveness of such reforms in reducing industrial compliance costs.[55] Like public investment analyses, they tended to be partial analyses used to justify and promote particular action proposals.

SUMMARY. By the time of Ronald Reagan's election as president in 1980, the EPA already had under way both a substantial program of regulatory reform initiatives to substitute economic incentives and marketable rights for direct regulation and enforcement, as urged by economists, and at least a rudimentary program of economic analysis to evaluate the costs and benefits, and effects on business, of alternative regulatory techniques. It can be argued that these techniques reflected a shift of philosophy that eroded the environmental goals established in the statutes; it can also be argued that some of those goals were speculative and ultimately unrealistic, their means costly and sometimes ineffective, and that the history of regulatory reform was therefore a reasonable accommodation with the reality of achieving half-loaves rather than none. The point here, however, is simply that these programs were already well under way long before the election of 1980 or Executive Order 12291.

Executive Oversight

From the public point of view, the expansion of social regulation by the federal government was a welcome and popular phenomenon. Its apparent benefits flowed mainly to the public in the form of a perception that the quality of life was being better protected; its costs were concentrated in a few sectors of business and industry, which had always been unpopular symbols of concentrated economic wealth and which were in any case the causes of the hazards regulated.

From those industries' point of view, however, the explosive growth of regulation not only inflicted unwelcome (if legitimate) costs of remedying past externalities but created new and serious externalities of their own. By 1977 there were some seventeen "social" regulatory agencies, the aggregate budgets of which nearly quintupled (from $1.5 billion to an estimated $7.3 billion) from 1970 to 1977; in the same period the annual number of pages in the *Federal Register*, which announces all federal rules and regulations, approximately tripled.[56] Some regulations included large and expensive margins of safety, either to hedge against unknown hazards or in some cases simply to satisfy political pressures (or to provide "bargaining chips" against future counterpressures). Some were frustratingly rigid, preventing businesses from using cheaper means even to achieve mutually accepted ends. All of them increased the overhead costs of reporting, monitoring, legal defense, and dealing with government and the public generally. Perhaps most important, regulation as a whole was increasingly unpredictable: many of the regulations were set at different times for different purposes yet affected the same basic industrial processes, so that inconsistencies among them confused compliance expectations and changes or new regulations might easily negate expensive capital investments undertaken to comply with previous ones.

Even as the regulatory revolution was beginning in 1970, therefore, the business community began mobilizing counterpressures not only against particular regulations but for tighter control over regulation as a whole, and through the 1970s each successive administration incrementally increased the level of such control.

QUALITY OF LIFE (QOL) REVIEWS. President Richard Nixon in 1970 established not only the Environmental Protection Agency but also a National Industrial Pollution Control Council (NIPCC) under the Department of Commerce. This council was composed exclusively of business leaders, and its meetings, in defiance of federal laws governing public access and advisory committees, were closed to nonmembers. In 1971, the Office of Management and Budget directed that all proposed "quality of life" regulations—regulations affecting health, safety, or environmental quality—be sent to OMB for review by other affected agencies before they were made public even in draft form for review and comment. Some such coordination process might well have been appropriate, given the cross-impacts of regulations noted above, had it been clearly intended to solve coordination problems through a publicly accountable procedure, especially because the just-enacted NEPA was providing such welcome public coordination of conflicting agency decisions of other sorts. As it was handled, however, OMB's directive originated with its environmental budget staff, who reviewed EPA's expanding regulatory mandate primarily as a threat to the budget; and it was widely perceived as a back-door avenue for business influence, using executive oversight to allow covert industry pressure on regulatory proposals through NIPCC before the public had equal opportunity to be heard. NIPCC was terminated in 1971 by congressional elimination of its budget; the QOL review process formally ended in January 1977, when Acting EPA Administrator John Quarles announced that the agency would no longer be bound by OMB's directive,[57] but by that time other instruments of executive oversight through analytical requirements were already in place.

COWPS AND INFLATION IMPACT STATEMENTS. President Gerald Ford's administration was dominated by the issues of inflation and recession, focused (and partially triggered) by the dramatic rise in oil prices at the time of the Arab oil embargo but rippling thence across the entire economy. To President Ford, curing these twin economic problems and seeking "energy independence" took precedence over virtually all other domestic issues. His "Whip Inflation Now" campaign and its "WIN" buttons symbolized this priority. Two major initiatives in this period were the creation by the Congress of a new Council on Wage and Price Stability (COWPS) in the Executive Office of the President and the requirement by the administration of an inflation impact statement (IIS) for every major legislative proposal, rule, or regulation recommended by federal administrative agencies. COWPS was created in August 1974, primarily to monitor private-sector actions that might add to inflation but also to review the activities and programs of the federal government to discover whether they had any inflationary impact.[58] The council's members were the secretaries of the principal economic agencies (Agriculture, Commerce, Labor, and Treasury), plus the director of OMB and the president's economic adviser.

From the outset, COWPS interpreted its mandate as requiring benefit-cost analyses of important regulatory actions. In its view, no single regulation would measurably affect aggregate indicators of inflation such as the consumer price index; so it simply asserted that any government regulation that generated benefits greater than costs was anti-inflationary (that is, it added to the aggregate supply of goods and services), whereas any regulation that did the opposite was by definition inflationary, and that, in addition, any regulation that was not cost-effective was to be defined as inflationary even if its benefits exceeded its costs.[59]

In November 1974 President Ford issued an executive order that required an inflation impact statement for every major rule or regulation and authorized OMB to develop criteria and oversee its implementation; OMB was also authorized to delegate responsibilities to COWPS.[60] OMB in turn—this time its management staff rather than the budget staff who had developed the QOL review process—issued a directive implementing the executive order, which charged each agency to develop its own IIS criteria and evaluative procedures within existing budget and personnel resources but subject to approval by OMB and COWPS.[61] In a memo of June 1975, OMB also established a numerical threshold of $100 million per year to define "major" regulations requiring an IIS.[62]

The IIS was clearly borrowed, in concept, from the environmental impact statement required by NEPA, and it shared the philosophy of seeking to influence administrative decisions by means of analytical documentation requirements. Its substantive intent, however, was clearly to reassert the influence of economic considerations in regulatory decisions whose primary emphasis had been health, safety, and environmental quality.

Moreover, its mechanism, like the QOL reviews but unlike the EIS, was once again internal oversight pressure rather than public debate: OMB and the agencies did not require the IIS and background analytical documents to be included in the decision record, or subject to public disclosure and judicial review, and a 1975 court decision confirmed that the IIS was simply "a managerial tool for implementing the President's personal economic policies and not . . . a legal framework enforceable by private civil action."[63] Not even the IIS criteria were published in the *Federal Register*, and according to COWPS's general counsel this low profile was deliberate policy to avoid the potential for judicial review that exists for EISs.[64] This policy removed key issues of methodology and assumptions—definition of costs and benefits, discount rate, and valuation of intangible benefits, for instance—from public scrutiny.

Under the COWPS statute and the IIS requirement, virtually all federal regulatory agencies came under the executive oversight authority of COWPS and OMB, and a small group of economists reviewed newly proposed regulations and commented on them. COWPS reviews under its own statutory authority normally were filed during the regular comment period as part of the agency's public decision record; but it also participated in selective off-the-record reviews under the IIS procedure and in response to requests by the Council of Economic Advisers and other aides to the president.[65] These oversight processes were direct forerunners of the system established by President Reagan's EO 12291, differing most significantly, first, in that they gave OMB or COWPS authority only to review and comment on regulations and their supporting analyses, not to compel or reject them; and second, that they did not establish efficiency as the criterion for regulatory decisions but only as a more explicit influence on those decisions.

In practice, COWPS not only commented on proposed regulations but intervened aggressively in agency proceedings to press its views on potentially inflationary impacts. In its most positive light, it thus generated a healthy creative tension with the agencies, raising questions and alternative assumptions that could, over time, improve the quality of analysis and ultimately of decisions. But it also created a time-consuming new review process that added to the agencies' administrative burdens and delayed them in their already understaffed implementation of statutory mandates (by 1978, for instance, OSHA had managed to promulgate only ten environmental health standards and EPA was also far behind statutory and court-ordered schedules for issuing many regulations).

Most important, like QOL reviews before it, the motives and objectives of the IIS process were distrusted. Was its bottom line really better analysis and more cost-effective pursuance of the agencies' missions, or was it a White House "thumb on the scale" weakening those missions? COWPS never produced a consistent methodology and criteria for IIS analysis but instead intervened by ad hoc critiques of agency proposals, using methods and assumptions that were no less arbitrary than the agencies' own. To its credit, it brought a new level of professionalism to White House oversight and a willingness to file its comments in the public record. But its critiques were done solely by economists, who had no particular expertise about nor demonstrated concern for the substantive objectives of the regulations in question, and by economists as part of an Executive Office staff whose objectives were inevitably to achieve the economic and political priorities of the White House rather than the particular balances of social benefits and costs mandated to the regulatory agencies by diverse statutes.

The record of the COWPS/IIS reviews is thus mixed. Most commentators conclude that the process had limited effect on agencies' decisions; but despite a wide variety of "guarded criticisms," the IIS was continued (renamed "economic impact statements") by a second executive order through the end of 1977.[66]

REGULATORY ANALYSIS, RARG, AND THE REGULATORY COUNCIL. President Jimmy Carter inherited not only the continued pressure to reduce inflation but also a rising tide of orchestrated business pressures to control and reduce federal regulations, asserting (in full-page newspaper and magazine attacks) vast costs to every family and small business from "government over-regulation" and "regulatory overkill."[67] In response, he not only continued the regulatory oversight instruments created during the Ford administration but carried them further with both a new executive order and two new oversight bodies, the Regulatory Analysis Review Group and the Regulatory Council.

President Carter's executive order of March 1978 required all agencies to prepare a "regulatory analysis" for every proposed regulation that would either cost the economy over $100 million per year or cause a "major" price increase in any industry, level of government, or geographic area; the agency must also discuss the economic consequences of alternative approaches and justify the option selected.[68] As under President Ford, OMB was directed to ensure effective implementation. In effect, this order not only ratified both OMB's previous oversight role and its threshold for defining "major" regulations; it also greatly expanded its authority to specify the content of regulatory analyses, to trigger the analysis on the basis of special hardship pleadings from particular industries and regions, and perhaps most significant, to require and review a detailed explanation of the actual balancing process that led the agency to choose each regulation over alternatives. This executive order gave much greater emphasis both to general standards, timetables, public accountability, and refinement of methods and to broader beneficial and adverse consequences than merely "inflationary impact." It also gave considerably broadened discretion to OMB to shape agency use of analysis. It thus came close to that of President Reagan, except in three crucial respects: it still did not attempt to establish economic efficiency as the explicit criterion for the agencies' decisions, it did not give OMB explicit authority to override the agencies, and it did require the agencies to publish their regulatory analysis procedures in the *Federal Register* for public review and comment.

At the same time he issued this executive order, President Carter created the Regulatory Analysis Review Group to review a limited number of regulatory analyses that might be especially costly, precedent-setting, or overlapping or conflicting with those of other agencies; it was chaired by the chairman of the Council of Economic Advisers, and its members included representatives of most of the executive branch agencies having either regulatory or economic functions. Its staff support was provided by the COWPS staff, thus continuing and further ratifying the oversight role of that agency[69] while targeting its effort selectively on ten to twenty major regulations per year rather than spreading it across all regulatory proposals. Its reviews were filed in the agencies' public records and could include dissenting opinions by RARG members.

The creation of RARG did not formally change the ultimate authority of the agencies to reach regulatory decisions, but informally it could exert heavy pressure on them, first, because it spoke with the authority of the Office of the President, and second, because it added to that authority the peer pressure of the other RARG members, the fellow agency heads of the other economic and regulatory agencies. Like COWPS before and alongside it, RARG did not develop a uniform policy for dealing with methodology and assumptions, and in practice these differed with the preferences of each staff analyst. In practice, too, its reviews exhibited persistent ideological preferences favoring "performance standards over design standards, incremental economic incentives over standards enforced by fixed penalties, and individual choice over government dictated outcomes, . . . [and opposing the use of social regulation to alter] the economic status quo . . . either [by] redistributing income or [by] impairing the economic status of regulated firms to solve a health, safety, or environmental problem."[70]

On the other hand, the strength of its influence depended heavily on continuing interest and emphasis by the president, an emphasis that was not in fact sustained. After a serious public embarrassment in 1978 over White House intervention in OSHA's cotton dust regulations, the president signaled that RARG was to "kibitz" rather than threaten superregulation by presidential override. By 1979 RARG had examined only nine of forty eligible proposals.[71]

In October 1978 in the wake of the cotton dust issue, President Carter created a separate and additional organization called the U.S. Regulatory Council, chaired by EPA Administrator Douglas Costle and including thirty-six executive branch and independent regulatory agencies. In contrast to RARG, whose mission was to serve as reviewer and thus adversary of selected regulations, the council's mission was to initiate positive steps at regulatory improvement: to coordinate regulatory programs, eliminate duplication and gaps, produce a semiannual calendar of regulations in progress, and provide a vehicle for developing common policies across agencies on cross-cutting regulatory issues (for instance, regulation of chemical carcinogens).[72] It was, in short, to provide visible leadership for President Carter's commitment to regulatory reform but also to restore positive initiative to the regulatory agencies themselves against the adversary pressures of RARG and COWPS.

OTHER CONTROL PROPOSALS. Presidential oversight through benefit-cost analysis was not, of course, the only way to control government regulation, and a wide range of others were debated and some enacted in the late 1970s. One other executive control instrument was the Paperwork Reduction Act of 1980, which gave OMB broad new powers to control the amount of paperwork inflicted by federal agencies on citizens and businesses. In reality, the tax forms of the Internal Revenue Service dwarf virtually all other paperwork requirements in aggregate; but the oversight authority given to OMB by this law further expanded its power over regulatory proposals as well because most regulations are implemented through reporting and recordkeeping requirements.[73]

The Regulatory Flexibility Act of 1981 sought to impose further requirements on agencies. As part of the analysis of regulations, this act required consideration of the effects on small entities—firms, organizations, or jurisdictions—so as to gauge whether disproportionately severe economic effects are being imposed on them. It, too, was delegated to OMB to implement.

Another executive control, proposed (and authorized in principle by EO 12291) but not implemented, was to establish "regulatory budgets" setting the maximum economic impact each regulatory agency could impose in a given year. This proposal was advanced by several well-placed policy scholars, one of whom became President Reagan's OMB staff director for regulatory affairs, but because of unresolved conceptual and methodological questions (as well as political and constitutional ones) it did not gather much momentum.[74]

Three forms of legislative control were also debated and in part adopted. One was to permit legislative vetoes of proposed regulations, either by one or both Houses or committees thereof. This idea was enacted in several environmental statutes (and many others) but was struck down by the Supreme Court in June 1983 as an unconstitutional breach of the separation of powers, and what if anything will replace it is unclear.[75] A second was so-called "sunset laws" that would terminate regulatory authorities on particular dates and thus trigger mandatory congressional review and reauthorization if they were to continue. This procedure has become relatively widely used, and although it has increased both the legislative work load and the frequency with which divisive issues must be reargued, it is constitutionally sound and probably desirable. A third is simply to require regulatory analysis by statute and accountable to the Congress rather than merely to the president; this proposal shares many of the practical and methodological problems of the present system, although accountability to the Congress would have different and perhaps preferable constitutional consequences (though in some forms it might simply ratify in legislation the expansive oversight power of OMB).[76]

Finally, legislation has been proposed to intensify judicial oversight of regulatory decision making by directing the courts to review each case on the merits of its decision record without deference to the agency's discretion or presumed expertise, thus forcing the agencies from a different direction to build an ironclad decision record in support of any regulatory proposal. This proposal has not been enacted but may still be under consideration.[77]

SUMMARY. As federal regulation for health, safety, and environmental quality expanded through the 1970s, so did demands for oversight and control of it, partly because of legitimate problems of excesses, rigidities, and inconsistencies, partly because of the costly and frustrating unpredictability of such a rapid transition, but partly also because of special pleadings and self-interested counterattacks by regulated businesses. Whereas the economic arguments of the early 1970s had stressed the efficiency benefits of internalizing externalities and making industries and their customers pay the full costs of air and water services, by the late 1970s a constant drumbeat of inflation rhetoric changed the subject, attacking government regulation as a whole and denouncing any increased business costs resulting from regulation as inflationary—no matter whether those costs were real or were internalizing previous real costs to others or were merely transfers to create a different (and possibly more efficient) mix of goods and services.

In response, each of the presidents in this period acted to create increasingly explicit requirements for analysis of expected economic impacts of major regulatory proposals and increasingly authoritative oversight agencies in the Executive Office of the President to review and comment on these analyses. These measures were intended to increase the "cost-sensitivity" of the regulatory agencies, and they did so, although those agencies continued to vary widely—in part for substantive statutory reasons, as discussed previously—in the weight they gave to these economic considerations in reaching their decisions. At the same time, the loyalties of Executive Office oversight agencies have always and inevitably been divided between encouraging good analysis for its own sake and promoting the particular priorities of the incumbent president, including sensitivity to special pleadings by particular industries and regions, and the very flexibility maintained by those agencies by not formalizing methods and assumptions for regulatory analysis left open the danger of corrupting benefit-cost analysis to serve ad hoc political purposes and mollify regulated firms.

Before President Reagan's executive order, however, the actions of these presidents stopped short of attempting either to assert economic efficiency as the final criterion for evaluating regulatory decisions or to give OMB outright veto authority over the agencies. Moreover, whereas the early forms of executive oversight operated as secret internal reviews of proposed regulations, later ones had deliberately shifted to public filing of comments on the decision record, apparently in the belief that such visible oversight was both more effective and more accountable.

Regulatory analysis itself was a direct descendant of both benefit-cost analysis and PPB as well as environmental impact statements, inheriting from BCA many of its principles as well as data and assumptions, but also from PPB its analysis of cost-effectiveness across alternatives, and from the EIS its emphasis on predicting impacts rather than merely netting benefits and costs. It continued to exhibit in practice all the unresolved problems of methodology and assumptions that had dogged public investment analysis, and in the attempt to apply it to regulatory decisions it added new ones as well.

First, were regulatory decisions even intended to serve an efficiency objective, or were they matters of equity, human rights, or other objectives? It is in the nature of rights such as freedom that they cannot be bought or sold and are at times admittedly inefficient but nonetheless justified by libertarian as well as pluralistic and humanistic arguments.[78] If the purpose of regulation is to secure statutory rights to certain levels of health or environmental quality, therefore,[79] regulatory BCA may have little to say and may in practice even distort the central issues. The same is true in practice if not in principle of the many alleged regulatory costs that are in fact merely transfers, substituting costs of abatement borne by polluters for costs of damage and avoidance borne by victims.

Second, the potential for bias in cost data was far more serious than for public investments because the costs of public investments were at least borne by government, whereas the costs of regulation were borne by myriad nongovernment parties, each of which had strategic incentives to overstate them. The temptation for agencies to exaggerate benefit estimates was probably no greater than for public investments, but perhaps no less either.

Third, and finally, benefit-cost analysis in practice has generally assumed static technology, yet many environmental regulations were intended to be (and have in fact been) technology-forcing, so that conventional BCA routinely overestimates expected compliance costs (while perhaps underestimating some others).[80]

The spreading requirements for economic analysis of regulatory decisions under executive oversight raised essential questions not only of methodology but also of ethics and politics and fundamentally of constitutional powers: what are the proper roles of the Congress, the president's office, and the regulatory agencies in balancing health, safety, and environmental quality against the economic effects of achieving them? By the time of President Reagan's election, the answers already given had opened a growing role for the Office of the President to wield ad hoc vetoes. The actual use of regulatory analysis, however, and of executive influence over such analyses, exhibited at least a publicly visible debate over issues and trade-offs in which presidential political preferences, although undoubtedly present, did not overwhelm either the clarity of regulatory agencies' ultimate responsibility or the effort to improve analysis for its own sake.

REAGAN, REGULATION, AND THE ENVIRONMENT

Although regulatory reform, analysis, and oversight mechanisms thus were well under way before the Reagan administration, the many still unimplemented statutory requirements of the 1970s laws continued to generate strong momentum toward additional federal regulations. The 1976 Resource Conservation and Recovery Act and 1980 Superfund laws were just being phased in, promising new costs for control of hazardous wastes; OSHA was now finally beginning seriously to regulate workplace health hazards, such as by its proposed generic carcinogen regulations; and yet to come were controls over toxic substances (TSCA), many hazardous air and water pollutants (CAA, FWPCAA), and a wide range of other substances— to which must be added the regulations of other agencies dealing with highway safety, consumer product safety, financial reporting, and others.

As the various elements of this process were added up, they formed a threatening picture of aggregate business regulation that coalesced many disparate business and conservative interests into a call for regulatory relief: not simply for market mechanisms as more effective techniques but stabilization and reduction of the aggregate burden of federal regulations of business.[81] As David Stockman stated in his famous "Economic Dunkirk" memo to President-elect Reagan in November 1980, "Unless swift, comprehensive, and far-reaching regulatory policy corrections are undertaken immediately, an unprecedented, quantum scale-up of the much-discussed 'regulatory burden' will occur during the next 18–40 months."[82]

The Reagan administration entered office with a commitment to regulatory relief as a fundamental theme of its domestic policy. This theme was timely in its appeal to businessmen and conservatives, Reagan's natural constituencies, and it fit perfectly with his own longstanding campaign against the images of "big government" and "bureaucrats."[83] It is not exaggerating to say that reduction in the size and growth of government— by deregulation, defederalization, and defunding—preoccupied Reagan to the exclusion of virtually everything else during the first year of his presidency.[84] Executive Order 12291 was a centerpiece of this commitment, "the support beam of his administration's framework for regulatory reform,"[85] and in this context it was at least a deliberate use of the language of economic analysis, coupled with an already emerging trend toward stronger executive oversight, as weapons to achieve a preconceived political purpose of general regulatory reduction.

Deregulation

The fundamental domestic policy of the Reagan administration was to reduce the size and scope of the federal government: to reduce taxes, to reduce domestic spending in all areas, to devolve as many functions as possible to state and local governments (if they wanted them, otherwise to let some of them simply disappear), and to reverse the growth of federal regulations and relax or eliminate them where possible.[86] Reagan was explicit in this policy redirection and that it was to override as much as possible the case-by-case arguments over particular programs and regulations. It was not that he was necessarily opposed to environment, health, or human services, but that he was so categorically antigovernment in domestic affairs that neither the specifics of the issues nor the real problems that had evoked regulation mattered: the issue was the size of government per se.

Regulatory Relief Task Force

One of Reagan's first acts as president (22 January 1981) was to create a Presidential Task Force on Regulatory Relief, chaired by Vice-President George Bush. This task force was to review not only major new regulatory proposals but also existing regulations and to recommend changes to the president to relieve businesses and state and local governments from federal regulatory burdens. Staff support was provided by the same OMB staff group, the Office of Information and Regulatory Affairs (OIRA), that oversees the Regulatory Impact Analysis process under Executive Order 12291 and its predecessor authorities as well as the "paperwork reduction" process authorized by 1980 legislation.

Just over a week later, President Reagan directed all eleven executive regulatory agency heads to postpone the effective dates of all pending regulations for sixty days and to issue no other new final regulations during that period; his purpose was to allow time for task force review of the so-called "midnight regulations," some 170 to 200 regulations issued in the final month of the Carter administration. Ultimately the majority of these were released, but some 30 to 72 of them (sources disagree) were pulled for reconsideration.[87]

The task force immediately began compiling a "hit list" of "burdensome" regulations for reconsideration, beginning with those pulled from the pending stream and then inviting nominations of others by businesses, trade associations, state and local governments, and anyone else who might feel burdened by them. By December 1981, 91 existing regulations and 9 paperwork requirements had been targeted for review; 60 percent of the regulations targeted concerned health, safety, or environmental quality, the vast majority of them from EPA and the National Highway Traffic Safety Administration, while less than 15 percent were economic (price or output) regulations.[88] By August 1983, when the task force declared its mission accomplished and disbanded, it had reviewed 119 regulations, nearly half of them from EPA and NHTSA; 76 of these had been revised or eliminated, including 17 completed and 5 more proposed for EPA. Three more were still under review. The number of final regulations issued had also been reduced by 22 percent and the number proposed by 34 percent.[89]

APPOINTMENTS. A second tactic of Reagan's deregulation policy was to hire ideological loyalists for all available positions, not only as agency heads but especially in key positions under them where priorities are sorted and filtered. This process was designed more than six months before the presidential campaign began to recruit people who were above all else loyal to Reagan's philosophy rather than to the particular subject matters or regulatory missions of their agencies, and it was closely controlled by the White House, even including lower-level appointments normally made by the agency head rather than the president.[90] It was further reinforced by such tactics as frequent cabinet meetings, periodic subcabinet pep talks, and deliberate isolation of administration appointees from agency career staffs.[91] In addition, regulatory jobs important to business were filled immediately, although key positions protecting health, safety, environmental quality, and other nonbusiness values were left unfilled for months (and particularly, until after the first year's budget cut decisions had been made without them); most of those ultimately appointed had both employment experience and personal records of opposition to their agencies' regulatory policies.[92]

The purpose and effect of this appointments policy were clearly to force the administration's deregulatory and budget reduction priorities into the daily processes of the agencies and to reinforce central presidential control of them by appointing people who would so reliably enforce these priorities—on "automatic pilot," so to speak—that direct White House control on particular issues would only occasionally be necessary.

BUDGET. Finally, Reagan and his staff deliberately used tax cuts and budget controls on a vast scale to exert downward pressure on nearly all domestic roles of the federal government, especially social regulation. They proposed cuts of more than 20 percent in the EPA's budget over two years and more than 30 percent in enforcement; OSHA's inspection staff was cut more than 25 percent, surface mine inspections by half, and critics have testified that the actual cuts are in fact far deeper than these official figures show. Several agencies (including EPA) also attempted to cancel regulations in anticipation of budget elimination of particular programs and to plead budget constraints as an excuse for abrogating consent decrees and other regulatory commitments.[93]

Consolidation of OMB Oversight Powers

Amid these many tactics used by the Reagan administration to reduce the federal role, a key one for the purposes of this chapter is an unprecedented consolidation of oversight powers in the Office of Management and Budget. This consolidation built upon several existing powers and two new ones added by Congress and the courts just before or during the Reagan administration, but Executive Order 12291 was a centerpiece of the expansion of influence over federal regulatory actions.

PREEXISTING POWERS. OMB has long exercised important influence through its supervision of the budget process, including both development of the president's budget vis-à-vis the agencies' requests and the allocation or impoundment of funds appropriated by Congress to each program. Less widely known, it clears all agencies' legislative proposals as being in accord or not in accord with the program of the president; it must approve all forms in which information is requested by federal agencies, from routine paper formats to survey research and the census; and it promulgates its own rules (circulars) governing the process and justification requirements for federal expenditures, such as benefit-cost analysis for water projects, state and regional clearinghouse review of local applications for federal funds, and faculty time accounting on federally funded research grants. OMB is, in short, not only a budget office but a regulatory agency itself, with broad powers and influence predating the Reagan administration.

ELIMINATION OF COMPETITORS. Among the early actions of the Reagan administration was to eliminate virtually all other Executive Office agencies that might compete or share oversight powers with OMB. The Council on Wage and Price Stability was eliminated and its staff functions absorbed by OMB's Office of Information and Regulatory Affairs. The Regulatory Council, established by President Carter to improve coordination among federal regulations, was abolished. The Regulatory Analysis Review Group was abolished and its functions absorbed by OIRA. A legislative battle would have occurred had Reagan tried to abolish the Council on Environmental Quality, so instead its entire staff was fired (secretaries included) and replaced, after a drastic budget cut, by a token staff of administration appointees with little experience or influence.

The only new Executive Office organization created was the Task Force on Regulatory Relief, and OMB functioned as the staff to that body. From the perspective of administrative efficiency and accountability, some of this streamlining has benefits over the diffuse coordination of RIA among OMB, RARG, COWPS, Regulatory Council, and others, but it does clearly increase the authority of OMB.

PAPERWORK CONTROL. The Paperwork Reduction Act of 1980—little noticed by the public—created OIRA and in addition gave OMB broad new controls over all federal reporting requirements. It directed OMB to reduce the burden of federal information collection by 15 percent by the end of fiscal year 1982 and another 10 percent by the end of FY 1983 and to relieve the burden associated with administering federal grant progams by 10 percent by FY 1982. Under this authority, OMB has set for each agency an information collection budget limiting the hours of paperwork that can be imposed on respondents for the collection of information; these budgets require a 17 percent reduction from 1980 to 1982.[94] OMB must also approve every form requesting such information. The legality of OMB's control over existing paperwork requirements has been questioned by the Justice Department and Internal Revenue Service and may be resolved only by litigation,[95] but its influence is clearly substantial. OMB claimed to have reduced federal paperwork by 13 percent by the end of FY 1982, and further substantial cuts were planned.[96]

ABOLITION OF LEGISLATIVE VETOES. In June 1983, the Supreme Court ruled in sweeping terms that laws authorizing a "legislative veto" of executive actions—such as regulations and perhaps budget impoundments—were unconstitutional.[97] This ruling was not directed at OMB, but one of its immediate effects will clearly be to reinforce the consolidation of OMB's power over the agencies through oversight of both budgets and rules, because that power—at least until and unless Congress changes the statutes and those changes are signed into law by a president—will be less subject to ad hoc congressional control.

REGULATORY ANALYSIS. Finally, of course, OMB's authority has been greatly expanded by Executive Order 12291.

Executive Order 12291

What does all this broad institutional history have to do with Executive Order 12291, a directive whose purpose, in its own language as well as in the minds of many advocates of economic analysis, is simply to ensure the common-sense purpose that government regulations have benefits to society greater than their costs? A great deal.

Executive Order 12291 has two major and distinct elements, both of which were built upon histories already developing but both adding significant new policy changes and both intended to serve the overall Reagan policy of deregulation.

EFFICIENCY TEST. The first element was the requirement not only that agencies prepare Regulatory Impact Analyses for every major proposed rule but also that these analyses demonstrate that the regulation's economic benefits exceed its cost. This requirement at face value looks similar to President Ford's inflation impact statements and President Carter's regulatory analyses, but in fact it went far beyond them. The Carter administration took pains to stress cost-effectiveness as a consideration in the pursuit of each agency's substantive mandate and not to appear to be imposing a benefit-cost test as the substantive criterion for regulatory decisions.[98] The reason for this policy was that each agency had substantive responsibilities mandated by statute, many of which—such as protection of health, safety, and environmental quality—were not reducible to economic efficiency either in principle or even practically by accepted analytical methods.[99] The Reagan order, in contrast, explicitly required that a benefit-cost test be applied and met in all cases in which it was not expressly prohibited by law; that the alternative that minimized the net cost to society be chosen; and that the agencies structure their priorities so as to maximize net aggregate social benefits.[100]

OMB CONTROL. Second, the executive order gave unprecedented oversight authority to OMB to control the regulatory process through supervision of these analytical requirements. OMB was authorized to review all RIAs prepared by the agencies; to designate other proposed or existing regulations as "major" and demand RIAs for them; to group rules for this purpose so that together they became "major"; and to delay publication of agency rulemaking proposals until they satisfy OMB. Moreover, it may exercise these powers off the public record of the agency's rulemaking and decision process and need keep no public record of its comments or the agency's response. The agency's only appeal is to the Task Force on Regulatory Relief or to the president himself.[101]

These oversight powers represent a significant break with all previous versions of regulatory oversight. In the words of Jim Tozzi, senior staff member of OIRA, "It has taken us nearly twenty years, through five administrations, to establish a central review office in OMB which has the authority to curtail the promulgation of onerous regulations."[102] The Congressional Research Service described it as "a formal, comprehensive, centralized, and substantively oriented system of control of informal rule-making that is without precedent."[103] Both the limits and the legality of this system are yet to be tested, in particular the extent to which OMB influence may inappropriately interfere either with the Administrative Procedures Act or with the substantive delegations of rulemaking authority to the agencies under their various statutes.

Summary

Executive Order 12291 embodies a conjunction of two partially conflicting histories: that of decades of effort to achieve better-reasoned formal analysis of government decisions and that of business pressures for, and the Reagan administration's commitment to, regulatory relief. Its formal elements bear the marks of the first history: George Eads has noted that it "borrows much of its procedure from Nixon's Quality of Life Review, many of its analytical requirements from Ford's Inflation Impact Statement program, and many of its analytical capacities from those established and initiated by Carter."[104] It also borrows its underlying principles from public investment economics, benefit-cost analysis, and PPB and some of its concepts from NEPA's environmental impact assessments. But it deliberately retreated from public accountability, did little at face value to encourage continued regulatory reform, and both by its tone and context implied once more—like PPB and other oversight procedures before it—the use of analytical requirements to serve White House politics, in this case a heavy a priori commitment to deregulation rather than to better analysis per se.

These two histories share several important common assumptions, the most important being that federal social regulation has expanded vastly over the past decade in ways that are at best uncoordinated—though many of them are directed at the same firms, processes, and substances—and at worst costly, sometimes ineffective, and at cross-purposes. Some better system of coordination was needed; some better analyses were needed; and some regulations might well not be needed if better coordination and analysis were done. But beyond these basic areas of agreement, the histories seek to use the same procedures and institutions to serve fundamentally different goals. The administration's regulatory reformers are in conflict with one another, conservative editor Antonin Scalia suggests, between "principled deregulators . . . who want market-based solutions, cost-benefit analysis, and so forth" and "business interests . . . who haven't given any thought to regulation in general, but know that in the past few years things have gotten out of hand."[105] The latter borrow the rhetoric and momentum of economic regulatory reform but in fact use it primarily as a political club against social regulations and use RIA simply as a handy weapon for deregulation—"paralysis by analysis," as environmental groups sometimes used the EIS—rather than for better analysis on the merits.

The conflicting pressures of these histories and contexts on those who must implement EO 12291 raise a series of important issues that will ultimately shape its value and effectiveness. It will probably be effective— it has already been effective—in blocking a small number of costly new regulations. But this is far from sufficient to make it an effective ongoing instrument of regulatory management: simply paralyzing the production of new regulations is not enough. Other questions must also be addressed.

THE EFFICIENCY CRITERION. Is a requirement that benefits exceed cost the appropriate criterion for social regulatory decisions? Michael Baram argues that it is not, saying that efficiency is only one among many regulatory objectives authorized by statute and that in practice it is simplistic, arbitrary in its assumptions, and likely to become merely a self-serving numbers game; cost-effectiveness analysis should be used as a tool in broader balancing, but the economic benefit-cost criterion should not be used as a rule.[106] Eads calls the efficiency test an "invitation to fraud" given the current state of its methodologies; he, too, advocates cost-effectiveness analysis only.[107]

DEREGULATORY BIAS. Should not the same analytical requirements apply to proposals to deregulate as to add new regulations? This question is a key test of the executive order's true objective. The response of OIRA's first director was that he would immediately waive RIA "on the basis of evidence, however sparse," that the proposal would reduce regulatory burdens.[108] The Supreme Court, however, has disagreed and unanimously overturned the Reagan administration's summary rescission of auto safety requirements (passive restraints) as "arbitrary and capricious," saying that agencies must follow the same analytical and procedural requirements when rescinding rules as when creating them.[109]

ACCOUNTABILITY. The EO 12291 approach in its present form raises serious questions of accountability for regulatory decisions. It creates unfettered authority for OMB to influence agency decisions without public scrutiny; it thus divides and confuses the ultimate responsibility for regulatory decisions in an untraceable way; and like the QOL reviews it creates a troubling prospect, especially in the context of OIRA's close working relationship with the president's Task Force on Regulatory Relief, of ex parte influences by special interests under the guise of executive oversight, without any safeguard of the integrity of the regulatory process or of the interests of the more general public.

COUNTERPRODUCTIVITY. The real issues in social regulation are how to ensure appropriate balancing of multiple objectives in regulatory decisions, how to ensure selection of the best regulatory instruments to achieve that balance, and how to coordinate and balance the aggregate effects of many regulations. Ironically, it is not clear that RIA under EO 12291 does any of these well, and it may even work against them. Substantive balancing requires faithfulness to particular statutes, not to presidential pressures, and often therefore can be changed only by statutory amendment. Selection of techniques is in principle improved by cost-effectiveness analysis, but the apparent failure of OMB to lead in developing consistent methodologies and its reactive role as ad hoc adversary to new regulatory proposals tend more to discourage new regulations than to improve them. And the RIA process gives no emphasis to better management of regulatory programs as a whole either within or across agencies yet places additional ad hoc documentation demands on the limited staffs that could otherwise do this.

Like NEPA's EIS, the RIA procedure uses documentation and review requirements as a crude and inefficient weapon to get the agencies' attention and to attempt in one sweeping administrative change a shift in myriad substantive balancing decisions that would otherwise—and may still—have to be sought through amendments to individual statutes.[110] The following chapters discuss its implementation in more detail.

But if not through executive oversight and RIA requirements, how can one address the genuine problem of regulatory burden, both in individual regulations and in their combined effects? One answer is substantive coordination rather than ad hoc deregulation: recreate the Regulatory Council or something like it and redirect OIRA and the task force to involve the regulatory agencies in substantive coordination—for instance, consistent treatment of carcinogens and other substances or coordinated regulation of particular industrial processes—rather than simply intensifying paperwork games and delays by reacting only as ad hoc adversary to particular regulations. Second, create an institutional mechanism to review and suggest hazard priorities, both to the executive branch and to the Congress and to be an advocate for substantive redirection of regulatory attention as appropriate.[111] Third, tackle the individual statutes as necessary to remove statutory impediments to appropriate balancing of the objectives at stake.[112] Finally, explore the potential of explicit negotiation and consensus-building procedures in developing regulations as an alternative to the artificial formalism of RIA, an alternative already widely used in other free-market industrial countries.[113]

There is no escape from the fact that regulatory decisions are ultimately fallible human judgments. There are better and worse ways of making such judgments, and analysis of the impacts and trade-offs involved among alternative choices is in principle one of the better ones. It is not clear on the face of it, however, that the broader administrative trappings imposed on this process by Executive Order 12291—efficiency tests, OMB authority, ad hoc adversary review, and deregulatory bias—will succeed in imposing that result on agencies that are unwilling or statutorily unable to do so. Like other executive oversight initiatives before it—water project review, PPB, QOL reviews, IIS, and so forth—it may simply create a new paperwork game rather than better analysis and divert attention from more important issues in regulatory management.

NOTES

1. 49 *Stat.* 1750. In practice it had actually been used by public works agencies at least since the late nineteenth century, but the 1936 law was the first to endorse it formally. See Baram, "Cost-Benefit Analysis," n. 17.
2. Maass, "Public Investment Planning in the United States," p. 219, n. 10.
3. U.S. Federal Interagency River Basin Committee, Subcommittee on Benefits and Costs, *Proposed Practices for Economic Analysis of River Basin Projects*; U.S. Bureau of the Budget, *Circular A-47*.
4. U.S. Congress, Senate, *Policies, Standards, and Procedures in the Formulation, Evaluation, and Review of Plans for Use and Development of Water and Related Land Resources*.
5. Testimony of Major General Frank P. Koisch, in U.S. Congress, House Committee on Governmental Operations, *Stream Channelization*, pt. 2, p. 557.
6. See Andrews, *Environmental Policy and Administrative Change*.
7. Maass, "Public Investment Planning," pp. 221–22.
8. U.S. Water Resources Council, "Principles and Standards for Planning Water and Related Land Resources."
9. U.S. Water Resources Council, "Economic and Environmental Principles and Guidelines for Water and Related Land Resources Implementation Studies." The other and unofficial criterion is, of course, politics: a key parameter of the analysis is state cost-sharing requirements, which Reagan administration officials decided to assess on a case-by-case basis in response to pressures from their constituents in western states. See *New York Times*, 19 June 1983.
10. Alain C. Enthoven, "The Planning, Programming, and Budgeting System in the Department of Defense: Some Lessons from Experience," and Alain C.

Enthoven and K. Wayne Smith, "The Planning, Programming, and Budgeting System in the Department of Defense: Current Status and Next Steps," in U.S. Congress, Joint Economic Committee, *The Analysis and Evaluation of Public Expenditures*, 3:901–8 and 955–69.

11. Keith E. Marvin and Andrew M. Rouse, "The Status of PPB in Federal Agencies: A Comparative Perspective," ibid., pp. 801–14.

12. Ibid.

13. See especially Haveman and Margolis, *Public Expenditures and Policy Analysis*, and Miller and Yandle, *Benefit-Cost Analysis of Social Regulation*.

14. Allen Schick, "Systems for Analysis: PPB and Its Alternatives," in U.S. Congress, Joint Economic Committee, *Analysis and Evaluation of Public Expenditures*, 7:817–34.

15. See, e.g., Krutilla, "Conservation Reconsidered." For a detailed case study critique of practice, however, see Feiveson, Sinden, and Socolow, *Boundaries of Analysis*.

16. See for instance Dorfman, ed., *Measuring Benefits of Government Investments*; and U.S. Congress, Joint Economic Committee, *Guidelines for Estimating the Benefits of Public Expenditures*.

17. 42 *U.S. C.A.* 4321 *et seq.*, sec. 102 (2)(C).

18. Andrews, *Environmental Policy*, chap. 7.

19. See *Calvert Cliffs Coordinating Committee* v. *AEC*, 449 F.2d 1109 (D.C. Circuit 1971).

20. Andrews, "NEPA in Practice."

21. See for instance Rourke, *Bureaucracy, Politics, and Public Policy*.

22. Maass, "Public Investment Planning."

23. See Environmental Law Institute, "Cost-Benefit Analysis and Environmental, Health and Safety Regulation."

24. U.S. Council on Environmental Quality, *Environmental Quality—1970*.

25. A good sampling of this literature may be found in Dorfman and Dorfman, eds., *Economics of the Environment*. Earlier works include Kapp, *Social Costs of Private Enterprise*; Kneese and Bower, *Managing Water Quality*; and Kneese, Ayres, and d'Arge, *Economics and the Environment*.

26. U.S. Council on Environmental Quality, *Environmental Quality*, annually since 1970.

27. Baram, "Cost-Benefit Analysis."

28. These costs, however, typically emphasize costs to those regulated, a more slippery political judgment than economic efficiency in its societywide meaning, which would subtract from these costs those that were merely transferred to other firms as individuals.

29. Baram, "Cost-Benefit Analysis," p. 496.

30. U.S. Council on Environmental Quality, *Environmental Quality—1972*.

31. Ibid., 1980.

32. U.S. Environmental Protection Agency, Science Advisory Board, "Economics in EPA."

33. U.S. Congress, Senate Committee on Governmental Affairs, *Study on Federal Regulation*, pp. 9–31.

34. See Weisbrod, "Problems of Enhancing the Public Interest: Toward a Model of Government Failures," in his *Public Interest Law*; and Wolf, "A Theory of Non-

market Failure," in Haveman and Margolis, eds., *Public Expenditure and Policy Analysis*, pp. 515–34.

35. Davies and Davies, *The Politics of Pollution*, pp. 52–56.
36. Jones, *Clean Air*.
37. Ashby and Anderson, *The Politics of Clean Air*, p. 32.
38. A. Allan Schmid, "Effective Public Policy and the Government Budget: A Uniform Treatment of Public Expenditures and Public Rules," U.S. Congress, Joint Economic Committee, *Analysis and Evaluation of Public Expenditures*, 1:579–91.
39. For example, Ruff, "The Economic Common Sense of Pollution"; Kneese and Bower, "Standards, Charges, and Equity," in their *Managing Water Quality*.
40. For example, Dales, *Pollution, Property and Prices*; Tietenberg, "The Design of Property Rights for Air Pollution Control"; and Rose-Ackerman, "Market Models for Pollution Control."
41. See Miller and Yandle, *Benefit-Cost Analysis*, p. 21.
42. U.S. Council on Environmental Quality, *Environmental Quality—1970*, p. 234.
43. Ibid., *1971*, pp. 113, 118, 134–39.
44. Ibid., *1973*, pp. 83, 109ff.
45. Ibid., *1975*, p. 495.
46. Ibid., *1976*, pp. 162–64.
47. Ibid., *1979*, pp. 644ff., esp. pp. 668–72.
48. U.S. Congress, Senate Committee on Governmental Affairs, *Study on Federal Regulation*, 6:206–8; Kelman, "Economists and the Environmental Muddle."
49. U.S. Congress, Committee on Governmental Affairs, *Study on Federal Regulation*, 6:206–8.
50. Ibid., p. 216.
51. Liroff, *Air Pollution Offsets*, pp. 6–7. See also Levin, "Getting There," pp. 59–92.
52. U.S. Regulatory Council, *Regulatory Reform Highlights*, p. 9.
53. Liroff, *Air Pollution Offsets*, pp. 23–26; U.S. Regulatory Council, *Regulatory Reform Highlights*, pp. 38ff.
54. U.S. Regulatory Council, *Regulatory Reform Highlights*, p. 41.
55. Ibid., pp. 43, 45.
56. Miller and Yandle, *Benefit-Cost Analysis*, p. 2.
57. For discussion of NIPCC and QOL reviews, see Andrews, *Environmental Policy*, chap. 3; and Baram, "Cost-Benefit Analysis," n. 148; and Eads and Fix, *Release, Not Reform*.
58. 88 *Stat.* 750 (1974).
59. Miller and Yandle, *Benefit-Cost Analysis*, p. 6.
60. Executive Order 11821, 3 C.F.R. 926, 27 November 1974; see also U.S. Congress, Senate Committee on Governmental Affairs, *Study on Federal Regulation*, 6:78ff.
61. U.S. Office of Management and Budget, *Budget Circular No. A-107*.
62. Baram, "Cost-Benefit Analysis," p. 504.
63. Ibid.
64. Interview with Vaughn Williams, general counsel, COWPS, 9 April 1976, quoted in Swaczy, "The Visible Paw and the Monkey Wrench."

65. Baram, "Cost-Benefit Analysis," pp. 504–5; Miller and Yandle, *Benefit-Cost Analysis*, p. 6.
66. Executive Order 11949, 3 C.F.R. 161; see also U.S. Congress, Senate Committee on Governmental Affairs, *Study on Federal Regulation*; Baram, "Cost-Benefit Analysis"; Liroff, "Cost-Benefit Analysis in Federal Environmental Programs," in Swartzman, Liroff, and Croke, *Cost-Benefit Analysis and Environmental Regulations*, p. 38.
67. Examples reproduced in U.S. Congress, House Committee on Interstate and Foreign Commerce, *Use of Cost-Benefit Analysis by Regulatory Agencies*, pp. 312–16.
68. Executive Order 12044, 3 C.F.R. 152, 23 March 1978.
69. Environmental Law Institute, *Cost-Benefit Analysis*.
70. Baram, "Cost-Benefit Analysis," p. 511.
71. Liroff, "Cost-Benefit Analysis"; Eads and Fix, *Release, Not Reform*.
72. Environmental Law Institute, *Cost-Benefit Analysis*.
73. For a good summary and discussion of regulatory control and oversight proposals see Clark, Kosters, and Miller, *Reforming Regulation*.
74. Ibid.
75. *Washington Post*, 24 June 1983, p. 1A.
76. Clark, Kosters, and Miller, *Reforming Regulation*; see also U.S. Congress, Senate Committee on Governmental Affairs, *Study on Federal Regulation*, pp. 83ff.
77. The so-called "Bumpers amendment," proposed by Senator Dale Bumpers.
78. Okun, *Equality and Efficiency*.
79. The interpretation of pollution as a matter of property rights was advanced among others by the second annual report of the Council on Environmental Quality (*Environmental Quality—1971*) and previously by several scholarly authors: see Paul Feldman, "Prescription for an Effective Government: Ethics, Economics, and PPBS," in U.S. Congress, Joint Economic Committee, *Analysis and Evaluation of Public Expenditures*, 3:878.
80. U.S. Council on Environmental Quality, *Environmental Quality—1980*.
81. See esp. Weidenbaum, *The Future of Business Regulation*.
82. Quoted in Mosher, "Reaganites, with OMB's List in Hand, Take Dead Aim at EPA's Regulations."
83. Cannon, *Reagan*, pp. 99–100.
84. Ibid., p. 318.
85. Scalia, "Regulation—The First Year," p. 19.
86. Cannon, *Reagan*, pp. 321–48; Nathan, "The Reagan Presidency in Domestic Affairs."
87. Federal Register 46 (1980): 11227; see also American Enterprise Institute for Public Policy Research, "Major Regulatory Initiatives during 1981," p. 64; and Conservation Foundation, *State of the Environment, 1982*, pp. 406–9 and notes.
88. U.S. President, Fact Sheet, "Year-End Summary of the Administration's Regulatory Relief Program."
89. U.S. President, Fact Sheets, "The Administration's Progress on Regulatory Relief," and "Reagan Administration Regulatory Achievements."
90. Nathan, "Reagan Presidency," pp. 37–41.

91. Interview with James Watt and Jeane Kirkpatrick, *Public Opinion*, February–March 1981.

92. Nathan, "Reagan Presidency."

93. Conservation Foundation, *State of the Environment*, pp. 389–92, 403–4, 408–9.

94. American Enterprise Institute, "Major Regulatory Initiatives," p. 66.

95. Ibid., p. 54.

96. U.S. President, Fact Sheet, "Administration's Progress."

97. *Washington Post*, 24 June 1983, p. 1A.

98. Eads, "White House Oversight of Executive Branch Regulation," pp. 180–81.

99. See Costle, "Bright Light in the Wrong Place."

100. Executive Order 12291; Eads, "White House Oversight."

101. Eads, "White House Oversight," pp. 181–83.

102. Letter from Jim J. Tozzi, "A Note to the Regulatory Relief Community," 29 April 1983.

103. U.S. Congress, House Committee on Energy and Commerce, *Presidential Control of Agency Rulemaking*, pp. 70–73.

104. Eads, "White House Oversight," p. 196.

105. Scalia, "Regulation," p. 38.

106. Baram, "Cost-Benefit Analysis," p. 523.

107. Eads, "White House Oversight," p. 191.

108. Quoted in ibid., p. 192.

109. *Washington Post*, 25 June 1983, p. A1.

110. Andrews, *Environmental Policy*, chap. 2.

111. See Ruckelshaus, "Science, Risk, and Public Policy."

112. Eads, "White House Oversight," p. 197.

113. Jasonoff, "Negotiation or Cost-Benefit Analysis."

3

ARTHUR G. FRAAS*

BENEFIT-COST ANALYSIS FOR ENVIRONMENTAL REGULATION

 THE primary role of the Office of Management and Budget under Executive Order 12291 is to assure that regulatory initiatives conform to the principles of the executive order. In carrying out this oversight function, OMB is a user of the information in the regulatory analysis. It also has a responsibility to assure that agencies conduct a high quality of analysis. In this chapter, I will discuss some of the practical problems in the preparation of these analyses and will indicate some of the likely implications for the role of analysis in decision making.

The first section outlines the basic requirements of the executive order and briefly discusses the experience to date. The second section considers OMB's oversight role under the executive order. The third section discusses some of the difficulties of preparing an analysis of environmental regulations.

THE PROCESS UNDER EXECUTIVE ORDER 12291

Under EO 12291, OMB is charged with reviewing all proposed and final rules of executive agencies before they are published in the *Federal Register*. The executive order requires that there be a demonstrated need for regulatory intervention and that the regulatory alternative selected by the agency should maximize net benefits to society. Major rules—that is, rules

*Economist, Office of Management and Budget, Washington, D.C. The views presented are mine alone and do not necessarily represent the views of the Office of Management and Budget. Thanks are due Elizabeth Pinkston, Paul Portney, and V. Kerry Smith for their comments on earlier versions.

that establish an important precedent, or have a significant effect on a specific sector or group, or have an annual benefit or cost effect of $100 million or more—must be accompanied by a regulatory impact analysis.

OMB's draft guidance on preparing RIAs requires a showing that there is adequate information concerning the need for and consequences of the proposed action; the potential benefits to society outweigh the potential costs; and of all the alternative approaches to the given regulatory objective, the proposed action will maximize net benefits to society.[1]

Under the executive order, as written and as it has been implemented to date, benefit-cost analysis is an analysis of last resort. It is necessary only if there is a showing of the need for federal regulatory intervention—that is, that there is evidence of market failure, that changes in the existing institutional arrangements will not adequately address the problem, and that federal intervention (as opposed to state or local action) is necessary to address the problem.

If a determination is made that federal intervention is needed, the agency must proceed with a benefit-cost analysis considering a variety of alternatives, including no regulation (regulatory failure may be worse than market failure); alternatives within the scope of the statutory provision (standards of varying stringency, varying dates for compliance); and other alternatives, including economic-incentive approaches (marketable permits, emission fees). The regulatory agency is directed to select the alternative maximizing net benefits to society. If statutory provisions prevent the agency from selecting this option, it is to select the regulatory alternative maximizing net benefits from those alternatives within the scope of the statute.

For environmental regulation, of course, the case can readily be made that regulatory initiatives address environmental problems arising from market failure and that there is a need for government intervention. As a result, the focus of analysis is largely concerned with the level of government intervention (federal versus state or local action), the nature of the intervention (for example, command and control versus marketable rights), and the net social benefits of the selected alternative.

The environmental statutes address to some extent each of these issues in a way that constrains the flexibility of the Environmental Protection Agency in developing a regulatory program. For example, the statutes prohibit, in some cases, the consideration of benefits or costs in setting specific environmental standards. One of the clearest and most important examples of such a statutory prohibition is the Clean Air Act requirement that EPA establish national ambient air standards without considering their cost. Of course, when specific provisions within the environmental statutes limit the agency's flexibility, it may be possible to achieve an efficient outcome only by amending these statutes.[2]

The Environmental Protection Agency, however, retains substantial flexibility under many specific provisions within these environmental statutes. For example, the language in many cases permits consideration of costs and benefits in setting standards.[3] Because of the flexibility allowed EPA under its operating statutes, analysis of various alternatives can make an important contribution to the regulatory process. In fact, in some important specific cases regulatory analysis has led to major adjustments in EPA's regulatory approach.[4] Even when the statutes constrain the outcome, regulatory analysis can assure that environmental regulation will not be any more inefficient than is required by the environmental statutes. Because environmental regulation is very expensive, these gains can be substantial.

Experience under Executive Order 12291

Under the executive order, OMB had reviewed approximately 5,400 rules by the end of 1982. Of these, 104 were classified as major rules and 70 were accompanied by RIAs. OMB has reviewed 7 major rules submitted by the Environmental Protection Agency. RIAs were submitted with 4 of these rules including Effluent Guideline Limits for the Iron and Steel Industry, National Contingency Plan under Superfund, Data Requirements for Pesticides Registration, and Standards for Disposal of High-Level Radioactive Waste.[5] Of the RIAs submitted by EPA, the best evaluation of benefits was developed in the analysis of technology-based water discharge limits (effluent guidelines) for the iron and steel industry. The others presented only qualitative descriptions of the likely benefits. In the case of the RIA for the disposal of high-level radioactive waste, for example, EPA argued that the rule would yield such benefits as facilitating the licensing of good disposal systems and providing residents in the vicinity of these facilities with "peace-of-mind."[6] In its RIA for the pesticides registration rule, EPA relied primarily on anecdotal information such as fish kills to characterize the likely benefits of the rule.

THE POLITICAL ECONOMY OF OMB OVERSIGHT

In evaluating the operation of the executive order process, one must recognize the extent to which regulatory activity is a political process. Major rules submitted to OMB under the executive order have had considerable political or legal momentum. In comparison with the political interests that are brought to bear on these regulatory initiatives, economic analysis is a relatively frail instrument.

The current oversight process established by the executive order has successfully raised some fundamental issues of regulatory approach, including the use of performance standards in place of design standards and the use of marketable permits in place of an administrative allocation of rights. The oversight process has also raised issues concerning the desirability of federal regulation as opposed to state or local action.

Enforcement of the executive order requirement that the selected regulatory option maximize net benefits has been relegated to a secondary role in the review process. In part, this has occurred because it is easier to raise fundamental issues of regulatory approach—for example, by advocating alternative approaches that rely on economic incentives or the return of more regulatory responsibility to state and local governments—instead of tackling the more technical issues that are vital to the quality of the RIA.

In addition, the role of benefit-cost analysis has been limited by the difficulty of developing high-quality analyses. As noted above, most of the analyses completed to date have presented only qualitative estimates of the likely benefits and, in the few cases in which benefits have been quantified, the range in the estimated benefits and the qualifications surrounding the estimates have been such that it has been difficult to use the results in making policy decisions.

The major role professional judgment plays in assessing the merits of the available studies and making the many assumptions necessary in developing these analyses is one of the more important factors contributing to the uncertainty of these estimates. Differences in professional judgment can have an appreciable effect on the magnitude of a "best" estimate. Differences that arise between the agencies and OMB over the likely effects of a given regulation often involve the exercise of professional judgment. Although these differences can have a substantial effect on the range of estimated benefits and costs, there is no suitable forum for resolving them. Instead, they are elevated to the political level, where they must compete for attention with a variety of other policy issues.

Finally, OMB's only means of securing better regulatory analysis is to return the rule and the RIA to the agency for reconsideration. Thus there are multiple objectives—policy objectives and the goal of improving regulatory analysis—and only one instrument for securing them. As a result, the return of a major rule because of an inadequate RIA has proved to be very difficult.

Because of the importance of the quality of the RIA to the executive order process, OMB needs to explore other ways of improving regulatory analysis. The exchange of informal staff memorandums may provide an alternative vehicle for an OMB critique of a regulatory analysis. When important issues concerning these analyses are raised either by OMB or outside parties, these issues could then be addressed by a panel convened by EPA's Science Advisory Board. EPA already relies heavily on panels of the Science Advisory Board and the Clean Air Scientific Advisory Committee for scientific judgments affecting its rulemaking activities.

GENERIC PROBLEMS IN BENEFITS ANALYSIS

The preparation of a regulatory analysis is a relatively new requirement emerging from the regulatory oversight initiatives of Presidents Ford and Carter. Executive Order 12291 establishes an even more ambitious analytical requirement. Under the earlier executive orders, for example, a regulatory analysis only rarely presented anything more than a qualitative statement of the likely benefits. Certainly EPA focused its attention on cost analysis. Benefits analysis and particularly its application to regulatory decision making is a new activity.

As a result, Executive Order 12291 establishes what I believe are best viewed as a set of "technology-forcing" requirements because the executive order requires an assessment of regulations that is substantially different from past procedures. For example, EPA has had little incentive in the past to develop information that is crucial to an understanding of the likely effects of its regulatory actions—for example, dose-response information for air pollutants such as carbon monoxide, ozone, and sulfur dioxide. In addition, the executive order requires a synthesis of this information in a way that has not been done before. In the case of ambient air standards, for example, it requires the development of a causal chain linking a set of control actions (reducing the total pounds discharged to the environment) to improved health and welfare. Thus the executive order requires important institutional changes in the way information is developed and organized in addressing regulatory issues.

Meeting the executive order requirements poses major analytical challenges, including developing the analysis in a timely fashion (often with limited funding), sorting out regulatory issues deserving review, and developing estimates with a level of precision that will inform the decision-making process. Because of the constraints on regulatory analysis (particularly of timeliness and budget), these analyses will necessarily depend on information in the available literature. There are some important problems

in framing the analysis and in translating results from the available literature to provide estimates of the benefits and costs of a regulatory action.
The discussion below concentrates attention on several of these difficulties,
including sorting out benefits attributable to cleanup by specific classes of
sources when environmental improvement is jointly dependent on cleanup
by multiple sources; translating the projected change in loadings (pounds
discharged) under the regulation into environmental changes affecting
health, recreation, aesthetics, and so forth; and sorting through the available literature for studies yielding reliable results and fitting these results to
address a specific regulatory issue. To help illustrate some of these problems, I have included as an appendix to this chapter a case study examining
EPA's analysis of its final rule establishing effluent guidelines for the iron
and steel industry.

The Narrow Focus of Most Rulemaking Initiatives

Under the current statutes, rulemaking activity is generally focused on a
very narrow set of issues—for example, setting technology-based standards
for individual industries or, in a somewhat broader context, setting ambient
standards for individual pollutants. This focus is much narrower than that of
most of the "benefits" studies in the existing literature and, often, too
narrow for sensible analysis.

As a consequence, a regulatory analysis for individual rules faces the
difficult task of sorting out the benefits and costs of controlling a single
class of sources or a single pollutant when environmental improvement is
jointly dependent on cleanup by multiple sources. In some cases, the
cleanup of discharges from a single source will be sufficient to meet air or
water quality objectives. This was largely (but not entirely) the case in
EPA's study of the effects of steel mill discharges on three particular rivers.
In general, though, an improvement in air or water quality requires the
cleanup of many sources. As a result, the cleanup of any single source is
likely to yield only relatively small changes in environmental quality, not
the larger, discrete changes that we generally associate with achieving, say,
"fishable" and "swimmable" waters.

This complexity regarding sources of pollution presents several problems in developing an estimate of benefits. The benefits of cleanup by an
individual source may depend both on the sequence in which other sources
reduce their discharges and on the extent of that cleanup. Thus, for example, the benefits of cleanup by a source may vary significantly depending on
whether the source is the first or the last to clean up its discharges. But even
if this problem can be resolved, it is difficult to identify and value the

generally small environmental effects of discharges from specific industrial plants.

A similar problem arises on the cost side. In its analysis of the cleanup of the Black River, EPA calculated the benefits of cleanup by the steel plant assuming that a nearby sewage treatment plant would also achieve a full cleanup of its effluents. In estimating the costs of cleanup, however, EPA considered only the cost for cleanup of the discharges from the steel plant, even though the benefits attributed to a cleanup of steel plant discharges were at least in part jointly dependent on cleanup by both sources. Similarly, EPA considers only the costs directly attributable to changes in the ambient standards in estimating the cost of national ambient air quality standards. Because emission standards for new stationary sources and for trucks and automobiles are subject to separate provisions of the Clean Air Act, the costs associated with controlling emissions from these sources are largely excluded from EPA's analysis of the cost of meeting ambient standards.

The answer to this problem, in the abstract, is simple—the focus should be adjusted to permit a sensible analysis. But given statutory constraints and institutional biases, this shift in the focus of analysis is difficult to accomplish.

The Scientific Uncertainty of "Fate" and "Effects"

Any analysis must begin with a scientific statement of the effect of a change in loadings or ambient concentrations on human health, environmental resources, and recreation and therefore requires knowledge of the "fate" and "effects" of pollutants. In the case of EPA's iron and steel study, for example, one needs to know the effect of discharges of pollutants such as ammonia, cyanide, and phenols on ambient water quality and ultimately on aquatic resources and recreation.[7] The issue extends across all areas of regulation, requiring knowledge of the effects of relatively small discharges of toxic pollutants (especially carcinogens), the effect of ambient concentrations of carbon monoxide, the "acid rain" effects of sulfur dioxide emissions, and the global effects of carbon dioxide and chlorofluorocarbon emissions. To varying degrees, there is disagreement within the scientific community about the magnitude—and in some cases, even the direction—of these effects.

In preparing a benefit-cost analysis, it is necessary to extract from the available scientific evidence a "best estimate" of the effect and a confidence interval. If there is substantial disagreement, and there often is, this is not easy to do. To some extent, scientific panels—such as those convened by the National Academy of Sciences—can provide a consensus statement. Often, though, there is no consensus statement. Regulatory analyses are limited from the beginning by the extent of the scientific uncertainty in the relationship between pollutant loadings and environmental effects.

Developing Benefits Estimates from the Available Literature

The relative ranking of alternatives in a benefit-cost analysis is generally sensitive to the various assumptions underlying the analysis. Clearly, assumptions about baseline conditions can be critical elements in an analysis. The characterization of various studies used (or not used) in the analysis and the assumptions necessary to transfer the results of these studies to a specific regulatory context can also have a critical effect on the relative ranking of regulatory alternatives. Thus professional judgment is an important ingredient in developing these estimates.

In any regulatory analysis, a number of such issues inevitably arise. The difficulty of evaluating individual analyses will be eased to the extent that some consensus can be reached on some of these issues. One of the problems deserving special attention is that of identifying promising methodologies to serve as the basis for benefits estimates.

In its iron and steel RIA, for example, EPA developed estimates of user benefits based on three different approaches—participation models, traditional "rule-of-thumb" planning models, and a contingent valuation study. User benefits estimates were then combined with an estimate of nonuser benefits for cleanup of each of the three rivers under study.

The problems with using willingness-to-pay estimates based on contingent valuation studies illustrate some of the methodological problems of using existing studies to develop benefits estimates for a specific regulatory issue.[8] The potential for bias in these studies is well known. In an effort to reduce this bias, researchers have developed a variety of survey techniques. Nevertheless, benefits estimates derived using this approach are likely to be biased upward, in my view, because they are not based on actual costs willingly incurred by households. In addition, we know that responses in these surveys can be sensitive to the way in which the surveys are conducted.[9]

Apart from questions of survey bias, it may be difficult to apply the results of contingent valuation studies in analyzing a specific rule. First, these studies must necessarily address large, discrete changes in environmental quality. For example, the respondents may be asked to value changes in water quality that make Mud Creek "fishable" and "swimmable." In practice, though, regulatory action may achieve relatively small changes in environmental quality that are far more subtle than can be conveyed to respondents in a survey format. For example, the reduction in loadings associated with more stringent discharge limits on a case-study watershed may reduce the number of twenty-hour-violations of EPA's ammonia standard from ten days to three days per year.

Second, it may be difficult to transfer the results of these studies to other sites. For example, can the results of a contingent valuation visibility study of the Grand Canyon be transferred to Zion Canyon or the Black Canyon of the Gunnison? Or, to get away from the unique features of these sites, can the results of a study of the value of achieving "fishable," "swimmable" status on the Charles River be transferred to, say, the Mahoning or Monongahela rivers?

Finally, it is difficult to know how well the survey baseline corresponds with existing environmental conditions at the case-study sites. The population living in the case-study watershed, for example, may consider the existing (baseline) water quality to be "fishable" and may value further improvements very differently from survey respondents living in the vicinity of the survey watershed.

Such questions do not, of course, break new ground in evaluating the contingent valuation approach. But the attempt to apply the results of these studies in a benefit-cost analysis raises some additional questions about their use. More broadly, this discussion suggests that when there are several available approaches for estimating benefits, more work should be done in the following areas: comparisons of different approaches to determine whether they yield consistent results; comparisons of the results of a single approach across sites to determine whether results are consistent; and follow-up studies to determine whether the models used in projecting user benefits yield plausible results in light of benefits actually realized from an improvement in environmental quality.

CONCLUSION

In selecting these several issues, I have tried to convey the vulnerability of the benefit-cost requirement. Clearly, the analysis is dependent on the validity of the underlying assumptions. Further, as a technology-forcing requirement, the executive order requires the application of benefit-cost analysis to regulatory decision making in areas in which it has not been used before. The attempt to develop these analyses will raise important methodological issues that must be resolved before we can accept the indicated results with any confidence. As a result, Executive Order 12291 is only one of the initial steps in the long process of improving environmental regulation.

APPENDIX

Case Study: Iron and Steel Discharge Limits under the Clean Water Act

EPA's analysis in the iron and steel rule followed two separate tracks. EPA's first approach—undertaken largely in response to an analysis sponsored by the American Iron and Steel Institute—was to compare a pro rata share of a national estimate of the benefits from cleanup of the nation's waters to the expected industrywide cost of meeting the discharge standards. EPA's second approach was to carry out a benefit-cost analysis of the cleanup of three specific streams—the Black River, The Mahoning River, and the Monongahela River.

There are, of course, important difficulties with a pro rata share approach. The national estimates were based in part on an extrapolation of stream-specific benefits estimates. The reasonableness of these national estimates, then, depends on the procedures for aggregation and the representativeness of the individual streams. EPA assigned a portion of the benefits to the cleanup of steel industry discharges using the fraction of total loadings originated by the steel industry. It is unlikely, though, that the damages of steel plant discharges are a linear function of pollutant loadings. Because the benefits of cleanup are site-specific, the required cleanup may have little effect on water quality, or the benefits of improved water quality may vary substantially across plants because of differences in population density or the availability of nearby water bodies. Finally, EPA added an estimate of the likely public health benefits on a pro rata basis resulting from cleanup of steel industry discharges. Public health benefits may well be limited, however, because there are few intakes for public water supply in the reaches immediately downstream of the discharge pipes for a steel mill.

In its case studies, EPA came much closer to the kind of benefit-cost analysis contemplated by EO 12291. In these three case studies, EPA examined the effects of requiring control at a level equal to Best Available Technology on three rivers: the Black River, the Mahoning River, and the Monongahela River. EPA and the states had conducted an extensive modeling exercise in developing permits for the steel plants discharging into these streams. EPA argued that these studies show that the water quality improvements associated with the cleanup of current discharges to meet the more stringent BAT limits would lead to important boating, fishing, and recreation improvements. In particular, the resulting improvement in water quality would support a sport fish population in stretches of these rivers that currently support only a rough fish population.

In developing its benefits estimate, EPA relied on studies in the existing literature on the benefits of a cleanup of water quality. EPA developed separate estimates of the likely benefits from studies of fishing and boating benefits to users using participation models, recreation planning models, and an estimate of users' willingness to pay based on Frederick W. Gramlich's survey for the Charles River. EPA added to its estimate of user benefits an estimate of the willingness to pay for cleanup on the part of nonusers. On the basis of its benefit-cost study for these three rivers, EPA concluded: "The findings outlined . . . show that for two of the three rivers the compliance costs lie within the respective estimated benefits ranges. . . . However, the costs are in the lower end of the benefits range, suggesting that net social benefits would more likely be positive than negative. . . . The figures also indicate that for the third river, the Monongahela, the benefits clearly outweigh the costs."[10]

Problems that arise when using the benefits analysis are translating a reduction in discharge loadings into water quality effects; allocating benefits of cleanup across sources; accepting benefits estimates derived from willingness-to-pay surveys; and fitting the benefit-estimating models to these site-specific cases.

Translating Discharge Loadings into Water Quality Effects

EPA argued that its studies—used in the permitting of steel plant discharges—supported the contention that the reduction in loadings required by BAT-level standards would result in significant water quality improvements. In addition, existing bioassay studies indicated that stream segments immediately downstream from steel plant outfalls do not support sport fish populations. Consultants for the steel industry argued that control of discharges would have no significant effect on water quality because of the limited additional reduction in pollutant loadings. On the Mahoning, this reduction was contrasted with the substantial loadings from other sources, especially nonpoint sources; on the Monongahela, this reduction changes the number of days ambient concentrations exceed water quality standards by only a small amount—say, from ten days to three days a year.

Benefits Estimates Derived from Willingness-to-Pay Surveys

In using a willingness-to-pay approach to estimate the benefits of cleanup, EPA relied on Gramlich's survey study of the willingness to pay indicated by families in the Cambridge, Massachusetts area for cleanup of the Charles River.[11] The estimates derived using this approach contribute significantly to EPA's estimate of the benefits of imposing BAT requirements on the steel industry, both because they are responsible for the upper bound of EPA's estimate of user benefits and through their contribution to the estimate of nonuser benefits (particularly on the Monongahela River).

I am concerned about the use of benefits estimates derived from such studies. First, they involve a subjective statement about the willingness to pay by the households participating in the survey. They are not based on the costs willingly incurred by these households and, as a result, the estimates derived using this approach are likely to be biased upward. In fact, we know that responses in these surveys are very sensitive to the way in which the surveys are conducted. Of course, apart from the questions of survey bias, it is also not clear how well the cleanup as represented in the survey correlates with the likely improvement in water quality for these three streams under the regulation. In addition, it is difficult to allocate the estimated benefits of cleanup where cleanup is jointly dependent on a more stringent control of the discharges from several sources.

Allocating Benefits of Cleanup across Sources

Assessment of the effect of more stringent discharge limits on steel facilities may also be contingent on cleanup of other plants discharging into the same water body.

In particular, in its analysis of the Black River, EPA's analysis recognizes that a full cleanup of the river would also require a more stringent control of the discharges from a sewage treatment plant upstream of the steel plant. But the analysis never confronts the problem of allocating the benefits of cleanup between the two facilities.

EPA's lower-bound estimates derived from the fishing and boating participation models assumed a cleanup of a limited segment of the river; the upper-bound estimates assumed that the sewage treatment plant cleaned up first and that all the benefits of a "fishable, boatable" river could be attributed to BAT cleanup by the steel plant. In developing an estimate based on the willingness-to-pay approach, all the benefits of the expected improvement in water quality were assigned to BAT-level cleanup by the steel plant, ignoring the cleanup required for the sewage treatment plant. The evaluation of source-specific standards when multiple sources contribute to an environmental problem is difficult because neither the biologic nor the economic models are well suited to sort out the incremental effects of a cleanup by a single source.

Fitting the Existing Literature to These Site-Specific Cases

In developing its benefits estimates for these case-study rivers, EPA used studies from the existing literature to derive a benefits estimate. There are inevitably questions about how well the models in the existing literature fit the specific case, for example: Can the Russell-Vaughan model of fishing participation be adjusted to reflect adequately the proximity of fishing opportunities on nearby Lake Erie?[12] Will an improvement in boating conditions result from BAT cleanup of steel mill discharges? If so, how should that cleanup be represented in the boating participation model EPA relied on in developing its benefit estimates?[13] Can Gramlich's study of the benefits of cleanup of the Charles River be transferred readily to the cleanup of three midwestern rivers?[14]

Of course, the problem is that the existing literature on the benefits of water cleanup is so thin that an analysis of benefits must force the few studies available to fit the case-study rivers. But it leaves a lot of room for second-guessing on whether the necessary assumptions are appropriate.

NOTES

1. U.S. Office of Management and Budget, "Interim Regulatory Impact Analysis Guidance."

2. Indeed, some have argued that the framework of these statutes is so seriously deficient that an efficient environmental regulation can be achieved only with a fundamental change in the political economy of the environmental statutes. This is Robert W. Crandall's thesis in Chapter 8 in this volume.

3. Often the statutory language is ambiguous, giving the agency some discretion in its reliance on such analysis in rulemaking. In some cases, though, the statutory language explicitly requires a balancing of benefits and costs in setting standards. For example, Section 1412(a) (2) of the Safe Drinking Water Act requires that standards be set to provide protection at the "extent feasible . . . (taking costs into consideration)."

4. Paul R. Portney outlines several of these changes in Chapter 9 in this volume.
5. The remaining three were rules governing the disposal of hazardous wastes under the Resource Conservation and Recovery Act. Although no RIAs were submitted with these rules, EPA expects to complete RIAs covering this program in 1983.
6. In a separate part of its rulemaking package (not in the RIA), EPA estimated that these wastes, if disposed as required under the proposed rule, would cause no more than one thousand premature deaths over ten thousand years. Changes in the stringency of these standards would yield modest changes in the expected number of premature deaths. All of the deaths associated with the disposal of these wastes would occur many hundreds of years from the date of installation. By contrast, EPA estimated that the natural ore bodies, if left unmined, would likely cause from three hundred to one million premature deaths over the ten thousand-year period (*Federal Register* 47 [29 December 1982]: 58196–206).
7. For example, EPA argued that under its rule the resulting improvement in water quality would permit the return of game fish species in stretches of river below the steel mills. The steel industry argued that more stringent discharge standards would not yield any significant change in water quality. EPA's analysis treated the projected improvement in water quality as "certain."
8. EPA is relying heavily on the contingent valuation approach in developing estimates of the benefits of environmental cleanup in several of its regulatory analyses.
9. See for example, Desvousges, Smith, and McGivney, *Alternative Approaches.*
10. U.S. Environmental Protection Agency, "Regulatory Impact Analysis of the Effluent Limitation Guidelines Regulation for the Iron and Steel Industry," 12 January 1982, p. 59.
11. Gramlich, "The Demand for Clean Water."
12. Russell and Vaughan, "Fresh Water Recreational Fishing."
13. Davidson, Adams, and Seneca, "The Social Value of Water Recreational Facilities Resulting from an Improvement in Water Quality."
14. Gramlich, "Demand for Clean Water."

4

ANN FISHER*

AN OVERVIEW AND EVALUATION OF EPA'S GUIDELINES FOR CONDUCTING REGULATORY IMPACT ANALYSES

As an early part of the Reagan administration's overall strategy to improve regulatory decision making, President Reagan signed Executive Order 12291 on 17 February 1981. This order requires sponsoring agencies to prepare Regulatory Impact Analyses for major rules[1] and submit them to the Office of Management and Budget for review before taking regulatory action. The Environmental Protection Agency's formal response was to draft guidelines on how to conduct an RIA for an environmental regulation. This chapter discusses the evolution and content of the guidelines, evaluates the legal and political constraints involved, and indicates how they compare with a "first best" set of guidelines from a conceptual perspective.

The first section briefly covers the process EPA used to draft its guidelines and their major components. Detailed discussions follow on how the efficiency aspects—benefits and costs—of a proposed regulation might be measured. The next section describes how the guidelines suggest that benefits and costs can be combined to get a net benefits estimate and the roles of time, uncertainty, distribution, and cost impact issues in an RIA. The chapter concludes with indications of how EPA's guidelines might have been improved and how effective they are likely to be.

*Benefits Staff, Economic Analysis Division, U.S. Environmental Protection Agency. I appreciate comments from Ralph Luken, Jeffrey Kolb, Alan Carlin, John Akin, and especially V. Kerry Smith. The views presented are mine alone and do not represent the views of EPA.

EPA'S GUIDELINES FOR PERFORMING REGULATORY
IMPACT ANALYSES: BACKGROUND

In the summer of 1981, EPA formed an agencywide work group to develop an internal policy for implementing EO 12291 and OMB's "Interim Regulatory Impact Analysis Guidance" (OMB's "Guidance"). This effort resulted in drafts of the "Guidelines for Performing Regulatory Impact Analyses" ("RIA Guidelines") and supporting appendixes with in-depth descriptions of issues and methodologies on benefits, costs, economic impact and distributional effects, and discounting.

These drafts were circulated informally for comment among analytical staffs in EPA's headquarters and regional program offices and were reviewed by a number of outside experts. A January 1982 revision of the "RIA Guidelines" was sent to EPA's associate and assistant administrators, to program offices, and to outside parties—including environmental organizations, industrial groups, private research organizations, university scholars, and government agencies such as OMB.

After incorporating feedback from these various sources, the "RIA Guidelines" finally became official EPA policy in December 1983. The appendixes to the "RIA Guidelines" are being revised to maintain consistency, and another appendix has been added, with two hypothetical sample RIAs to illustrate how the "RIA Guidelines" and its appendixes could be applied.[2]

EPA's "RIA Guidelines" summarize the relevant components of EO 12291 and OMB's "Guidance," and describe the analytical methods and procedures to use in preparing an environmental regulation's RIA. They state the goal toward which EPA will strive in developing RIAs: to present the benefits and costs to society of alternative courses of action and to explain these and other implications of the recommended alternative.

For some RIAs, off-the-shelf methodologies and studies can provide the basis for benefit and cost analyses. One example is the adoption of existing studies to estimate benefits in the RIA for iron and steel effluent guidelines. Off-the-shelf research results also can be useful for many aspects of cost estimation, especially inasmuch as EPA has more experience with this type of analysis. On the other hand, more analysis of both benefits and costs will be necessary to fill conceptual and empirical gaps in many cases. For some of these, EPA's program offices, Office of Research and Development, and Office of Policy, Planning, and Evaluation (OPPE) are coordinating efforts to provide inputs for upcoming RIAs.

Even so, the "RIA Guidelines" recognize that particular RIAs will vary in their level of detail and quantification and in their degree of certainty.

These differences will result from variations in the nature and quantity of underlying data, in the adequacy of the available analytical methodology, and in resource or time constraints, or because the particular environmental problems or control methodologies do not lend themselves to quantification. In the early stages of developing an RIA, program offices are encouraged to reach informal agreement with EPA's OPPE and with OMB about the appropriate procedures, extent of detail, and degree of quantification.[3]

Organizationally, the "RIA Guidelines" outline factors and methodologies to be considered in stating the need for the proposed regulatory action, examining alternative approaches to the problem, quantifying benefits and costs and valuing them in dollar terms (when feasible), and evaluating the findings on benefits and costs.[4] Although the appendixes provide more background and suggest how to proceed with the analyses, they do not set forth additional requirements. The following sections highlight key features of EPA's "RIA Guidelines." They discuss benefits, costs, and how to combine them to assess the net social benefits of a regulatory proposal.

COMBINING BENEFITS AND COSTS

Assessing Benefits

Because the benefits of environmental regulations typically are not exchanged in markets, their measurement and valuation is more difficult than for ordinary commodities. Decreased pollution leads to improvements in health and aesthetics and reductions in damages to plants, animals, and materials. In some cases, it is possible to trace the release of a particular pollutant to its impact on ambient environmental quality, resulting exposures, and adverse effects, and ultimately to what people would pay to avoid those effects. Possible mitigating behavior, such as material or crop substitution and medical care, make this chain of effects difficult to model. Thus, particularly when there is substantial uncertainty as to the magnitude or effects of pollution impacts, it may be more feasible to examine the value people place on reducing the discharge itself (because of their concern about potential risks).

QUANTIFYING HEALTH EFFECTS. Because EPA's primary mission is to protect public health, the most important component of its RIAs usually is an analysis of health benefits. This section of the "RIA Guidelines" has created the most controversy, both in the method of quantifying health effects and in placing a dollar value on them.[5]

The "RIA Guidelines" recommend pushing the state of the art in quantifying health effects. Limited understanding of disease mechanisms and of the relation between releases of substances and their path into the human body leads to major uncertainties in health risk assessment. In line with EPA's past approach, and with much of the toxicological literature, health risk assessment is viewed as a two-stage process: first, identification of risk, or the discovery that a substance can cause adverse effects; and second, risk estimation, which combines measurement of the likelihood that alternative exposure levels will cause particular adverse effects with estimation of the probability that these exposures will occur.

Information in four main areas can assist with the identification of a toxic substance and the prediction of the degree of harm for particular exposure levels: epidemiological evidence on actual human response; animal (*in vivo*) experiments; short-term *in vitro* tests; and structure activity analysis. EPA uses one or a combination of the first two, when data are available. Although the latter two are helpful as screening devices, there is no well-accepted procedure for their use in predicting human response to various amounts of specific substances.

Table 4.1 gives a brief outline of the features, advantages, and disadvantages of this information.[6] There are several major problems. Very few epidemiological data are available. Although animal studies are the most widely used, they are costly and time-consuming (more than $500,000 and three years per substance), and there are substantial uncertainties associated with using animal data to predict human responses to specific exposure levels. Another major hurdle is to predict the changes in exposure, particularly for relevant subgroups, that would occur from a particular regulatory action.

The "RIA Guidelines" treat carcinogens and noncarcinogens separately.[7] This approach is consistent with much of the biomedical literature, which finds that many carcinogens do not appear to have a threshold, but most noncarcinogens do have a threshold dose below which there are no adverse health effects.[8] This classification typically reflects a difference in data availability as well. For both carcinogens and noncarcinogens, more effort has been devoted to risk identification than to risk estimation. Substances identified as potential (or confirmed) human carcinogens often have been studied in lifetime animal experiments, however, so that some data are available for constructing dose-response functions.[9] Frequently, data for noncarcinogens are far more limited, precluding construction of dose-response functions.

Given these difficulties, the "RIA Guidelines" call for evaluating a substance for each potential adverse effect, analyzing the likelihood that a substance has been falsely identified as harmful, and calculating relative risk for various population groups. It is recognized that the ability to perform these analyses will vary substantially. To account for each stage of uncertainty, best estimates should be accompanied by confidence intervals whenever possible.

The present version of the "RIA Guidelines" allows a variety of models to be used for both dose-response and exposure estimates. EPA currently is reviewing its policy for assessing cancer risk. As refinements are adopted, they will be incorporated in the "RIA Guidelines."

For noncarcinogens, health risk assessment often is more difficult. EPA has proposed guidelines for assessing mutagenicity risk. Until they are finalized, current methodologies (based primarily on radiation studies) are recommended when data are available. There are no currently agreed-upon methods for quantifying teratogenic risk. The present approach is to demonstrate a no-observable-effect level (NOEL) in mammalian tests and then apply a margin of safety. This approach is similar to that used for substances that cause acute or chronic toxic effects but have no evidence of carcinogenicity.[10] Safety factors are applied to account for uncertainties in the difference in sensitivity between test animals and humans (that is, in the conversion of animal dose to an equivalent human dose) and the susceptibility of more sensitive subpopulations and sometimes to account for chronic rather than subchronic exposure. The resulting safe exposure levels are designed to have zero risk and do not account for the possibility that substantially larger doses also could have zero risk. When the data permit, a dose-response function for noncarcinogens should be developed. When the data are inadequate for estimating dose-response functions or exposure, however, a method relying on experts' assessments of all available data to predict risk levels can be used, as described in the benefits appendix of the "RIA Guidelines."

VALUING HEALTH EFFECTS. Because EO 12291 calls for quantification and monetization whenever possible, the "RIA Guidelines" address the issue of valuing health effects. The willingness-to-pay concept is recognized as the appropriate approach, but data limitations and political realities limit its use. The costs-avoided approach is recommended for reductions in morbidity. These costs would include medical costs, loss of work and earnings, and impact on productivity. The "RIA Guidelines" mention that this approach understates the benefits of reduced morbidity by ignoring pain and suffering and the value of time for people who are not in the labor force.

Table 4.1. Data Sources for Determining Dose-Response Functions

HUMAN DATA

Clinical Studies (for example, for sulfur dioxide):

A planned research experiment is conducted, with controlled exposure levels.

Ethical considerations and legal restrictions limit the use of this approach.

The data are generally for a pollutant's impact on an index of organ function rather than for disease (and clearly not death).

Cohort Studies (prospective or retrospective)

Groups with different exposures to a suspect substance are followed over time to determine differences in response.

Large samples, long follow-up periods, and statistical analysis to account for other influences are required.

It is difficult to detect rare effects, especially for retrospective studies with poor exposure records.

Case Control Studies

A group with a disease is compared to a control group without it to see if exposure differs between the two groups.

Studies may be macroepidemiological* in which aggregate mortality and morbidity rates are related to characteristics of relevant population groups or microepidemiological† in which analyses are based on data for particular individuals.

They can adjust for other influences such as sex, race, smoking, income, diet, and exercise.

Sample sizes can be smaller than for cohort studies, but finding a suitable control group may be difficult.

Data usually do not consider lag between exposure and adverse health effect.

Current exposure typically is assumed to be the same as past exposure for cumulative health effects.

Results can be biased by population migration or mitigating actions that make actual exposure differ from apparent exposure.

Results from occupation-related studies may not be applicable to the much lower doses expected in the environment, especially for people with varying sensitivities compared with workers.

Episodic Studies (for example, methylmercury poisoning from contaminated grain in Iraq)

These studies depend on accidents, so investigators are unprepared, control groups may not exist, and therapy takes precedence over research.

ANIMAL DATA

Animal (in vivo) *Experiments*

Controlled laboratory setting permits isolation of effects from a specific substance.

The full effects of the substance can be examined because animals can be permitted to get a disease and die.

Response identification often is not clear-cut.

Shorter life spans for animals yield results faster than for cohort studies of humans.

Table 4.1 continued

Uncertainties arise in predicting response at much lower environmental exposures, based on high test doses.

Uncertainties arise with respect to translating animal response into predictions of human response for equivalent exposures.

A controlled experiment may show no response to the isolated substance, whereas a realistic setting may involve synergism with other substances.

Short-term in vitro *Tests*

Bacteria, mammalian cell cultures, or small organisms are observed (after exposure) for a few days to a few weeks.

Tests are far less costly than lifetime animal experiments.

Tests have been developed for relatively few endpoints.

Concordance between the results of short-term tests and lifetime animal studies is imperfect for the (relatively few) substances that have been compared.

STRUCTURE ACTIVITY ANALYSIS

Molecular structures of suspect substances are compared with substances whose toxicity and metabolic pathways are well known.

The data base is weak for some classes of chemicals in this relatively new field.

---

*See, for example, Lave and Seskin, *Air Pollution and Human Health.*
†See Ostro, "Effects of Air Pollution on Work Loss and Morbidity."

For reductions in mortality risk, no value is assigned. When all benefits and costs other than reductions in mortality risk have been quantified and monetized, any net costs could be divided by the expected reduction in statistical deaths to find that regulation's cost per life saved. The resulting implicit value per statistical life may then be compared with the results of market behavior studies showing that people appear to demand compensation for small risks to life such that a single expected fatality is valued at $400,000 to $7,000,000 (in 1982 dollars).

These figures are based primarily on studies of wage premiums in risky occupations, which show that differing groups of individuals require $400–$7,000 in additional annual income voluntarily to accept increased annual job-related risks of death of about one in a thousand.[11] A regulation that reduces risk of death to each of a thousand people by .001 would save one life in expected value terms. The increased safety would then be worth $400,000 to $7,000,000. Although this is an a priori analytical measure of the value of safety to one thousand people, among whom one person—unidentifiable in advance—is expected to die, rather than an ex post measure of compensation for a particular death, many people find it ethically unacceptable to place a dollar value on human life.[12] When combined with the shortcomings of the studies used to determine the $400,000 to $7,000,-000 range, this view supports the implicit valuation approach adopted in the "RIA Guidelines." This range is conservative; some studies have yielded higher empirical estimates.[13] The "RIA Guidelines" point out that this implicit valuation approach—of examining the cost per life saved—breaks down when there are several types of nonmonetized benefits.

NONHEALTH BENEFITS. Quantification and monetization may be more feasible for nonhealth than for health effects. Nonhealth effects range from aesthetics to preservation of ecosystems to enhanced agricultural productivity and materials performance. One technique that can be used is the damage function approach, which examines physical effects and then accounts for economic behavior such as mitigation and substitution. Because several steps are involved by the time dollar benefits are calculated, however, considerable uncertainty may exist in the final benefit figures. When this consideration is combined with time and budget constraints, it may be desirable to use alternative techniques that study economic responses directly rather than relying on the physical damages approach.

Some techniques consider market goods that are closely tied to environmental conditions. Examples would be the direct cost approach (which relies on estimates of cost savings to various groups as a result of environmental regulation[14]), the hedonic approach (in which property values or wages are related to the relevant attributes of the parcel or job, including environmental amenities), and the travel cost approach (which relates the value of a recreation site to the expenditures associated with visiting that site). In addition, recent studies have related the economic effect of pollution to entire sectors of the economy.[15] Each of these approaches has difficulties in practice. In some cases, an environmental benefit is not tied closely enough to any market commodity (for example, visibility in western national parks or preservation of a species), or market data do not yet exist (for example, related to the risk of a new chemical). In such instances, contingent valuation surveys asking people about their willingness to pay for hypothetical levels of environmental quality may be the only available alternative.

Rather than specifying a particular approach for each situation, the "RIA Guidelines" indicate that each of these techniques has shortcomings and that the one most appropriate depends on the affected group, the nature of the environmental commodity, and connnections between the environmental good and related markets. Generally, the direct cost approach can be used for commercial effects, such as reduced damages to fisheries, forests, and agriculture and building or machinery lifetimes. Travel costs and property value studies can be used for recreation and some aesthetic benefits. For intrinsic effects, such as aesthetics or the existence and functioning of ecosystems, it may be necessary to rely on contingent valuation surveys.

Analyzing Costs

For some time, EPA has generated cost estimates during the rulemaking process. These estimates have tended to focus on compliance costs for private parties directly affected by regulation. The "RIA Guidelines" define a broader concept of the total opportunity cost to society, including the value of goods and services lost by society resulting from the use of resources to comply with a regulation, the use of resources to implement a regulation, and any reduction in output in lieu of compliance. These costs fall into four general categories: private-sector real-resource costs, deadweight welfare losses, government regulatory costs, and adjustment costs. As in the case of benefit assessment, uncertainty should be accounted for by including upper- and lower-bound estimates as well as best estimates of costs.

Firms' compliance costs (investment costs and the present value of regulation-related variable costs) for most regulations will account for nearly all the costs to society. These costs are already estimated by EPA, relying primarily on engineering cost estimates.[16] In addition, many program offices now include monitoring, enforcement, and other government regulatory costs in their analyses. The "RIA Guidelines" state that efforts to estimate remaining components of total social costs should vary with their importance, depending on the specific regulation. For both costs and cost impacts (which are discussed in the next section), it is recognized that more information and analysis are worthwhile only if their value exceeds their costs. Budget limitations can be expected to direct more RIA analytical efforts toward proposed regulations with potentially high costs, strong controversy, and large uncertainties.

Although a dynamic, general-equilibrium framework is the ideal way to trace the direct and indirect social costs over the full adjustment period, practical considerations lead to recommending a static, partial-equilibrium approach for estimating compliance costs and net welfare losses incurred by producers and consumers because of decreased output.[17] Minimal effort should be expended in measuring the deadweight welfare loss (because it generally will be small), except for such programs as TSCA that give EPA the power to ban substances and prohibit or limit specific uses.

Government regulatory costs include litigation, enforcement, permitting, monitoring and reporting (if not already measured in compliance costs), and any other costs related to that regulation and incurred by federal, state, or local agencies. Only postpromulgation costs should be included because costs incurred before that point are sunk costs.

A cost analysis should include adjustment costs for displaced resources because some of them fail to be reemployed elsewhere in the economy, because there are resource reallocation costs (such as time and money spent job-hunting and moving), and because society expends resources to operate programs to help the unemployed. The partial-equilibrium framework tends to overstate these adjustment costs, but this is mitigated to some extent by measuring lost wages rather than lost production because it is likely that nonlabor inputs will be reallocated relatively quickly. The focus on adjustment costs in this portion of the RIA is to examine their net effect on total social costs. The equity effects of the cost impacts, including transfers as well as real resource costs, are discussed in the next section.

The "RIA Guidelines" also call for an assessment (usually qualitative) of a regulation's effect on product quality, productivity, innovation, and market structure. The cost appendix provides suggestions for estimating the costs associated with unconventional regulatory alternatives. These include pollution charges (such as emission fees, user charges, and product charges); recycling, reuse, and disposal incentives (subsidies for pollution reduction and refundable deposits); trading pollution entitlements (bubbles, offsets, and marketable permits); pollution indemnity (so that injured parties may be more readily compensated); information and labeling rules (for specific substances or contaminated sites); and government cost-sharing (for example, in pollution-control equipment).

Putting It All Together

Choosing a discount rate is crucial in calculating the present value estimate of net benefits required by EO 12291, particularly inasmuch as many of EPA's regulations require large initial outlays and have long gestation periods before benefits are realized. The 10 percent figure mandated in OMB's "Guidance" may not reflect the opportunity costs associated with each of the many ways of financing public investments, differences in their riskiness, differences in the form of the benefits and costs, and differences in their distribution. Since OMB's "Guidance" does allow the use of other rates to test the sensitivity of results, the discount rate appendix summarizes the rationale behind each of four approaches for selecting social discount rates for benefit-cost analyses of environmental programs: shadow price of capital, opportunity cost, weighted average, and social rate of time preference.

The approach using the shadow price of capital appears to be the soundest theoretically, but it may be difficult to implement because benefits and costs must be adjusted by their opportunity costs before discounting by the social rate of time preference. For this reason, and because there is not yet a consensus among economists as to the best approach, program offices are allowed to choose the one most appropriate for each regulation.[18] The discount rate appendix implies that a real rate of return between zero and 5 percent generally will be appropriate.[19] If the discount rate accounts for risk-averseness, then risk-free regulations would be discounted at the lower end of that range.[20]

Benefits and costs that are most sensitive to the discount rate—those expected to occur many years in the future—also are likely to be the ones most difficult to predict. Thus particular care should be taken to ensure that discounting does not inadvertently oversimplify or distort the evaluation of a proposed rule. Discounting applies only to benefits and costs that have been monetized, and important unquantifiable and nonmonetized benefits and costs should not be neglected in the regulatory decision.

The net benefit calculation should be accompanied by a presentation and evaluation of all benefits and costs that can be quantified but not monetized as well as those that are unquantifiable. Economic impact and distributional issues are evaluated in the RIA's section on net benefits. For all benefits (monetized, quantified only, and unquantifiable), the benefit schedule should show the type of benefit, to whom it will accrue, and when it will accrue. Similarly, the cost schedule should identify the type of cost, who will bear it, and when it will be incurred. The intratemporal part of the schedule, showing "to whom," relies on the type of economic impact analysis EPA has performed routinely. The intertemporal part, however, showing "when," relies on a new form of intergenerational equity analysis.

The primary economic impacts are those on prices, production, industry profitability and capital availability, and employment. Secondary effects, including influences on secondary employment, the community, the balance of trade, and energy, should be examined if primary effects are substantial or if there is reason to believe that any of these impact categories are likely to be important in the decision process. Although many effects will be detrimental, some may be positive (such as expanded production of pollution-control equipment or of substitutes for the pollution-related product). The appendix on distribution and economic impact analysis details how to evaluate these effects.

Equity impacts are likely to be small and transitory for regulations with a time horizon of less than one generation. Transfer payments or taxes can be used to mitigate important undesirable effects. For regulatory actions with intergenerational impacts, however—time horizons exceeding the twenty-five- to thirty-year range—the economic efficiency criterion is less suitable as a guide for decision making.[21] For example, disposal of long-lived hazardous wastes raises issues of the equitable distribution of benefits and costs across generations.

There is no entirely satisfactory method for examining the sensitivity of intergenerational distribution of benefits and costs to alternative social discount rates. The "RIA Guidelines" recommend, however, that for regulatory alternatives with negative net discounted benefits because of their long horizon, the analysis should include the number of years until net undiscounted benefits become positive and the number of years and amounts by which they remain positive. Accepting a proposed regulation on this basis would be consistent with the overtaking principle.[22] Alternatively, undiscounted benefits to future generations can be compared directly with costs to the current generation.

The "RIA Guidelines" stress that monetizing as many benefits and costs as feasible allows the administrator to concentrate on the importance of remaining costs and benefits, to judge whether they are significant enough to change the decision indicated on the basis of the net benefit estimate. An RIA is broader than a traditional narrowly defined benefit-cost analysis that examines only efficiency. In addition to considering efficiency, an RIA explicitly is to describe and evaluate nonmonetizable and unquantifiable benefits and costs, as well as the distribution of benefits and costs.

In some cases, legal constraints prevent the comparison of benefits and costs from playing a role in the choice among regulatory alternatives. For example, the 1977 Clean Air Act Amendments specify that primary standards for criteria air pollutants should be set to protect public health. Then risk assessment procedures can be used to determine exposure levels that will eliminate risk, but the value of this risk reduction (that is, the benefits of improved health) cannot explicitly enter the standards decision. Although an RIA is still required in such instances, it should explicitly state that benefit-cost analysis cannot be used in the regulatory decision and explain the legal basis for that determination.[23] This RIA also would provide cost-effectiveness analysis of several alternatives that would achieve essentially the same predetermined regulatory goal. Unless this goal happens to be the one that maximizes net social benefits, the evaluation of a proposed air standard (returning to the example above) from the health benefit perspective is likely to lead to different conclusions compared with its evaluation based on health effects.

EVALUATING EPA'S "RIA GUIDELINES" AND APPENDIXES

One way to evaluate the "RIA Guidelines" is to compare them with those available for other benefit-cost analyses. The Department of Transportation (DOT) is the only other federal agency identified as developing guidance in response to EO 12291.[24]

For many issues, the treatment in "Guidance for Regulatory Evaluation" (DOT's "Guidance") is similar to that in EPA's "RIA Guidelines." Obvious differences occur on the basis of separate mandates for the two agencies. Examples would be DOT's conceptual basis for accident risk assessment compared with EPA's discussion of health risk estimation and DOT's concern about savings in travel time compared with EPA's interest in improved visibility and recreation. Other differences are the result of varying interpretations of the executive order and of the benefit-cost analysis literature.

Table 4.2 summarizes major divergences between the two sets of guidance. For example, although DOT's "Guidance" recommends that the figure be used with caution, a value per fatality of $340,000 is suggested. This figure is based on societal (not personal) losses and a 10 percent discount rate. DOT's figure can be compared with an implied value-per-statistical-life range of $400,000 to $7 million in EPA's "RIA Guidelines." Although this range is less precise, it has the advantage of being more closely related to the willingness-to-pay concept.

Another important difference between these two sets of guidance regards the discount rate. DOT's "Guidance" accepts OMB's 10 percent, although the sensitivity analysis section mentions that one parameter that might be varied is the discount rate. EPA's guidelines go further, recommending the use of justifiable lower rates in the sensitivity analysis. These lower rates may be closer to society's rate of time preference. Their use for environmental decisions with some very long-term impacts may be more crucial than for transportation regulations, for which benefits and costs are likely to follow similar time paths.

Other differences have to do with the information provided with each agency's document. For example, DOT's "Guidance" includes a checklist for implementation, whereas EPA's "RIA Guidelines" include sample (hypothetical) RIAs. On the basis of the above comparison, EPA's "RIA Guidelines" appear to be closer to the conceptually ideal approach than DOT's "Guidance."

Table 4.2. Major Divergences between Regulatory Impact Analysis Guidance for Two Agencies

DOT's "Guidance for Regulatory Evaluations"	EPA's "RIA Guidelines"
Value per fatality: $340,000, based on societal losses and a 10 percent discount rate	$400,000 to $7,000,000 (1982 dollars)
Discount rate: 10 percent, although a sensitivity analysis could vary this rate	Discount rate: 10 percent, with lower rates in a sensitivity analysis, possibly including an adjustment for uncertainty
Sensitivity analysis: Expected value approach, best case/worst case approach, or high, medium, and low cases approach	Sensitivity analysis: expected values and confidence intervals are recommended over best case/worst case approach
Checklist for elements of a regulatory evaluation	Sample (hypothetical) RIA's included as appendixes

From a policy viewpoint, the ultimate question is whether EPA's "RIA Guidelines" will result in improved decision making with respect to the criteria set forth in EO 12291 and OMB's "Guidance." On balance, the answer seems to be a qualified "yes." The "RIA Guidelines" will lead to better analyses, although they could be tightened in some areas.

Aside from more overall emphasis on examining the benefits of environmental regulations, the language on health risk assessment in the "RIA Guidelines" reflects progress. Traditionally, scientific caution and the agency's mission to protect public health led to worst-case risk estimates as the basis for regulation. Although this approach may ensure safety, it can lead to overregulation. For example, EPA's Cancer Assessment Group (CAG) previously reported only the upper 95 percent confidence level on carcinogenic risk for a specific dose. When combined with exposure estimates (that also might reflect upper confidence levels), this would give an upper bound on the number of lives "expected" to be saved (or risk units avoided) if exposure were reduced to that level. In turn, this would lower the cost-per-life-saved (or cost-per-risk-unit-reduced) figure for that regulation, making it appear to be a better bargain than best estimates would indicate.[25]

In addition, the "RIA Guidelines" suggest the use of whatever dose-response function fits the data best for carcinogen risk assessment. Because alternative dose-response functions often imply vastly differing risks at the low doses likely to occur in the environment, this can be viewed as license to choose the one that gives the "desired" answer (not necessarily the correct answer). More optimistically, this may reflect genuine uncertainty about the biomedical mechanisms causing cancer and be a step toward recognizing that some carcinogens may have thresholds.

Having a more definitive recommendation about the appropriate discount rate for environmental regulations would be convenient, but the ongoing controversy among economists makes this unlikely in the near future. The "RIA Guidelines" allow program offices to select discounting procedures that match the circumstances of the regulation under consideration. This flexibility may lead to different discount rates across RIAs. Rather than indicating inconsistency, this policy can be viewed as a recognition that when the economic effects of environmental regulations differ, the use of different discount rates may be justified. On the other hand, it could permit the selection of rates to support a predetermined end, rather than in response to specific features of the regulation. The oversight effectiveness of OPPE and OMB will determine the outcome with respect to these possibilities.

The evolution of the "RIA Guidelines" sometimes led to potential weak spots and other times resulted in improvements. For example, in identifying health risks, the "RIA Guidelines'" language calls for "a discussion of the likelihood that the substance may be harmful to humans" (p. 7). Program offices may interpret this statement as permitting a qualitative evaluation, rather than requiring a probability statement as to the correctness of the harmful classification. An early draft explicitly required a probability statement, but critics wanted the entire concept eliminated. Negotiation led to the compromise outlined above.

Some reviewers may criticize the "RIA Guidelines'" lack of direct valuation of mortality effects, particularly because the implicit valuation technique breaks down when there are nonmonetized benefits or costs in addition to reductions in mortality risk. It is politically unpopular, however, even to do risk assessments that could lead to "body counts," or the number of statistical lives saved by a proposed regulation. As a result, one version of the "RIA Guidelines" did not require estimation of the number of people who may be made ill or die. Instead it provided for an alternative expression of health risk in terms of risk units, in which one risk unit equals a 10^{-6} change in lifetime risk for one person. Although it is possible to convert risk units into statistical lives, the risk unit notion might be more acceptable, because it is intuitively closer to the decision being made. That is, an environmental regulation reduces the health risk to each person by a small amount. This concept also is closely related to the measures used (the value of small reductions in the probability of death) in studies that have estimated the value of a statistical life. The final version, however, relies on the statistical-lives-saved concept.

In the future, it may be desirable to move toward weighting larger risks more heavily. This would be consistent with the literature indicating that people place higher values, for example, on a reduction of .001 for a risk of 10^{-2} than on that same reduction associated with a risk of 10^{-3} [26] In a similar vein, it may be possible to narrow the range of values per statistical life mentioned in the previous section. There are a number of shortcomings in the studies upon which that range is based, and most of the studies did not examine environmental risks explicitly. With increased research, it may be possible to argue that the value of reducing mortality risk from environmental pollution lies within a particular range, whereas the value of the same risk reduction from, for example, a traffic death lies in some other range.[27]

A general limitation of the "RIA Guidelines" and appendixes stems from the attempt to develop a concise document that would be applicable to the diverse programs and regulations for which EPA is responsible. More attention is given to this problem in the appendixes, but it may be necessary to develop additional background papers for specific programs or regulations. This will be facilitated by EPA's view that the "RIA Guidelines" will require periodic updating to reflect refinements in various agency policies (such as the cancer policy and mutagenicity guidelines).

Although early drafts of the "RIA Guidelines" required cost-effectiveness analysis in all circumstances, the final language is consistent with EO 12291 and OMB's "Guidance." It requires cost-effectiveness analysis for several alternatives when some can achieve essentially the same regulatory goal at lower cost or when many benefits are not easily quantified. The "RIA Guidelines" point out that cost-effectiveness analysis does not tell how much control is optimal, so that it must begin with an external policy goal of a desired level of effect or a cost limit.

There is limited evidence as to the effectiveness of the RIA requirement and of EPA's guidelines for implementing that requirement. So far, the regulations that have been sent to OMB have had positive net economic benefits. This may reflect program offices' reluctance to send forward "bad" regulations for fear that they might be sent back. From a realistic point of view, it is still too early to assess the long-term impacts of EO 12291 and of EPA's "RIA Guidelines."

These long-term impacts largely depend on how regulatory impact analysis fits into EPA's overall process of rulemaking. During 1982 and

1983, several program offices worked to make their RIAs conform to the draft guidelines. Nevertheless, the guidelines lacked the authority of agency policy as long as they were in draft form.

Now that the "RIA Guidelines" are official EPA policy, their effectiveness will depend on the availability of resources to conduct RIAs and on enforcement within the agency and by OMB. Available evidence indicates that substantial resources are being devoted to RIAs as part of the regulatory development process. The importance of the findings in an RIA is not yet clear. The internal debate over the supporting analyses for the particulate matter national ambient air quality standards RIA indicates that the process has led to more detailed documentation of the implications of alternative levels for these standards. Thus internal oversight appears to be consistent with the intent of the executive order. On the other hand, it is too early to assess how stringently OMB will interpret EO 12291; thus far, EPA has submitted only RIAs in which showing positive net benefits was relatively straightforward.

In summary, arduous negotiations were a key in the process of developing EPA's "RIA Guidelines." Nevertheless, the overall result has the potential to lead to analyses that pay more attention to the relationship between a proposed regulation's monetizable benefits and costs. This should not downplay the significance in the decision process of nonmonetizable and unquantifiable benefits and costs or of distributional considerations. The ultimate effectiveness of the "RIA Guidelines" will depend on enforcement both within EPA and by OMB. In turn, their enforcement will be affected by whether or not the benefit-cost requirement for significant rulemaking is given statutory force, as has been proposed (S. 1080 and H.R. 746, 97th Congress).

NOTES

1. EO 12291 defines "major rule" as "any regulation that is likely to result in:
    (1) An annual effect on the economy of $100 million or more;
    (2) A major increase in costs or prices for consumers, individual industries, Federal, State, or local government agencies, or geographic regions; or
    (3) Significant adverse effects on competition, employment, investment, productivity, innovation, or on the ability of the United States-based enterprises to compete with foreign-based enterprises in domestic or export markets."
    Varying interpretations of this definition may require substantial analysis for a "nonmajor" justification. The director of OMB has the authority to order that a rule or set of related rules be considered as a major rule.
2. Copies of the "RIA Guidelines" and appendixes are available through EPA's Office of Policy, Planning, and Evaluation.
3. In addition to decisions about how to handle these uncertainties, such negotia-

tion will establish expectations for regulations dealing with generic information-gathering, testing, and procedural rules (for which EPA's "RIA Guidelines" are less readily applicable).

4. Incremental benefits and costs of all alternative actions will be compared against a baseline. The baseline employed should be an estimate of the situation in the absence of taking steps to mitigate the problem at hand, but multiple baselines may be needed to account for uncertainties in what might happen without the proposed regulation.

5. That is, the damage function approach is emphasized for health effects.

6. For more detail on these approaches, see Fisher, "The Scientific Bases for Relating Health Effects to Exposure Levels," or the benefits appendix of "RIA Guidelines."

7. Noncarcinogens include mutagens, teratogens, and substances that cause any other acute or chronic toxic effects. Although carcinogens sometimes have multiple adverse health effects, cancer generally shows up at lower doses than noncancer effects.

8. The use of the threshold concept may depend on the definition of an adverse health effect. Small doses of some substances cause physiological changes without creating any noticeable illness or disability. In such cases, the finding of an adverse health effect depends partly on an arbitrary designation along the continuum from "no effect" to "death." An alternative interpretation is that indications of thresholds result from our limited analytic tools because the adverse effects from low-level exposures may get lost in the "noise."

9. Of course, interpreting these dose-response functions for human risk is compounded by the fact that high doses used in animal experiments often fit several functions equally well, yet these functions imply widely differing risks at the low doses expected in the environment. Additional uncertainties arise in translating from animal doses to human equivalents and in accounting for sensitive population subgroups.

10. For example, the NOEL approach was used to set water quality criteria for 27 of the 64 criteria pollutants (U.S. Environmental Protection Agency, "Water Quality Criteria Documents").

11. Bailey, *Reducing Risks to Life*; Blomquist, "The Value of Human Life"; Graham and Vaupel, "Value of a Life"; Thaler and Rosen, "The Value of Saving a Life"; and Viscusi, "Labor Market Valuations of Life and Limb."

12. Kelman, "Cost Benefit Analysis."

13. Olson, "An Analysis of Wage Differentials Received by Workers on Dangerous Jobs"; and Broder and Morrall, "The Economic Basis for OSHA's and EPA's General Carcinogen Regulations."

14. These estimates may come from damage functions.

15. Manuel et al., *Benefits Analysis of the Alternative Secondary National Ambient Air Quality Standards for Sulfur Dioxide and Total Suspended Particulates.*

16. Engineering cost estimates tend to be less accurate when it is necessary to extend the engineering production functions beyond the range of existing systems, as is the situation for many environmental regulations. They also may fail to include changes in the production process in lieu of pollution control equipment or changes in the overall market situation.

17. When the short-term response to regulation is thought to be substantially differ-

ent from and more costly than the long-term response, a dynamic model may be approximated by using static models to analyze several equilibrium points.

18. When benefits and costs have similar time profiles, the benefit-cost analysis will be insensitive to the use of alternative discount rates. In such cases, the RIA should make this clear, and no further effort need be devoted to supporting a particular discount rate. Similar statements apply when the benefits so outweigh the costs (or vice versa) that changes in the discount rate would not influence the policy implications of the analysis.

19. Higher rates (8–15 percent) corresponding to the opportunity cost of capital would apply to short-term regulatory actions that primarily displace private investment.

20. The riskiness of any public investment that absorbs a small fraction of national income depends on the covariance of the investment's returns with national income, when risk can be efficiently distributed. That is, rather than focusing on the returns to a particular project, the project should be viewed from the larger perspective of how it affects the returns to society. Then most environmental projects are either riskless or reduce risk. For example, the uncertainty over the likely impact of chlorofluorocarbons (CFCs) on the atmosphere (and ultimately on climate, health, and the environment) imply uncertain returns to reducing the use of CFCs. Viewed more broadly, regulation would reduce the potential variability in outcomes (and society's risk) created by the use of CFCs. Thus the discount rate for such a proposed regulation would have a negative, rather than a positive, risk factor.

21. According to Freeman ("Equity, Efficiency, and Discounting"), an efficiency viewpoint indicates that discounting should be used for intergenerational effects. Page ("Discounting and Intergenerational Equity" and "Intergenerational Justice as Opportunity") agrees that this defines the intergenerationally efficient set of projects but argues that equity considerations then should determine the choice among efficient programs.

22. Page, "Discounting," and Mishan and Page, "The Methodology of Cost Benefit Analysis."

23. Even when the regulatory decision cannot be based on the RIA, knowing the cost of reaching a statutory goal could lead to legislative change when that cost is viewed as too high (Hopkins, "E.O. 12291 and OMB Regulatory Impact Analysis Guidance").

24. Another potential candidate for comparison is the Water Resources Council's "Principles and Standards for Planning Water and Related Land Resources," although these deal primarily with nonhealth issues (physical aspects of water supplies, hydropower, navigation, recreation). In contrast, a major emphasis in EPA's RIAs will be on health effects. In addition, the "Principles and Standards" have been revised and await President Reagan's signature to repeal the existing guidance and implement the new version (to be called "Principles and Guidelines"). Given the difference in focus and their present state of flux, the "Principles and Standards" seem inappropriate as a basis for comparison.

25. When the estimates must be based on animal data, CAG still plans to report only the upper 95 percent confidence bound (with the lower bound understood to be zero). When epidemiological data are available, the best estimate will be reported along with the upper and lower bounds.

26. On the other hand, recent experiments indicate that people place higher values on a unit of risk reduction when the base risk is low, rather than high (Weinstein, "Decision Theoretic Approaches to Evaluating Health Risks"). Further research may resolve this apparent inconsistency, perhaps on the basis of the type of risk involved or because the reductions in low-level risk are often to the certainty level of zero risk. See also Jones-Lee, "The Value of Changes in the Probability of Death or Injury"; Linnerooth, "The Value of Human Life"; and Weinstein, Shepard and Pliskin, "The Economic Value of Changing Mortality Probabilities."

27. It may be important to consider age, or "quality-adjusted-life-years" lost (Arthur, "The Economics of Risk to Life"; and Zeckhauser and Shepard, "Principles for Saving and Valuing Lives"). Such an implication follows from the work of Litai, Lanning, and Rasmussen ("The Public Perception of Risk"), which shows that differing risk levels are perceived as equivalent, depending on such characteristics as the degree of voluntariness, familiarity, and catastrophe, and from earlier work by several others, such as Fischhoff, Solvic, and Lichtenstein ("Weighing the Risks").

Part II

EXPERIENCE WITH
REGULATORY IMPACT
ANALYSES UNDER
EXECUTIVE ORDER 12291

5

W. NORTON GRUBB*
DALE WHITTINGTON
MICHAEL HUMPHRIES

THE AMBIGUITIES OF BENEFIT-COST ANALYSIS: AN EVALUATION OF REGULATORY IMPACT ANALYSES UNDER EXECUTIVE ORDER 12291

PRESIDENT Reagan wasted no time establishing his program of regulatory relief. Within two days of his inauguration, he created the Task Force on Regulatory Relief, chaired by Vice-President George Bush. On 17 February 1981, President Reagan signed Executive Order 12291, which established the dominance of benefit-cost principles for the evaluation of subsequent regulations. Although this executive order is a natural extension of the interest in benefit-cost analysis that has grown since the 1940s, EO 12291 also served a special political purpose for President Reagan: benefit-cost analysis might provide a mechanism that could confirm his contention that the "regulatory machine has run amuck" and has imposed "excessive and inefficient" regulations whose costs to society outweigh their benefits.

The adoption of EO 12291 raises a number of different questions. One

*W. Norton Grubb, Associate Professor, Lyndon B. Johnson School of Public Affairs, University of Texas at Austin; Dale Whittington, Assistant Professor, Department of City and Regional Planning, University of North Carolina at Chapel Hill; and Michael Humphries, Department of Economics, University of Texas at Austin.

The preparation of this chapter was partially supported by a grant from the Sloan Foundation to the Lyndon B. Johnson School of Public Affairs and a Junior Faculty Development Award from the University of North Carolina. An earlier version was presented at the 1982 meetings of the Association for Public Policy Analysis and Management. Helpful comments were made by Kerry Smith, Jack Wells, Stephanie Chimenti, David Warner, Susan Hadden, Jurgen Schmandt, Tom McGarity, Richard Nelson, Richard Andrews, Tom Snyder, Dan Sokoloski, Robert Leone, and Emil Malizia.

of these is administrative and managerial: given a potentially large number of benefit-cost studies, what procedures should be adopted to ensure that these studies will be competently performed, consistent in their assumptions, and seriously considered in the final regulatory decision? Another important question involves the quality of benefit-cost analysis and whether the executive order has managed to improve the level of economic analysis in federal agencies. The larger questions center on the interaction of analysis and politics, especially the issues of whether political considerations have influenced the benefit-cost analyses performed and whether these analyses have had any weight in the final regulatory decisions.

Although Executive Order 12291 is still in the early stages of its implementation, some real dangers have already emerged, along with some apparent successes. In fact, the early analyses completed in response to EO 12291 reflect all the ambiguities that have always been part of benefit-cost analysis and of its use in evaluating regulations. Some analyses appear to have modified political positions, but many others show obvious ideological biases. Some have struggled adequately with the familiar problems of quantifying benefits and costs; others—especially in the environmental area—have failed completely, just as critics of benefit-cost analysis claimed they would. EO 12291 presents real opportunities to improve the economic analysis underlying regulatory changes, but there is no guarantee that these opportunities will be realized as the executive order is currently being implemented.

In this chapter we examine the early benefit-cost analyses that have been prepared under EO 12291, paying special attention to three analyses for environmental regulations, and comparing these analyses to the generally accepted best practices that have emerged in the past forty years. Because EO 12291 has developed from previous efforts to impose benefit-cost analysis, we first review the history of these efforts and the relationship of the executive order to earlier reforms. We then describe the implementation of EO 12291, contrasting OMB's efforts to manage and coordinate benefit-cost studies with the conventional economic planning model that has developed in the project evaluation literature. We next discuss the quality of the benefit-cost analyses performed in the first year of EO 12291, identifying some of the most common analytic problems. The following section examines more closely several analyses prepared by the Environmental Protection Agency, illustrating some of the general limitations of benefit-cost analysis in the difficult environmental area. We conclude with some tentative conclusions about the role of benefit-cost analysis in regulatory reform and the possible consequences of EO 12291.

EO 12291 IN THE HISTORY OF COST-BENEFIT ANALYSIS

Executive Order 12291 is the most recent in a long line of attempts to rationalize budgetary and regulatory practice through the use of economic analysis. The U.S. Flood Control Act of 1936 initiated the practice of benefit-cost analysis within the federal government. The act required that "the federal government should improve or participate in the improvement of navigable waters or their tributaries, including watersheds thereof, for flood control purposes if the benefits to whomsoever they may accrue are in excess of the estimated costs, and if the lives and social security of people are otherwise adversely affected." This wording appears again in slightly modified form in the initial OMB instructions to agencies concerning the implementation of Executive Order 12291: "A schedule of benefits should be included that would show the type of benefit, to whom it would accrue, and when it would accrue."

The Natural Resources Planning Board began the task of conducting benefit-cost studies of federal water projects in the late 1930s, but there were no benefit-cost manuals in print. As the Corps of Engineers and other federal agencies tried to implement the Flood Control Act of 1936, it was only natural that advocates of particular projects developed procedures to make the benefits large and the costs small. Some of these attempts were ingenious and took the economics profession considerable internal wrangling to evaluate, a process that continues in such controversial areas as the treatment of income distribution, uncertainty, and secondary benefits.

During the 1940s it became apparent that it made no sense for each analyst or agency to develop its own procedures for estimating benefits and costs. In 1946 a Subcommittee on Benefits and Costs was established by the Federal Interagency River Basin Committee (consisting of the departments of Agriculture, Army, and Commerce; the Federal Security Agency, the forerunner of Health and Human Services; Labor; and the Federal Power Commission) for the purpose of developing common principles and procedures for evaluating water resources projects. The subcommittee's report of May 1950, which became known as the "Green Book," was essentially a set of guidelines to implement the Flood Control Act of 1936 and covered the measurement of benefits and costs, interest and discount rates, price levels, risk allowances, periods of analysis, treatment of taxes, and cost allocation for multiple-purpose projects.

During the 1950s the subcommittee and its staff, as well as other government bodies, continued to revise and develop these evaluation procedures and in 1958 issued a new edition of the "Green Book."[1] The introduction contains a subsection on economic analysis and public policy in which the authors acknowledge the problems of coordinating benefit-cost analysis with national economic policy:

> There are problems of Government economic policy which are beyond the responsibility of resource development agencies, but which affect, and are affected by, resource development programs. Likewise, the total size of a national public works program at any particular time is determined in the light of fiscal and other factors which are independent of the considerations pertinent in the analysis of individual projects. Such questions are appropriately handled at a higher level of government. This report does not suggest means of integrating broader economic policies with resource development programs. While such integration is highly desirable, and while the procedures in this report are of use in such analysis, those matters are beyond the scope of this report. [2]

The Bureau of the Budget's active participation in the Interagency Committee on Water Resources and its own publication in 1952, *Circular A-47*, requiring uniform procedures that would permit comparison among projects, also indicated a growing awareness of the relationships between benefit-cost analysis and the budgetary process.

During the 1960s the use of benefit-cost analysis became widespread, extending beyond the water resources field to transportation, health, and many other areas of public policy. Robert McNamara introduced benefit-cost principles to the military establishment under the jargon of PPB. The basic conceptual framework was readily adopted in the field of defense, in which long-range strategic planning was obviously needed. The Defense Department still remains one of the only federal government agencies in which it is ideologically acceptable to undertake long-range planning similar to corporate strategic planning, in part because there was never any question of the market providing the country with a national defense.

With the publication in 1962 of *Design of Water Resource Systems* by Arthur Maass and others, academic interest in project evaluation was increasingly drawn to multiple-objective approaches. Analysts evaluating water resource projects realized that the focus of benefit-cost analysis on the single objective of maximizing net benefits, or national income, was inadequate to capture other social and political concerns such as income distribution, environmental quality, and full employment. Dissatisfaction with the traditional cost-benefit framework resulted in the publication of the Water Resources Research Council's (WRRC) "Principles and Standards for Planning Water and Related Land Resources" in 1973.

The "Principles and Standards" established two primary objectives for water resources projects—national economic development and environmental quality—and required that accounts be established for both. The report also acknowledged the importance of regional development and social well-being. There would thus no longer be a simple benefit-cost test but rather a series of trade-offs among several competing objectives. Multiobjective planning and evaluation procedures grew in popularity throughout the 1970s, and there are now several major textbooks in the field which combine the multiobjective formulation with mathematical programming and systems analysis.[3]

The environmental legislation of the early 1970s furthered the replacement of benefit-cost analysis with multiobjective approaches. The National Environmental Policy Act of 1969 required a new form of project analysis—the environmental impact statement—to examine the effects on the environment of any federal project or policy, regardless of its benefits. Environmental impact statements could not, however, replace the need for a more structured analytical approach to project and policy evaluation. In 1979 the Council on Environmental Quality issued regulations on how to implement the procedures of NEPA (including the preparation of environmental impact statements). The regulations specifically incorporated benefit-cost analysis:

> If a cost-benefit analysis relevant to the choice among environmentally different alternatives is being considered for the proposed action, it shall be incorporated by reference or appended to the statement as an aid in evaluating the environmental consequences. To assess the adequacy of compliance with section 102(2)(B) of the Act the statement shall, when a cost-benefit analysis is prepared, discuss the relationship between that analysis and any analysis of unquantified environmental impacts, values, and amenities. For purposes of complying with the Act, the weighing of the merits and drawbacks of the various alternatives need not be displayed in a monetary cost-benefit analysis and should not be when there are important qualitative considerations. In any event, an environmental impact statement should at least indicate those considerations, including factors not related to environmental quality, which are likely to be relevant and important to a decision.[4]

Thus the efforts to incorporate multiple objectives into decision making have come from two different directions. On the one hand, the multiobjective approach advocated by the WRRC in 1973 established a separate environmental objective in addition to a benefit-cost analysis. Environmental impact statements, on the other hand, focus primarily on the environmental "account," but can legitimately incorporate a traditional benefit-cost analysis.

During the 1960s and 1970s, benefit-cost analysis and multiobjective evaluation became widely adopted by international funding agencies and national planning organizations in developing countries. Bankers and financial analysts appreciated the analytical rigor of benefit-cost analysis and its apparent similarity to financial analysis. Many planners in developing countries, on the other hand, were attracted to the premise of benefit-cost analysis that market prices might not be adequate measures of social value, a popular perspective when the terms of trade were moving against many raw material exports from the Third World.

Several major benefit-cost manuals addressed the issues of evaluating investments in developing countries. *Manual of Industrial Project Analysis in Developing Countries* (1969) by I. M. D. Little and J. A. Mirrlees was prepared for the Organization for Economic Cooperation and Development (OECD) to standardize and upgrade its project evaluation procedures. *Guidelines for Project Evaluation* (1972) by Partha Dasgupta, A. K. Sen, and Stephen Marglin was prepared for the United Nations Industrial Development Organization (UNIDO) for a similar purpose. The World Bank also sponsored a benefit-cost manual, *Economic Analysis of Projects* (1975) by Lyn Squire and Herman G. Van der Tak. The OECD and UNIDO manuals have been particularly influential because they were able to synthesize clearly the voluminous and often tedious literature on cost-benefit analysis that appeared during the 1950s and 1960s.

The use of benefit-cost analysis by international funding agencies and developing countries again focused attention on the planning issues of coordinating and managing large numbers of benefit-cost studies and integrating national economic planning objectives with the results of project evaluations. The UNIDO *Guidelines* present a stylized framework, which outlines the information flows between the central planning office (CPO)—by which is meant the institutional arrangements with the responsibility for national economic planning and management of public-sector investments—and project analysts scattered among various ministries and regional offices. The CPO sends two types of information to the project evaluators: rules or procedures to ensure consistency among the project evaluations, and national parameters or shadow prices for particular items that should be determined centrally. Examples of such national parameters include the social rate of discount, the social value of investment, the shadow value of labor, the value of life, and the weights to be given to income distribution and regional equity objectives. The project evaluators are to send project appraisals back to the CPO, which then decides which investments to make based on the entire portfolio put together by project analysts. In this process the CPO would fund projects that maximize the present value of net benefits subject to a budget constraint.

The planning problem facing the CPO, however, is more complex than simply specifying individual input values. The CPO must ensure that the outcomes of some investments do not violate the input assumptions of other studies. Benefit-cost analysis is a partial equilibrium analysis, which assumes that everything else stays constant while an incremental project or policy is undertaken. This is clearly an unrealistic assumption for a national government to make because the benefit-cost studies of one agency may be influenced by the regulatory actions or investment projects contemplated by other agencies (as we will see in the analysis of environmental regulations in the section on the quality of RIAs).

Despite the complex planning issues involved in managing and coordinating thousands of benefit-cost studies, every president since John F. Kennedy has felt compelled to improve management and program evaluation procedures, often relying heavily on benefit-cost analysis. President Johnson attempted to institute PPB throughout the federal government. This effort met with little success, largely because of the lack of strong support from the White House and a failure to recognize the dimensions of the task, both of which have been persistent problems for efforts at budgetary and regulatory reform. Richard Nixon revived the interest in management efficiency and management by objectives (which had been eclipsed by the Vietnam War) and established a leading role for the new Office of Management and Budget. But then Watergate overshadowed concerns for efficiency in government. Gerald Ford made an ill-fated foray into the field of economic analysis and government regulation with his WIN (Whip Inflation Now) buttons and inflationary impact statements.[5]

Jimmy Carter tried to bring zero-based budgeting to Washington, patterned after a scheme he had used in Georgia state government. Zero-based budgeting was essentially another attempt to bring economic efficiency criteria into the budgetary process based on the assumption that entire programs rather than marginal program expenditures should be evaluated. Zero-based budgeting also failed to get off the ground, partly because of the Carter administration's poorly executed attempts to apply benefit-cost analysis to water resources projects popular with significant segments of Congress and also because of the excessive analytical burden it imposed on the federal bureaucracy.

In the regulatory area Carter strengthened the oversight role of the Council on Wage and Price Stability. On 23 March 1978, he issued Executive Order 12044, which introduced an informal brand of cost-effectiveness and benefit-cost analysis. Executive Order 12044 applied only to "informal" rulemaking in the executive branch, not to regulations issued in accordance with the formal rulemaking provisions of the Administrative Procedures Act. Many other types of regulations were also exempted, such as those dealing with military or foreign affairs, agency management or personnel, and federal government procurement. Executive Order 12044 specifically required public participation and an open rulemaking process. Agencies were required to notify parties affected by the regulation and to give the public at least sixty days to comment on proposed regulations classified as "significant."

The methodology and procedures agency heads were to follow in preparing regulatory analyses were left vague. There were no references in Executive Order 12044 to formal benefit-cost analysis or concepts derived from welfare economics, though there was a requirement that every RIA analyze the "economic consequences" of each alternative and that the "least burdensome of the acceptable alternatives" be chosen. Although the executive order assigned OMB the responsibility for implementation, agency heads were instructed to establish their own procedures for developing regulatory analyses. In practice the oversight role fell to the Council on Wage and Price Stability, staffed by professional economists, who used more formal economic analysis to review proposed regulations and regulatory analyses.

President Reagan's EO 12291, issued almost three years after Carter's EO 12044, is in many respects similar to the earlier order.[6] The specific requirements of Executive Order 12291 are described in earlier chapters, and we will not reiterate them here.

Like Executive Order 12044, Executive Order 12291 exempted various categories of regulations, including those issued under formal rulemaking procedures, those issued with respect to a military or foreign affairs function of the United States, and those related to agency organization, management, or personnel. Executive Order 12291 also gave OMB responsibility for implementing its provisions. The order provided no specific information on how to prepare Regulatory Impact Analyses, though it did give OMB authority to "develop procedures for estimating the annual benefits and cost of agency regulations, on both an aggregate and economic or industrial sector basis, for purposes of compiling a regulatory budget." Both executive orders stressed the need to reduce paperwork and the regulatory burden and to estimate the administrative costs of implementing and enforcing the regulation.

Rather than representing a radical shift in policy, Reagan's Executive Order 12291 in places seems to be a minor rewrite by a professional economist of Carter's Executive Order 12044. There are, however, two important differences. One is that the explicit requirement for "early and meaningful" public participation in EO 12044 is missing from EO 12291. The other is that Executive Order 12291 explicitly adopts a formal benefit-cost rule for evaluating proposed regulations. The OMB "Interim Regulatory Impact Analysis Guidance," issued 6 June 1981, elaborates on the normative theory of government action underlying Executive Order 12291 and Reagan's program of regulatory relief:

> The statement of the need for and the consequences of the proposed regulatory change should address the following questions: (a) What precisely is the problem that needs to be corrected? (That is, what market imperfection(s) give(s) rise to the regulatory proposal? Causes, not just symptoms, should be identified.) (b) How would the regulatory proposal, if promulgated, improve the functioning of the market, or otherwise meet the regulatory objective(s)? Since regulatory failure may be a real possibility, is it clear that the proposed regulation would produce better results than no regulatory change? (Imperfectly functioning markets should not be compared with idealized, perfectly functioning regulatory programs).[7]

This directive clearly espouses the convention of public goods theory that market failure is the justification for government intervention in the market.[8] Other conventional justifications for government intervention— equity considerations and moral arguments, for example—have no role under EO 12291.

In many ways, then, EO 12291 is the legacy of efforts over forty years to use benefit-cost analysis in evaluating projects and regulations. But the order ignores two recent developments in project and program analysis. First, it is relatively explicit in rejecting multiobjective approaches: although the OMB "Guidance" specifies that the recipients of costs and benefits should be identified, the order itself states that maximizing net benefits to society is to be the sole criterion for regulation, unmodified by distributive, environmental, or other noneconomic objectives. Second, neither the executive order nor the OMB "Guidance" nor the OMB's actions since 1981 have recognized the importance of the managerial issues involved in directing and coordinating a large program of economic analysis. As a result, the practice of benefit-cost analysis in the federal government remains relatively haphazard and inconsistent.

MANAGEMENT AND COORDINATION OF BENEFIT-COST ANALYSES IN THE FEDERAL GOVERNMENT

The overall process of managing and coordinating the multitude of benefit-cost analyses prepared in different federal agencies is critical to EO 12291's objective of fostering efficient regulation. Otherwise, inconsistencies are certain to arise. For example, the EPA might reject one regulation and the Department of Interior accept another simply because the two agencies used different values for a life saved or different discount rates.

The simple framework presented in the UNIDO *Guidelines* is useful for understanding some of OMB's difficulties in implementing EO 12291. Although OMB is essentially assuming the role of the central planning office, OMB has not sent the agencies any detailed rules and procedures to ensure minimal consistency among RIAs.[9] The five-page OMB "Guidance" of 6 June 1981 consists primarily of generalities similar to those in EO 12291; it could not possibly be construed as a substitute for a benefit-cost manual. Although writing another basic benefit-cost manual would not have been necessary or useful, technical flaws common to the existing RIAs—which will be reviewed in the next section—indicate that agency analysts need a more detailed, explicit set of rules and procedures. From a historical perspective, the failure of OMB to issue appropriate instructions is particularly unfortunate because one of the principal functions of the central planning apparatus is educational—to teach agencies what good analysis entails. A more aggressive approach would have included an extensive training program for agency analysts on how RIAs should be prepared.

For example, further OMB guidance seems necessary for calculating the resource costs of designing, administering, and implementing regulations, one aspect of the "regulatory burden" which both President Reagan and OMB have emphasized. This complex cost-allocation problem has not been addressed in any RIAs so far, probably in part because agency analysts do not know how to tackle the calculation. Another example of an area in which OMB guidance is needed is in the allocation of resources to the preparation of different RIAs. Presently, the preparation of some RIAs is very costly (on the order of several hundred thousand dollars); others reflect no more than an afternoon's work. Some RIAs are prepared by outside consultants; most are done internally. Although more resources should be allocated to RIAs for those important regulations for which the analysis is most likely to make a difference, there is no indication that the existing level of effort committed to different RIAs reflects such considerations. If an agency is free to spend $500,000 on one regulation and $500 on another, there is a great potential for decisions—and the quality of different RIAs—to be based on political grounds.

Not only did OMB fail to issue detailed instructions on methodological approaches, it also failed to issue information on "national parameters" necessary to ensure consistent evaluation. The only national parameter which OMB directed agencies to use was a 10 percent real rate of discount, a value based on existing OMB practice but relatively high compared to other methods of calculating the discount rate.[10] Nothing was forthcoming from OMB on the value of life, the shadow value of labor or investment, macroeconomic conditions, population projections, or future relative prices for energy or raw materials.

Given this lack of direction from OMB, most agencies issued procedural instructions on how an RIA was to move through the internal bureaucracy, largely describing who had to sign off when. The question of what an RIA should be was largely left to an agency's or individual's interpretation of the executive order and assessment of what would be acceptable to the individuals who were to approve the RIA at various stages of the internal review process. Under these circumstances many bureaucrats would naturally try to issue perfunctory, noncontroversial RIAs and see if they would be acceptable. In 1981 OMB rarely rejected an RIA as inadequate on technical grounds, and thus the strategy of perfunctory compliance would probably be successful. In other instances, the individuals responsible simply repackaged a regulatory analysis prepared under Carter's EO 12044 as an RIA.

Two agencies—EPA and DOT—have prepared benefit-cost manuals of their own, effectively assuming OMB's responsibility in this area. Neither EPA's nor DOT's benefit-cost instructions could be construed as comprehensive. EPA's is twenty pages long (although there are numerous, lengthy technical appendixes); DOT's is twenty-eight pages long. Neither approaches the breadth and sophistication of the UNIDO or OECD manuals, or even the "Green Book." In fact, the DOT benefit-cost handbook sensibly refers the reader to Ezra J. Mishan's *Economics for Social Decisions: Elements of Cost-Benefit Analysis* (1973). Given the history of benefit-cost analysis in the federal government, it is not surprising that EPA's benefit-cost guidelines are technically superior to those of any federal agency, as well as those of OMB.[11] Although EPA has certainly not developed a reputation as a bastion of believers in economic analysis, the tradition of benefit-cost and multiobjective analysis in the water resources field and the experience of the 1970s with environmental impact statements have fostered an awareness of formal analytic methods often lacking in other federal agencies. EPA's and DOT's manuals are most notable because of the absence of similar documents from OMB and other agencies. The current situation is in some respects similar to that of the 1940s, when different agencies and analysts conducted benefit-cost analyses without any central direction or guidance.

The most important practical issue in OMB's management and coordination of RIAs has been the process of granting exemptions to EO 12291. Of the 2,803 regulations and proposed regulations reviewed by OMB between 17 February and December 1981, only 62 were designated "major." Of these, 43 were published in final or proposed form by 31 December, but only 22 required an RIA. The other regulations were exempted.[12] RIAs were prepared for less than 1 percent of all regulations in the first year of EO 12291 and thus are rare events, even among rules designated "major." Benefit-cost analyses could not, of course, have been prepared for all of the 2,803 regulations released in 1981, but the widespread practice of exemptions is a potential source of bias.

The largest exemption—that RIAs are required only for "major" rules—reflects the reasonable conclusion that thorough analyses ought not to be done for trivial, routine, or noncontroversial changes. The boundary between major and nonmajor rules is unavoidably arbitrary, and the $100 million threshold seems reasonable. It is sometimes difficult, however, to tell whether a rule has substantial effects because a rule can be declared nonmajor without any supporting documentation. The Carter administration declared a large number of rules to have consequences of $90 to $95 million, suspiciously close to the $100 million limit.

In determining which regulations are "major" and thus require an RIA, agencies have concentrated on the definition of an annual effect on the economy of $100 million or more and ignored the other two definitions of "a major increase in costs or prices" and "significant adverse effects on competition [and] employment." In practice, agencies have often interpreted "an effect on the economy of $100 million or more" as the agency expenditure required, rather than as either the costs or the benefits to groups outside the government.[13] Of course, the $100 million limit may have been intentionally set lower than desired so as to counter this tendency. In other words, OMB might well be satisfied to limit the requirements of the executive order to regulations with impacts over $500 million.

Other ambiguities surround this conception of "major." For example, the Department of Transportation declared a rule limiting traffic in Washington's National Airport "nonmajor" because the net costs were under $100 million, even though DOT estimated that passengers would lose $218.4 million (23). (The RIAs that we have consulted are listed in an appendix at the end of the chapter, and we refer to them in the text by the numbers in that list.) In this and several other cases, RIAs have been prepared even though the agency has declared the rule "nonmajor." In fact, a preliminary benefit-cost analysis must be performed to determine whether a rule is major because the $100 million boundary presumably refers to the calculation of net social benefits (or costs), not financial expenditures. Several agencies in fact perform such preliminary studies before deciding whether an RIA is necessary.

Another problem with the category of nonmajor rules is that, although rules may be individually insignificant, groups of similar rules can be collectively important. An example is the Department of Agriculture's set of RIAs for its price support programs. A closely related problem is the case in which an agency declares a marginal change or each of a series of marginal changes in an existing program to be nonmajor rather than examining the costs and benefits of the entire program. Zero-based budgeting is addressed at precisely such problems.

Some rules that are nonmajor have a concentrated effect in a small geographic area. OMB has generally exempted regulations "which are directed largely or entirely at individual firms or other entities, and thus do not meet the executive order's definition of a regulation as a statement of general applicability" and has given a blanket exemption to many state implementation plans that often grant waivers to individual firms.[14] Although the effects of such regulatory changes may not be of "general applicability" and may generate less than $100 million of costs and benefits, their influence can be serious in a particular region.[15]

In addition to exemptions for nonmajor rules, OMB has granted many general exemptions to EO 12291. In addition to exemptions for regulations that are "essentially nonregulatory" and those that affect individual firms, OMB has provided a blanket exemption for regulations "which relax or defer regulatory requirements, or which delegate regulatory activity to the states." Under this exemption, approval of state plans covering mining reclamation, water, solid waste management, and air, noise, and radiation standards does not require an RIA. Similarly exempted are all Department of Transportation rules that delay compliance dates of existing regulations; EPA rulings that delete chemicals from the list of toxic pollutants under section 307(a) of TSCA; suspensions of toxic testing requirements under the National Pollutant Discharge Elimination System (NPDES); hazardous waste delisting petitions under the Resource Conservation and Recovery Act (RCRA); and actions regarding pesticide tolerance and food additives "*except* those which make an existing tolerance more stringent."[16] The deregulatory bias in this pattern of exemptions is obvious; there is not even a pretense of subjecting deregulatory efforts to an "objective" benefit-cost test.

Other general exemptions include regulations governing international trade and those related to expenditure programs such as food stamps, Aid to Families with Dependent Children, and Medicaid. Many of the changes in such expenditure programs have concerned eligibility and payment practices and have been designed to reduce federal spending for social welfare programs. Because these are essentially transfer programs, benefit-cost analysis would normally find there to be zero net benefits unless redistributive consequences were considered as benefits. In two respects, however, the exemption of welfare programs violates the spirit of EO 12291. First, welfare programs have efficiency effects such as disincentives to work, and some of the changes made by the Reagan administration have been widely criticized for increasing disincentives to work. An RIA would have revealed the magnitude of these efficiency losses, which could have potentially been more than the savings. Second, EO 12291 specifically directs agencies to consider alternative methods of achieving program goals. In the case of welfare programs, alternative measures might produce equivalent savings to the federal government but with smaller efficiency losses and less damage to the redistributive effects of these programs.

Another category of exemptions involves regulations declared to have emergency status. Examples include Department of Agriculture rules on price supports and EPA rules on pesticide tolerances, "which must be issued promptly at the beginning of the growing season in order to avoid large crop losses." Although provisions must obviously be made for exemptions during emergencies, the determination of what constitutes an emergency may be essentially a political decision.

Perhaps the most important consequence of the current OMB practice of granting exemptions to EO 12291 is the chilling effect it has on the development of new regulations. On the one hand, OMB has tended to exempt changes that deregulate from the requirement of preparing an RIA; on the other hand, OMB has shown no sign of exempting changes that make regulations more stringent. Any effort to make a regulation more stringent will certainly require the time and expense of an RIA. The OMB implementation of EO 12291 thus slows and complicates a regulatory process that has already become lengthy and cumbersome. Several individuals working in federal agencies have reported to us that the prospect of having to perform a benefit-cost analysis has discouraged them from proposing new regulations.

The deregulatory bias does not fall evenhandedly on all regulatory efforts. The chilling effects of EO 12291 are especially serious in cases in which new regulations involve benefits that are difficult to quantify, or there is not enough experience to quantify benefits. For example, DOT withdrew the rule for transporting anhydrous ammonia by pipeline.[17] The regulation would have required 20 percent water content by weight; the purpose was to reduce the risk of stress and corrosion of the pipeline. Industry response during the comment period was favorable, but the rule was withdrawn because the Materials Transportation Bureau could not quantify the benefits. If this pattern becomes widespread, OMB's implementation of EO 12291 will bias the regulatory process against regulations for which the benefits are difficult to measure or are uncertain, such as efforts to protect wildlife and scenic areas or to enhance the quality of life.

Were it to follow the model of the central planning office, OMB would assure the quality of analysis and make effective use of the information it receives from federal agencies. To date, OMB has shown little interest in doing either. The most important information OMB has sent the agencies has been in the form of exemptions, rather than national parameters or guidelines for analysis. OMB has generally let the agencies interpret the executive order and the OMB "Guidelines" and then occasionally criticizes the results. This approach has not enabled OMB to correct technical errors in the RIAs, in part because the only action OMB can take at this stage in the regulatory process is to return the rule, which is often not politically feasible.

To be sure, OMB is often in a politically weak position relative to federal agencies, and its Office of Regulatory Analysis is not staffed well enough to scrutinize carefully the thousands of regulations issued each year. Nevertheless, in the absence of the political will and the resources necessary to make OMB function more like a central planning office, the implementation of EO 12291 has been uneven at best. As a result, the quality of the RIAs in the first year of EO 12291 has been highly variable.

THE QUALITY OF BENEFIT-COST ANALYSIS IN THE REAGAN ADMINISTRATION

The RIAs performed in 1981 under EO 12291 constitute a set of examples, ranging across agencies and including both controversial and noncontroversial issues, that allows us to examine how benefit-cost analyses are currently performed in the federal government.[18] It is important to remember, however, how few RIAs have been performed so far because of the myriad exemptions from EO 12291. One obvious implication is that the image sometimes conveyed by the Reagan administration that benefit-cost analysis is widely used to determine precisely which regulations should be promulgated is inaccurate because RIAs are the exception rather than the rule.

Our major conclusion from a review of all RIAs prepared in 1981—which will be surprising only to cynics who assume that all analyses under EO 12291 are post hoc justifications of decisions made on purely political grounds—is that the range and sophistication of the different studies is enormous. This variation may reflect the substantial differences in resources committed to RIAs. Not surprisingly, some RIAs are purely perfunctory. For example, the RIA for the Rural Electrification Agency's specifications for filled telephone cable (5) describes the changes but fails to analyze any consequences. Analysis was also perfunctory for the RIA forbidding procedures on oil and gas leases in the Alaska National Petroleum Reserve (15). Although this RIA mentions the considerations necessary for a complete benefit-cost analysis—including issues of uncertainty, income distribution, and discounting—it fails to carry out any of the analyses.

At the other extreme, the RIA for a proposal to create a marine sanctuary including the Channel Islands and Point Reyes presented four different ways of estimating benefits, used three different discount rates, and included an extensive discussion of such difficult issues as valuing the preservation of wildlife and the treatment of uncertainty (12). Other RIAs with thorough coverage of economic issues include three from the Department of Transportation: one covering different standards for automatic seat belts (21), one covering different bumper standards (22), and one investigating the consequences of fewer flights at Washington National Airport (23).

The best of the RIAs provide extensive information, even when they commit serious analytical errors; the worst of them are uninformative and misleading. Despite this wide variation in the quality of the RIAs, six problems emerge consistently, all of them familiar to students of benefit-cost analysis.

THE RELATIVE NEGLECT OF BENEFITS. The most prevalent weakness in the RIAs has both ideological and technical causes. In his program of regulatory relief, President Reagan has consistently stressed the costs of regulations and the savings (especially to business and industry) that deregulation will bring, without mentioning the benefits of regulation such as cleaner air and water, occupational injuries avoided, automobile fatalities avoided, and better-informed consumers.[19] Consistent with this lopsided view of benefit-cost analysis, many of the RIAs prepared under EO 12291 have spent a great deal of energy estimating the reduced costs to corporations from deregulation, while virtually ignoring the reduced benefits to consumers and workers.

For example, the RIA analyzing affirmative action requirements for government contractors (16) devotes much effort to calculating the reduced costs to employers and the government of limiting affirmative action requirements to larger employers. It makes no effort to estimate the effects on women and minority workers of exempting small firms. The RIA concludes, without any supporting evidence, that these regulatory changes would "result in substantial cost savings for both contractors and the Government without significantly affecting employee protections."[20] This claim might be true because of the legendary ineffectiveness of the Office of Federal Contract Compliance (OFCC), but the RIA considers neither the effects on employees nor the obvious alternative of strengthening the OFCC.

As another example, the Department of Agriculture's RIA on changing the labeling and content requirements for mechanically deboned meat—an extremely controversial measure among consumer groups—develops extensive estimates of the reduced costs to the meatpacking industry (1). The RIA assumes these costs will be largely passed on to consumers because of the presumed competitiveness of the food sector; the RIA does not present a comparable discussion of the consequences for consumers of decreased meat quality. More generally, in a study of fifty-seven regulatory analyses, GAO investigators found twenty-three analyses without any estimates of benefits, while only eight lacked estimates of costs.[21] The U.S. Regulatory Council's interviews with analysts in the agencies revealed that procedures to estimate benefits are often crude and imprecise; yet another source of bias is that many analysts believe agency cost estimates tend to be overestimates, especially when agencies are uncertain of their data.[22]

As another indication of the apparent tendency of agencies to search harder for evidence on costs than on benefits, the Department of Education's *Deregulation Tool Kit* contains a section on ways to calculate cost savings from deregulation and completely ignores the calculation of benefits foregone.[23] Several proposed rules have specifically asked for public comment on cost savings but failed to mention benefits. It sometimes appears that uncertain benefits or those difficult to quantify are simply valued at zero; for example, when the Treasury Department rescinded labeling requirements for beer, wine, and liquor, the assistant secretary for enforcement and operation defended the decision on the grounds that the costs were relatively clear and easy to calculate but the benefits were speculative.

The valuation of the benefits of regulation—or the costs of deregulation—is often exceedingly difficult, and previous administrations have also been faulted for their relative neglect of benefits.[24] Some benefits take the form of consumer information and quality standards, as in beef grading and the labeling of mechanically deboned meat. Other benefits, notoriously difficult to value, take the form of lives saved or injuries prevented, as in the case of automatic seat belt standards and OSHA's regulations on occupational noise exposure. Still other regulations involve aesthetic benefits such as the creation of wildlife sanctuaries. In the first round of RIAs under EO 12291, however, there appears to be no relationship between the technical difficulty of valuing the reduced benefits to consumers and workers from deregulation proposals and the effort to estimate benefits. Some of the most difficult cases—such as the wildlife refuge in the Channel Islands and Point Reyes (12), the consequences of different seat belt standards (21), and the effects of reduced traffic at Washington National Airport (22) on surrounding communities—have some of the most elaborate and detailed RIAs. Conversely, brief treatment of benefits often occurs in cases for which the calculation of foregone benefits would have been relatively less difficult, such as meat grading.

In summary, although EO 12291 and the OMB "Guidance" are evenhanded in their discussion of costs and benefits, it seems that the emphasis of the Reagan administration on deregulation has not been lost on many agencies.

VALUATION OF COSTS AND BENEFITS. A second general area of difficulty is substantially more technical. Although it is hardly surprising that RIAs fall short of perfection in valuing costs and benefits, two elementary errors occur with disturbing frequency. The first is a tendency to include transfer payments among the costs (or benefits) rather than including the real efficiency losses resulting from the transfers. For example, the Department of Agriculture's analysis of the trigger price for farmer-owned wheat reserves notes that one "benefit" of the trigger price selected is higher wheat prices and a higher return per planted acre compared to the alternatives, never mentioning that these price increases are costs to consumers, nor distinguishing between transfer payments and efficiency losses. The real efficiency effects that would arise from reduced consumption by some consumers and from some marginal producers entering the market would require an analysis of consumers' surplus and economic rent.

As a second example, the Department of Labor's (DOL) analysis of reducing wage standards in service contracts to the federal government (17) and on construction projects coverd by the Davis-Bacon Act (18) treats the reduced wages paid by the government to contractors as benefits, failing to consider these lower wages as simultaneous costs to workers. The real efficiency effects of lower wages in government contracts—for example, the possibilities of attracting less skilled or less stable workers or even causing shortages of labor—are never mentioned. The Department of Transportation's analysis of the costs of automatic seat belts (and air bags, although in a less detailed manner) includes both the manufacturers' and dealers' profit as real costs rather than ignoring them as transfer payments (21).

Only one RIA explicitly recognizes the difference between transfer payments and real resource costs. The Department of Labor's analysis of suspending benefits for retired workers who continue working (19) treats pension benefits as transfers and concentrates on measuring the disincentives to working that would result from permitting pension plans to disallow benefits—assuming young workers cannot be substituted for retired workers. Thus even within one agency the treatment of transfer payments varies. The inappropriate inclusion of transfers in many RIAs as costs or benefits means that the analyses are often more like benefit-cost analyses to the federal government or industry rather than to society as a whole (as EO 12291 explicitly requires).

The second major problem in valuing costs and benefits concerns a fundamental premise of formal benefit-cost analysis—that market prices may not be accurate reflections of social value and should be adjusted for market imperfections such as monopoly pricing and for consumers' surplus and economic rents. The RIAs performed so far have not developed any shadow prices to use in place of market prices. In only one case has there been a recognition that consumer surplus ought to be used to measure benefits. The analysis of changing standards for mechanically deboned meat (1) assumes that cost decreases will be passed on to consumers in the form of lower prices and recognizes that the benefits to consumers should include the increase in consumer surplus on the meat sold. But the RIA ignores the issue of economic rent, partly because cost reductions are assumed (rather than demonstrated) to be passed on to consumers and partly because the supply of beef is assumed to be inelastic in the short run. This omission is critical because from the consumers' standpoint the changes would allow meat packers to substitute mechanically deboned meat for hand-boned meat, potentially reducing the meatpackers' costs with no benefits to consumers. If cost reductions are not passed on to consumers, the meatpackers capture most of the benefits through increased economic rent.

More sophisticated analyses, which attempt to adjust market prices and use measures of consumers' surplus and economic rent, are difficult and time-consuming, and in some cases the greater accuracy may not be justified. These issues are, however, the heart of formal benefit-cost analysis, and the absence of any recognition that market prices might not be appropriate measures of social value suggests that many of the individuals actually preparing RIAs in the federal government know little about the theoretical or methodological foundations of what they are doing.

DISTRIBUTIONAL ISSUES. The question of how best to handle distributional issues within a benefit-cost framework is a source of continuing controversy within the project evaluation literature. Indeed, a principal impetus for the development of multiobjective analysis was a desire to incorporate distributional issues explicitly in the decision criteria. Although it fails to adopt a formal multiobjective approach, the OMB "Guidance" on EO 12291 states that the recipients of costs and benefits should at least be identified.

In several RIAs this instruction has been followed in ways that are appropriate and illuminating. The analysis of the Washington National Airport (23) indicates that communities will benefit from reduced noise and airlines will benefit from restricting flights by using planes close to their capacities; passengers will be net losers because of the cost and inconvenience of landing at more distant airports. The Farmers Home Administration's analysis of alternative income limits for low-income and moderate-income housing loans (4) explicitly considers the distributional consequences of different limits, by geographic area, race, and income. In one case (6) the agency decided to choose the option that concentrated the subsidized loans on the poorest possible recipients, who would be least likely to qualify for subsidized loans. The DOL analysis of pension benefits (19) not only calculates the aggregate costs but also checks to see whether there will be severe costs to a few employers.

Sometimes an RIA recognizes that distributional consequences exist but does not analyze their importance. For example, the RIA covering oil and gas leasing in the Alaska National Petroleum Reserve (15) mentions that development may impose costs on local Eskimos while generating national benefits for energy consumers, though it fails to specify how serious the effects on the Eskimos' traditional way of life would be.

Most often, however, the RIAs do not mention the distribution of costs and benefits, even when the winners and losers are relatively obvious. For example, the principal beneficiaries of agricultural price supports are farmers, and the principal losers are consumers and taxpayers. The winners under the revised wage standards are taxpayers and government contractors; the losers are construction and service workers. The redistribution resulting from some programs is the result of legislative intent, but in other cases a more detailed analysis of the distributional consequences involved would be closer to the spirit of the OMB "Guidance."

CONSIDERATION OF ALTERNATIVES. EO 12291 requires "a description of alternative approaches that could substantially achieve the same regulatory goal at a lower cost." The OMB "Guidance" states that "the RIA should show that the agency has considered the most important alternative approaches to the problem," including the alternatives of no regulation, "market-oriented ways of regulating" such as providing consumers with additional information on performace rather than changing design standards, and economic incentives. In practice, such a wide range of alternatives is often inappropriate. In some cases a regulatory role is legislatively prescribed, eliminating the alternative of no regulation (as with farm price supports and Ocean Thermal Energy Conversion [OTEC] plant regulation). In other cases, alternative methods of achieving the same goals have already proved impossible. For example, the Post Office's decision to adopt a voluntary nine-digit zip code followed years of efforts to develop alternative ways of routing mail mechanically (20).

Some RIAs do consider several alternatives. The Department of Agriculture's (USDA) analysis of alternative meat standards compares one standard proposed by the meat industry, one proposed by consumer groups, and a third suggested by the USDA itself (8). The RIA on OTEC plant regulation (10) considers three levels of complexity; the analyses of farm price supports often compare the chosen price level with one slightly lower and one slightly higher. The Department of Labor's analysis of suspending pension benefits (19) in effect considers the entire continuum of possible standards, from allowing firms to suspend benefits when pensioners work one additional hour per month to allowing suspension only with full-time work.

Many of the RIAs performed in 1981 fail, however, to consider some clear alternatives, for seemingly obvious reasons. Alternatives that might more effectively meet regulatory goals but would involve more stringent regulations or higher costs to firms are not considered because of the bias toward deregulation in President Reagan's program of regulatory relief. One such example is the case of automatic seat belt standards. Despite evidence that "use-enhancing features" on seat belts (such as ignition interlocks, which prevent a car from starting until seat belts are fastened) increase seat belt use considerably, the RIA (21) fails to consider such requirements. Similarly, the costs and benefits of air bags are not evaluated on the grounds that the automobile companies have not planned to offer them.

The Department of Labor's analysis of affirmative action requirements for federal contractors (10) fails to consider whether there are alternative ways of reducing the costs of complying with affirmative action regulations short of exempting contractors. The Department of Agriculture's analysis of mechanical deboning (1) provides an extensive evaluation of an alternative suggested by the meat industry but fails to give equally serious consideration to an alternative suggested by consumer groups.

Because OMB does not enforce the requirement of examining a full range of alternatives, agencies appear to have ample latitude to restrict alternatives considered. In particular, the possibility of more stringent regulation (which might yield the greatest net social benefit) is rarely examined. The notion that benefit-cost analysis is an impartial judge of all the alternatives is thus undermined.

UNCERTAINTY. Uncertainty takes several forms in the regulations analyzed under EO 12291. The estimated values of benefits and costs are often uncertain. Many of the RIAs cope with this problem adequately through the use of sensitivity analysis. The RIAs for the Channel Islands–Point Reyes marine reserve (12) and for alternative bumper standards (22) are noteworthy for the variety of estimation techniques used. At the other extreme is the Post Office's analysis of the nine-digit zip code, which presents no alternative estimates of costs and benefits (20).

In several cases knowledge is so poor that no estimates of costs and benefits are possible. For example, the analyses of ocean thermal energy conversion plants (10) and deep seabed mining regulations (11) provide little more than a description of the types of costs and benefits that might exist because the absence of experience with these activities makes the estimation of costs and benefits impossible. In a similar vein, the analysis of oil and gas leasing procedures in the Alaska National Petroleum Reserve (15) argues that simple rather than complex bidding procedures should be used because of the unavoidable uncertainties about the discoveries that will be made, the costs of recovery, and the future price of oil.

These cases provide examples of a more general problem in performing benefit-cost analyses of proposed regulations. Often regulations propose novel activities or change drastically the economic incentives or choices firms and consumers face. Lacking prior information of how firms and consumers may react, it may be impossible to do more than speculate about the costs and benefits that may result. The RIAs just mentioned do a good job of describing possible outcomes in situations of real ignorance. In other cases—such as the proposals to add water to pipelines transporting anhydrous ammonia—uncertainty may bias the regulatory procedure against new regulations.

It is often possible to reduce uncertainty by gathering further information, either from conventional research or experimentation.[25] Developing new information to reduce uncertainty is obviously expensive and thus requires a difficult allocation decision, but this alternative is rarely considered in the existing RIAs. In the case of automatic seat belt standards, this was a serious omission. For example, there is surprisingly little information on the reasons why people do not wear seat belts and on whether automatic belts would result in substantially greater use. What data do exist can be interpreted in several ways. Although experiments with automatic seat belts would be comparatively simple to devise and inexpensive— particularly compared with the number of lives that could potentially be saved—the Department of Transportation has apparently never conducted such experiments, and the RIA (21) does not consider such an alternative. This is a particularly glaring oversight given the experimentation the Department of Transportation has performed in other areas such as testing the effects of different bumper standards and crash testing automobiles, and it highlights the need for explicit consideration of the value of reducing uncertainty.

A second uncertainty is individuals' experiences even when the probabilities of alternative outcomes are known. For example, the net benefits to individuals of different bumper standards and seat belt standards are uncertain, even if they are known in the aggregate, because each individual faces a probability rather than a certainty of an accident. One argument is that uncertain benefits should be valued at their certainty equivalent or the value of the expected outcome plus a risk premium. In the case of alternative seat belt standards, more effective seat belts lead not only to fewer deaths and injuries but also to a lower probability of death or injury to every individual, whether or not he or she is in an accident. Risk-averse individuals should be willing to pay some amount (a risk premium) for this reduced change, and if so this risk premium should be included among the benefits as a measure of the value of greater safety. Although the consideration and calculation of such a risk premium is both difficult and controversial, the existing RIAs have not recognized this element of uncertainty, even in cases of safety standards for which the essential point is to reduce common risks.

CHANGES IN RELATIVE PRICES AND THE DISCOUNT RATE. Perhaps surprisingly, the discount rate is rarely an issue in the RIAs because regulations are assumed to generate benefits and costs that continue at the same level year after year. The RIAs never attempt to model either the process of implementing the regulations or changes in the relative values of costs and benefits over time. In effect, the RIAs look at the equilibrium condition after the regulation is in place and there is full compliance and then examine the annual costs and benefits. Only under these assumptions are the costs and benefits in any one year an accurate reflection of the relative magnitude of the present values of the time stream of costs and benefits.

For example, creation of a wildlife marine sanctuary generates environmental benefits and costs of foregone oil exploration, which continue into the indefinite future. The RIA (12) assumes that the relative prices of environmental protection and oil remain constant over the future, and thus a comparison of annual costs and benefits is sufficient. Similarly, rescinding the requirement of automatic seat belts generates costs through lives lost and benefits through reduced expenditures on safety restraints. These annual costs and benefits remain the same only as long as driving habits and the costs of automatic restraints remain the same. In these two cases, as well as most other RIAs, the main reason for estimating costs and benefits over time and then discounting these streams to the present would be to speculate about how future changes in relative prices might affect the present value of a proposed regulatory change.[26] None of the RIAs performed in 1981 have attempted to estimate future changes in relative prices and their influence on future costs or benefits.

A few RIAs have, however, used a discount rate. The proposed voluntary nine-digit zip code would entail current costs in the form of automated handling equipment and the conversion of mailing lists to the new codes and would yield future returns in decreased costs of handling volume mail.

In its analysis (20) the Post Office used real discount rates of 10, 15, and 20 percent and calculated an internal social rate of return of 31 percent, indicating positive net benefits under any reasonable discount rate. The Department of Transportation seems to have used an 11 percent discount rate to calculate the present value of net benefits of restricting flights at Washington National Airport (23). Although the present value of net benefit is positive with an 11 percent rate, a more realistic, lower rate might put more weight on future costs because the costs of restricting flights increase over time with increasing traffic to the Washington area. The choice of the discount can thus be important, and OMB's specification of a relatively high 10 percent real rate may be inappropriate.

In examining these six types of errors in the existing RIAs, the only consistent bias that emerges is the expected one: the deregulatory emphasis of President Reagan's program has apparently influenced the benefit-cost analyses performed to date. Greater attention has been paid to costs than to benefits, and the alternative of more stringent regulation has not been considered. Otherwise, the technical flaws are those which have always been the most prevalent and controversial in benefit-cost analysis: the calculation of costs and benefits, the distinction between transfer payments and efficiency losses, the treatment of uncertainty, the consideration of distributional consequences, and incorporation of relative price changes.

THE QUALITY OF REGULATORY IMPACT ANALYSIS IN THE U.S. ENVIRONMENTAL PROTECTION AGENCY

Although none of the RIAs in our 1981 sample were prepared by the Environmental Protection Agency, by October 1982 EPA had completed RIAs for the effluent guidelines for the iron and steel industry (24), the hazardous wastes Superfund (25), and pesticide registration (26). These three RIAs are among the most ambitious and detailed that have been prepared in the federal government to date; each is several hundred pages long, including appendixes and supporting documents. This large resource commitment is consistent with the tradition of using economic analysis in evaluating environmental projects and regulations. Yet despite the substantial effort involved in these RIAs, they are not helpful for regulatory decision making or policy formulation. Not surprisingly, they reveal the limitations of benefit-cost analysis in complex areas with uncertain costs, intangible benefits, and interdependent government decisions. Better than any other RIAs, those performed by EPA reveal the problems generated when there is no coordination among the different analyses necessary for government regulations and when multiobjective approaches are abandoned in favor of an all-encompassing benefit-cost standard.

The first RIA, released in March 1982, analyzed wastewater effluent limitation guidelines for the iron and steel industry. The 1977 Clean Water Act Amendments require EPA to develop several levels of technology-based effluent limitations for the iron and steel industry, including Best Practicable Control Technology Currently Available, Best Available Technology Economically Achievable, and New Source Performance Standards. The RIA focuses on BAT because 80 percent of the iron and steel industry is currently in compliance with BPT standards. The RIA examines the incremental costs of the BAT standards, which Congress intended to be more stringent than the BPT standards, and the incremental benefits of reduced effluent discharges associated with BAT.

The EPA must make three decisions when setting the industrial effluent guidelines: how to subcategorize the industry, which pollutants to regulate, and how stringent to set the standard for each pollutant. "Subcategories" can refer to both different stages of a given production process (for example, cokemaking and steelmaking) and to different production technologies. For each subcategory, EPA identified about three to five levels of wastewater control technology and the effluent levels associated with each technology for approximately ten pollutants such as ammonia, toxic metals, and cyanides. To determine which level of control should be selected as the BAT standard, EPA developed cost estimates for each. Based on a professional judgment of which one was cost-effective, EPA then selected one of the control levels as the BAT standard. For five of the twelve subcategories, EPA set the BAT standard equal to the BPT standard. In the remaining seven subcategories, EPA selected one of the least stringent levels of control; the most stringent level of effluent control was not selected for any of the twelve subcategories. EPA acknowledged in the RIA that these BAT standards represented a substantial relaxation of previously proposed BAT standards, noting that determination was largely based on comments from industry.

Thus the initial flaw in this RIA is that BAT standards were chosen with an informal cost-effectiveness technique; the RIA then proceeds to analyze only the standards chosen, rather than the range of alternatives. The EPA estimated that the effects of moving from BPT to BAT limitations would be to reduce toxic organic pollutant loadings by 90 percent and toxic metals by 50 percent and that the annual costs for existing iron and steel facilities in the United States would be $17 million. These cost estimates are based on market prices with no attempt made to incorporate shadow prices for capital, labor, or materials. The question addressed in the RIA is whether this reduction in pollution is worth the costs. This is not the same as asking whether the BAT regulation is justified for a given steel and iron facility. The answer to this question would depend upon the marginal costs of pollution control for the specific plant and the marginal benefits of the improvements in water quality in a specific water body. The marginal benefits would in general depend upon how much other dischargers on the water body reduce their pollution. A benefit-cost analysis of the proposed effluent guidelines for the iron and steel industry must thus assume a certain level of pollution reduction by other dischargers.

A serious methodological problem, not addressed in this RIA, is thus posed, which reflects the general difficulties of coordinating analyses by a central planning organization. If EPA were to prepare different RIAs for each of the twenty-one primary industries for which effluent guidelines are required by the 1977 Clean Water Act, each of these twenty-one RIAs should be consistent with what is assumed about the level of pollution from the other twenty industries (as well as from municipal discharges) because many water bodies receive the effluent from more than one source. Because the benefits associated with water quality improvements are often a highly nonlinear function of pollutant levels, the sum of the benefits from twenty-one separate benefit-cost studies—each of which assumed the other twenty industries were in compliance with BPT and BAT standards—could seriously overestimate the total benefits resulting from the water pollution control program.

Assuming that the problem of coordinating assumptions in the RIAs could be resolved, the correct approach to estimating the benefits of specific national effluent standards would be to determine the value of the water quality improvements in each water body into which an iron and steel plant discharges effluents. The national benefits would be obtained by summing the benefits associated with each such water body. But even the most advanced analysis linking effluent discharges to water quality and then linking improvements in water quality to increased recreation and public health benefits can now generate only crude approximations of total benefits. The available data and methodologies are presently not good enough to distinguish among the alternative subcategory effluent guideline options contained in the RIA.

Given the difficulty of estimating benefits, EPA tried two different approaches in the RIA. First, three rivers were selected (Mahoning, Black, and Monongahela); for three stream segments the benefits of achieving BAT were estimated and compared with the specific costs for the iron and steel dischargers on the given stream segment. For the Black and Mahoning river case studies, however, the water quality benefits were calculated for reductions in effluent discharges by all pollutant sources, not simply the iron and steel industry. Second, the EPA estimated total national benefits from water pollution control and allocated a portion to the iron and steel industry based upon its estimated percentage of total pollutant loadings. EPA was well aware of the limitations of both approaches, observing that "all these benefit estimates have a large degree of uncertainty associated with them." But there is no further discussion of the problem of extrapolating results from case studies to the nation, though it would have been relatively simple to have judged the representativeness of the three rivers analyzed. The RIA simply concludes that "the analysis does indicate that there is a high probability that the societal benefits of the regulation do significantly outweigh the costs."[27]

Another major problem in this RIA is predictable: because of the difficulty in quantifying the health benefits of pollution standards, the benefit calculations concentrate on the recreation benefits of the proposed BAT standards. The resulting figures therefore underestimate true benefits. The inability to develop useful estimates of health benefits would be particularly serious if the RIA had performed benefit-cost analyses of several technological alternatives available (rather than cost-effectiveness analyses) because without a way of translating different pollutant loadings into health effects it is impossible to judge whether more stringent standards are worth their higher costs. The result, in effect, is that benefit-cost analysis is never really used in setting the effluent guidelines for the iron and steel industry: the BAT standards are selected with an informal cost-effectiveness technique filtered through industry comments, and the choice of these standards is then justified ex post through an inexact benefit-cost analysis. EPA could have taken greater care in its benefit estimates and could have chosen its BAT standards with a different procedure, but the fundamental problem remains the impossibility of applying benefit-cost techniques in areas for which the most critical benefits still cannot be calculated.

The technical difficulties in this particular RIA are enormous, but ironically the information from a benefit-cost analysis may be irrelevant in any case. EPA has argued that the primary determinant of the BAT standard should be the technological capability for effluent reduction rather than economic considerations; in practice this argument gives EPA wide discretion in choosing the effluent limitations for a subcategory. This discretion and EPA's interpretation of its legislative authority have been continuously challenged by both environmental groups such as the Natural Resources

Defense Council (NRDC) and the iron and steel industry. The establishment of effluent guidelines for the iron and steel industry has entailed a long and tedious rulemaking process, which has already lasted more than ten years. The initial effluent guideline development documents were completed in 1974, and the EPA promulgated the guidelines in two phases in 1974 and 1976. In 1975 and 1977 the Third Circuit Court remanded these regulations. A 1976 settlement agreement between EPA and NRDC set court-ordered schedules for final promulgation of the effluent guidelines. The EPA subsequently modified these schedules. In October 1979 revised draft development documents were published, followed by proposed development documents and an accompanying economic impact analysis in December 1980. Over the period May 1981 to January 1982, EPA prepared the RIA for the proposed effluent guidelines. The RIA was issued in March 1982, and the final effluent guidelines were published in the *Federal Register* in May 1982. These final rules were challenged again in court by both the Natural Resources Defense Council and the American Iron and Steel Institute, and a final consent agreement was reached in February 1983, which set a December 1983 deadline for the promulgation of BAT standards.

To date the RIA has not had any discernible impact on this rulemaking process, and it seems likely that it may remain irrelevant for two reasons. Most obviously, the recent litigation has arisen because of the intense conflict between industry on the one hand and environmentalists on the other, a conflict involving distributional issues that cannot be resolved through benefit-cost analysis. Second, because the Clean Water Act does not require EPA to quantify benefits or to balance the costs of pollution controls against the expected benefits, it is possible that the potential conflict between the legislation and the executive order could generate more litigation.[28]

The limitations of the RIA for the iron and steel effluent guidelines also characterize the RIA for revisions to the Comprehensive Environmental Response, Compensation, and Liability Act (CERCLA, also referred to as Superfund). The president is required to revise the National Oil and Hazardous Substances Pollution Contingency Plan (NCP), and the RIA attempts to assess the incremental costs and benefits of two alternative NCP revisions (25). Virtually all of the technical errors common among other RIAs can be found in this study—transfer payments confused with real resource costs, employment consequences valued improperly, discounting calculations done incorrectly, benefits double-counted because of confusion between stocks and flows. This RIA is unique, however, in explicitly stating, "While the dominant analytical technique in an RIA is benefit-cost analysis, that technique is not used in these analyses." One reason given is that "Congress made the judgment that the benefits of cleanup activities under Superfund would outweigh the costs of the CERCLA tax"; a second reason is that "the benefits are highly intangible."[29]

As is typical of past economic impact analyses prepared by EPA, most of this RIA is concerned with the financial implications for the affected industries and the macroeconomic effects of the proposed regulations. The real efficiency costs of the required cleanup operations are never presented except for the claim that they are small in regard to changes in output and prices. Instead, there is an extended discussion of the incidence of cleanup costs among industries, firms, and governments. The macroeconomic "analysis" consists of such irrelevant comparisons as the annual Superfund expenditures as a percentage of GNP.

The RIA focused on two alternative allocations of Superfund money for the cleanup of hazardous waste sites but does not address the costs and benefits of the funding mechanism specified in the authorizing legislation. The two regulatory alternatives are poorly specified in the RIA. One supposedly "characterizes the objectives of the NCP revisions as the protection of public health, welfare, and the environment, with an emphasis on possible public health concerns"; the other "enlarges the scope of the program by giving greater emphasis to public welfare and the environment, thereby increasing the likely costs of response at each site."[30] Although the relationship of the alternatives to these objectives is never made clear, the operational distinction between the two is that one assumes a larger number of remedial actions (170 versus 115 per year) and a lower average cost per site ($4.5 million versus $6.75 million) than the second. By confining the analysis to these two alternatives, the RIA can judge only whether fewer, more intensive cleanup efforts are more valuable than more, less intensive efforts. Although this trade-off is an important issue, the larger questions of whether the total cleanup effort should be expanded or contracted and whether other regulatory alternatives might be more desirable are never addressed.

The only strength of the RIA is its straightforward and repeated admission that the benefits of cleaning up hazardous waste dumps are unknown:

> No quantifiable estimate of the magnitude of the environmental benefits accruing from the revised NCP response actions can be developed at this time . . . the difficulties in estimating environmental benefits stem not only from uncertainties about the nature and extent of cleanup that the

revised NCP will bring about, but also from the difficulties inherent in developing units of measurement that adequately communicate some idea of the social worth of reduced harm to the environment.

No estimate of the number of people who will be spared adverse health effects by the NCP can be developed at this time.

No measures of the reduction in risk of chemical exposure through surface water contamination were developed, although such benefits . . . may be sustainable.[31]

As an alternative to measuring benefits, the RIA presents calculations of the reduction in the population at risk resulting from the two alternatives. These estimates do not reflect the fact that higher cleanup costs at a given rate might reduce the risk for the surrounding population: "It is assumed that all remedial actions are equally effective at reducing populations at risk of exposure."[32] The RIA's estimate of reduced population at risk thus cannot distinguish between the benefits of the two alternatives, and of course the lack of any benefit estimates makes the comparison of overall benefits and costs impossible.

The third EPA RIA, analyzing data requirements for registering pesticides (26), suffers primarily from an inability to measure either the benefits of protecting the public from inadequately tested pesticides or the costs associated with preventing needed pesticides from reaching the market in a timely fashion. The objective of the Federal Insecticide, Fungicide, and Rodenticide Act is to reduce the adverse effects from pesticide use to "acceptable" levels. EPA's Office of Pesticide Programs regulates the distribution, sale, and use of pesticides through a registration process for new products, new uses of registered products, and reregistration of existing products. EPA's decision on a pesticide registration application is currently based on data supplied by the manufacturer.

Unlike the iron and steel and Superfund RIAs, this RIA on pesticide registration was able to identify a reasonable range of options. The RIA attempts to examine the costs and benefits of five regulatory alternatives defined in terms of the data requirements to register a pesticide:

1. EPA issues nonbinding ("nonregulatory") guidance.
2. EPA issues regulations on the data required from manufacturers but waivers are permitted and tiered testing is employed.
3. Manufacturers must certify that their products do not cause unreasonable adverse effects (self certification).
4. EPA issues data requirements for all pesticide products; waivers and tiered testing are prohibited.

5. Manufacturers are permitted to sell new products on a limited basis after submitting short-term studies to EPA; full registration occurs after all studies are completed.[33]

The more stringent alternatives reduce the risk of exposing the public to chronic adverse effects from pesticides but also increase compliance costs and reduce the benefits from using pesticides by keeping "good" pesticides off the market longer than "necessary." The RIA provides substantial information on the compliance costs associated with the five regulatory alternatives and attempts to measure changes in consumers' surplus and economic rents associated with the resulting increases in pesticide costs.

The authors of this RIA obviously struggled with the recurrent problem of comparing these cost estimates with benefits they could not quantify. The RIA states: "The results of the analyses are highly impacted by outcomes of a qualitative nature. Relatively few factors were capable of being fully quantified and/or monetized as is suggested by EO 12291." Presumably under pressure to produce quantitative results and without the time or resources to conduct basic research on benefit estimation, the RIA concocts a "benefit-cost rating technique" in order "to bring the results of the analysis into net benefit terms." The procedure used is summarized as follows:

1. A total of 100 points is allocated to benefit factors.
2. A total of 100 points is allocated to cost factors.
3. The points within the benefit and cost areas are allocated to the various benefit and cost factors in proportion to the importance attached to the items by the management of the program. The more important the cost or benefit factor, the more points it receives and vice versa.
4. The points for each factor are allocated to the regulatory options in accordance with the quantitative and/or qualitative outcomes of the impact analysis as reported in earlier sections of the report.
5. The points allocated to each of the alternatives in each row are assigned independently from row to row with respect to benefits and costs.
6. The benefit ratings and cost ratings are totaled, giving an overall benefit rating and cost rating for each alternative. These ratings in turn are subtracted to give a net benefit rating and are divided to give a benefit-cost rating ratio.
7. Intuitively, the alternative having the highest net benefit rating or highest cost-benefit rating ratio would be the preferred alternative and vice versa.

Although noting that this procedure is not a benefit-cost analysis, the authors of the RIA argue, "It seems a reasonable method of summarizing the various quantitative and qualitative benefit and cost factors."[34] There is no theoretical basis for this procedure of using subjective weightings assigned to various categories of costs and benefits and therefore no support for the conclusion in the RIA concerning the selected alternatives. The RIA does present a sensitivity analysis on the subjective weightings but provides no information on possible uncertainties in the chronic health and ecosystem effects of the different alternatives because all that is available is a subjective rating of what these effects might be.

The most charitable interpretation of this RIA is that it illustrates the overwhelming problem with subjecting a complex environmental decision to benefit-cost analysis, in an area in which the effects are largely unknown and the benefits include improved health and fewer disabilities, both notoriously difficult to estimate and value. The effort to develop a "benefit-cost rating technique" shows ingenuity and desperation, but it is in no sense an approximation to benefit-cost analysis. Beyond the value of this technique in forcing an analyst to specify the kinds of benefits and costs that should be considered, this approach cannot provide much help in regulatory decision making.

The first RIAs performed by the Environmental Protection Agency illustrate the problems with benefit-cost analysis that other agencies have experienced under EO 12291, though EPA's RIAs are extreme cases because of the special difficulties of performing benefit-cost analyses in the environmental area, in which many industries affect specific water bodies and air quality regions. The inability to analyze the long-term health effects, common to other RIAs, is another constant problem, but especially serious because ignoring the health effects of environmental regulations amounts to giving up the major purpose of such regulations.

Finally, as in other agencies, the usefulness of RIAs in the environmental area has been limited by the narrow focus of the questions posed and the limited alternatives considered. Many policy or regulatory problems have very large numbers of possible solutions, and much of the art of policy analysis involves selecting a few alternatives that should be examined in more detail. The application of benefit-cost techniques to a specific regulation, rather than to a range of alternatives, is often of little use in designing appropriate policy. If the analysis concludes that benefits are greater than costs, this means that the regulation is better than nothing, not that it is the best available. For many classes of pressing environmental problems, this is a trivial conclusion. On the other hand, if analysis concludes that the benefits are less than the costs, the RIA may yield little insight into the alternatives that might produce net benefits.

Given the complexities of many environmental issues, analytical resources—including those associated with benefit-cost analysis—would often be better spent on policy and program design rather than ex post analyses of a few regulations. Benefit-cost analysis is not now powerful enough to handle these complexities. The requirements of EO 12291 may force an improvement in benefit-cost techniques, but for the moment they add little to the regulatory process.

CONCLUSIONS: HAS EO 12291 IMPROVED REGULATION?

Executive Order 12291 is still relatively new, and many federal agencies have not yet adjusted their regulatory procedures to incorporate its requirements fully. Its influence on the regulatory process is not yet clear because so few regulations have been reviewed under EO 12291 and because the process itself is still evolving. Nevertheless, it is worth raising the question of what its long-run effects are likely to be. Like benefit-cost analysis itself, EO 12291 has so far generated contradictory results and provides ammunition for both supporters and critics of benefit-cost analysis.

The first question to ask is whether EO 12291 has improved the quality of benefit-cost analysis performed in the federal government. The answer depends on which agency is involved, how the agency views benefit-cost analysis, and what resources it puts into analysis. For example, we reviewed a set of analyses prepared by the same individuals in the Department of Agriculture for both the Carter and Reagan executive orders and found no substantial differences. In both cases the analyses were perfunctory and tended to describe rather than evaluate the proposed change. The numbers in the analyses which support the proposed regulatory change are in both cases incomprehensible. Even within the Department of Agriculture, however, the quality of regulatory analysis varies considerably. The RIAs covering the price support programs are much worse than those for regulating meat processing and those governing Farmers Home Administration loans.

Of course, EO 12291 has generated many benefit-cost analyses of remarkably low quality, but the requirement of an RIA has also resulted in some studies that are more thorough than any we have seen from the Carter administration. The RIAs for the Channel Islands–Point Reyes marine sanctuary, for changes in beef grading standards, for different bumper standards, for the regulation of pensions, and for restrictions at Washington National Airport all provide substantial amounts of relevant information and represent well-reasoned defenses of the final position chosen. Even when the logic of the final position is at odds with the economic analysis (most notably in the RIA for automatic safety restrictions), the RIA presents enough information to allow an independent assessment.

More important than the absolute number of high-quality analyses under EO 12291—which is small by any standard—is the fact that benefit-cost analysis seems to be taking its place in the routine procedures associated with the regulatory process.[35] The consciousness that costs and benefits need to be analyzed rather than assumed, that alternatives need to be considered, that information is uncertain and may require sensitivity analyses, that the claims of external interest groups need to be independently checked—all these views are implicit in EO 12291 and are present in the best RIAs that have been performed so far. Compared to President Carter's EO 12044, which required only a weak form of cost-effectiveness analysis, EO 12291 at least requires a full consideration of regulatory alternatives and a specification of winners and losers.

To be sure, the spread of more sophisticated economic analysis could be undermined by capricious and biased implementation of EO 12291 by this or any other administration. OMB's performance to date does not provide grounds for much optimism, particularly because of its widespread granting of exemptions and its apparent lack of interest in coordinating and improving the quality of analysis. Even under these conditions, however, the executive order gives some support to federal administrators who want to carry out more sophisticated economic analyses.

In evaluating EO 12291, a related question is whether the order has made any difference in the regulations actually promulgated. One way to address the question is to see whether the RIAs support the regulatory alternative choosen. In most cases they have, though RIAs may be written to confirm a decision previously reached rather than used to determine or influence the decision. But even the small number of RIAs performed so far provide at least three examples of the final decision differing from the recommendations of the RIA. In the case of alternative beef grading standards, the RIA (8) concludes that the standards chosen would not reduce the costs to the industry in the short run and suggests (without any evidence) that costs might decrease in the long run. Given a documented decline in the palatability of beef, it seems clear that the costs of the proposed standard outweigh the benefits. For the Channel Islands–Point Reyes marine sanctuary, the RIA (12) concludes that no matter what method of valuing benefits is used, the sanctuary is worthwhile. Despite this conclusion, the final rule has been suspended.[36]

Finally, the RIA covering automatic safety restraints (21) presents detailed information (including an appendix, which places a value on lives lost and injuries and displays present values with different discount rates at different levels of seat belt use) that supports the value of automatic seat belt standards under all but the most extreme assumptions.[37] The RIA's conclusion and the proposed rule, however, stress the uncertainty of the information used and rescinded automatic seat belt standards on the grounds that "most of the anticipated benefits have virtually disappeared because of the uncertainty about incremental seat belt use," despite a good deal of evidence to the contrary in the RIA.[38]

An alternative approach to examining the effects of EO 12291 is to see whether the rules promulgated so far have differed from those one might expect to have emerged on purely political grounds. By this test EO 12291 does seem to have made a difference in some cases. For example, in the case of beef grading standards, the evidence presented in the RIA (8) caused the Department of Agriculture to adopt grading standards intermediate between those proposed by consumer groups and those proposed by the meat industry. In the regulation of pension plans, the RIA (19) presented well-reasoned evidence that the proposal made by many pension plans— that they be allowed to reduce pensions if a retired person performed any work—would cause disincentives to work and thus efficiency losses. The Department of Labor, in fact, rejected the industry's position. In its analysis of bumper standards, the Department of Transportation ended up reducing bumper standards based on the evidence in the RIA (22), but it did not eliminate the standards as the automobile industry wanted. In the analysis of alternative ways of registering pesticides (26), EPA's analysis explicitly rejected the least stringent alternative of self-certification. In these examples economic analysis appears to support the efforts of federal agencies to reject the industry's deregulation position in favor of a compromise.

Even if the effect of EO 12291 on regulations remains small, there is another important benefit from the requirement of economic analysis. As in the case of environmental impact statements, RIAs provide additional information to those outside the government about the issues and the rulemaking process. This information can provide the basis for comments and criticism; in fact, several proposed rulemakings have requested information from the public on various elements of costs and benefits that were uncertain or unknown to the agency. In at least one case the analysis in the RIA facilitated a successful court challenge to the regulatory change. The Department of Transportation's decision to rescind the requirements of automatic restraints in automobiles has been successfully challenged in

State Farm Mutual Automobiles Insurance Co. v. *Department of Transportation*, and the judge's decision noted the evidence produced by the National Highway Traffic Safety Administration. The judge also faulted the agency for the lack of evidence supporting its contention that seat belt use would not increase and criticized its failure to analyze alternatives such as air bags.[39] Thus challenges based on the Administrative Procedures Act can use information generated by RIAs. (This decision was upheld by the Supreme Court in June 1983.)

Of course, the final verdict on Executive Order 12291 cannot be pronounced for several years. On the one hand, there is clearly plenty of leeway in EO 12291 for ideological bias, especially in the process of exemptions but also in the content of RIAs and the relative neglect of benefits. The implementation of EO 12291 has contained an obvious bias for deregulation and may have a chilling effect on new regulations. The initial efforts by OMB to manage the executive order have been inept and reflect no understanding of the constructive role that a central agency might play in improving consistency and quality of economic analysis. In ignoring the development of multiobjective approaches, EO 12291 is perhaps twenty years out of date and ignores the fact that previous attempts to impose economic efficiency as the single policy objective have been short-lived. There is, of course, nothing that EO 12291 can do about the well-known, inherent limitations of benefit-cost analysis, including its inability to encompass ethical issues and noneconomic values, the difficulties in quantifying costs and benefits, and the problems with partial equilibrium analysis, uncertainty, and forecasting. These inherent limits have led many analysts to reject benefit-cost as a part of regulatory reform.[40]

On the other hand, EO 12291 has produced some analyses of high quality and has in still other cases provided valuable information about the basis for public decisions. In a few cases ideological positions seem to have been tempered by economic analysis. There appears to be a new consciousness of benefit-cost analysis as a normal part of the regulatory process, with some agencies (though not all by any means) making substantial efforts to commit resources to the improvement of RIAs.

There are several ironies surrounding the implementation of EO 12291 that allow speculation about the direction the order may take. One is that an administration committed to decentralization of power and hostile to government planning has initiated a form of analysis that, to be successful, requires greater centralized control by an agency such as OMB and more national planning, in the sense of developing coordinated procedures and national parameters. Although OMB in the Reagan administration may be able to muddle along without playing such a role, sooner or later the inconsistencies and inequities generated by a decentralized system of analysis are likely to increase the pressure for a more centralized planning function.

Still another irony is that an administration often distrustful of public participation in government decision making—one that has moved to restrict the Freedom of Information Act and to extend classification of government documents, for example—has promoted an executive order that may increase public participation in regulatory rulemaking and public scrutiny of agency decisions. Whether such an outcome occurs will depend on how citizens and interest groups participate in the regulatory process under EO 12291 and on whether OMB makes its own internal procedures more visible. But the potential for the executive order to increase public participation is substantial; indeed, the notion of expanded use of economic analysis in regulatory decisions without some public accountability for the quality of the analysis—conveying the image of a technocracy making decisions insulated from politics—is likely to be unacceptable to all parties.

A final irony of Executive Order 12291 is that the Reagan administration, which has adopted benefit-cost anlaysis as a vehicle for reducing regulations, has in some cases given ammunition to those who oppose deregulation and who have little political power compared to the regulated industries. In fact, the Reagan administration is currently being attacked by the New Right and the members of the business community for OMB's failure to push its deregulatory agenda more aggressively; the members of these groups are not interested in the slow process of preparing Regulatory Impact Analyses. Of course, benefit-cost analysis is inescapably susceptible to political manipulation; but as an analytic technique it does have its own rules and standards and thus provides a method for opponents of deregulation to object legitimately to political decisions.

The general perception today that benefit-cost analysis has a reactionary bias is the result both of President Reagan's conservative agenda and his use of EO 12291 to promote deregulation and of the use of benefit-cost analysis by the Army Corps of Engineers to justify water projects of doubtful economic value and with serious environmental consequences. This perception is somewhat ironic, however, because benefit-cost analysis was originally a way to emphasize the public interest in projects inspired by local political interests. In principle, benefit-cost analysis provides an analytic method that can be used against both the false claims of regulated industries, who are often accused of capturing the regulatory process, and the zeal of consumers, environmentalists, and bureaucrats, who are often charged with forcing the regulatory machine to run amuck. Whether benefit-cost analysis can do either of these in practice depends on how it becomes politicized and on whether the results are actually used in the regulatory process.

Executive Order 12291 has the sweep of fifty years of analytic efforts behind it, though it has ignored several of the important lessons of that history. Unavoidably, it is heir to the common problems with benefit-cost analysis as well as to the inflated claims made on its behalf. The long-run success of EO 12291 depends on the participation of various groups and organizations: of OMB (or some other centralized office) to give some direction and coordination to the enterprise; of the economists and others who believe in regulatory analysis within the federal bureaucracy to instill an ethic supportive of economic analysis that cannot easily be swept away by purely political concerns; and of various publics outside government to scrutinize agency decision making and ensure that public values are not swept aside by a wave of misplaced utilitarianism. Otherwise, it will take its place as another in a long series of failed efforts at regulatory reform.

APPENDIX: REGULATORY IMPACT ANALYSES

Department of Agriculture

1. "Preliminary Regulatory Impact Analysis of Proposed Change to MP(S)P Regulations," Food Safety and Inspection Service, Appendix to Proposed Rule, *Federal Register* 46 (1982): 39297–352.

2. "Final Impact Statement: Proposed Amendments to the Redesignation of Regulations Covering Section 502 Rural Housing Loan Policies, Procedures and Authorizations," Farmers Home Administration, 1 August 1981.

3. "Final Regulatory Impact Analysis: Revision of Definition of Low Income for Section 502, 504, and Approved 515 as Required by P.L. 96-153," Famers Home Administration, 14 September 1981.

4. "Final Regulatory Impact Analysis: Moderate Income Limits for Farmers Home Administration Rural Housing Programs," 14 September 1981.

5. "Regulatory Impact Analysis: REA Bulletin 345-89, REA Specifications for Filled Telephone Cable with Expanded Insulation, P.E. 189," Rural Electrification Administration, 23 September 1981.

6. "Final Regulatory Impact Analysis: Interest Credit (Subsidy) to Moderate Income Borrowers," Farmers Home Administration, 3 October 1981.

7. "Final Impact Analysis Statement: Establishing New Area-based Low and Moderate Income Limits for Farmers Home Administration (FMHA) Rural Housing Program," Farmers Home Administration, 11 December 1981.

8. "Summary of the Preliminary Regulatory Impact Analysis of Proposed Changes in the United States Standards for Grades of Carcass Beef and Slaughter Cattle," Appendix to the Proposed Rules, *Federal Register* 46 (1981): 63071–75.

9. "Final Regulatory Impact Analysis: Interim Final Rulemaking–Puerto Rico Nutritional Assistance Grant," Food and Nutritional Service, 4 March 1982.

Department of Commerce

10. "Ocean Thermal Energy Conversion: Final Regulatory Impact Analysis," National Oceanic and Atmosphere Administration, Office of Ocean Mineral and Energy, July 1981.

11. "Final Regulatory Impact Analysis and Final Regulatory Flexibility Analysis for Regulations to Implement Public Law 96-283, The Deep Seabed Hard Mineral Resources Act," National Oceanic and Atmospheric Administration, Office of Ocean Mineral and Energy, September 1981.

12. "Regulatory Impact Analysis on Regulations Affecting Hydro-Carbon Operations with Channel Islands and Point Reyes National Marine Sanctuaries."

Department of the Interior

13. "Occupational Noise Exposure: Hearing Conservation Amendment," Occupational Health and Safety Administration, *Federal Register* 46 (1981): 42722–38.

14. "Final Regulatory Impact Analysis of Options to Change the Application Fees and Rental Structures of the Noncompetitive Portion of the Federal Onshore Oil and Gas Leasing Program," January 1982.

15. "Final Regulatory Impact Analysis for Regulations Governing Competitive Oil and Gas Leasing in the National Petroleum Reserve in Alaska," Bureau of Land Management, 30 April 1982.

Department of Labor

16. "Preliminary Regulatory Impact Analysis on Proposed Office of Federal Contract Compliance Regulations," undated.

17. "Preliminary Regulatory Impact Analysis of Proposed Service Contract Act Regulations," undated.

18. "Preliminary Regulatory Impact and Regulatory Flexibility Analysis on David-Bacon Related Regulations," undated.

19. "Regulatory Impact Analysis: Suspension of Pension Benefits upon Reemployment of Retirees," undated (20 CFR 2530203-3).

Postal Service

20. "Final Regulatory Impact Analysis," Appendix to Final Rule, "Amendments to ZIP Code Provisions to Explain the ZIP + 4 Code," *Federal Register* 46 (1981): 33253–68.

Department of Transportation

21. "Final Regulatory Impact Analysis, Amendment to FMUSS 208, Occupant Crash Protection: Rescission of Automatic Occupant Protection Requirements," National Highway Traffic Safety Administration, Office of Program and Rulemaking Analysis, October 1981.

22. "Final Regulatory Impact Analysis: Part 581 Bumper Standards," National Highway Traffic Safety Administration, Plans and Programs, Office of Program and Rulemaking Analysis, May 1982.

23. "Final Regulatory Evaluation of Metropolitan Washington Airport Policy," Federal Aviation Administration, Office of Aviation Policy and Plans, October 1981.

United States Environmental Protection Agency

24. "Regulatory Impact Analysis of the Effluent Limitation Guidelines Regulation for the Iron and Steel Industry," Office of Water Regulations and Standards, 17 March 1982.

25. "Regulatory Impact Analysis of the Revisions to the National Oil and Hazardous Substances Pollution Contingency Plan," Draft Report, ICF, Inc., 16 February 1982.

26. "Regulatory Impact Analysis: Data Requirements for Registering Pesticides under the Federal Insecticide, Fungicide, and Rodenticide Act," Office of Pesticide Program, August 1982, EPA 540/9-82-013.

In addition to the above Regulatory Impact Analyses, we have reviewed the following brief RIAs prepared for regulations from the Department of Agriculture's price stabilization programs:

"Final Impact Statement, 1981—Crop Rice Loan and Purchase Rates for Whole Kernels by Class and Broken Kernels for all Classes," Agricultural Stabilization and Conservation Service, 14 April 1981.

"Final Impact Statement, 1981—Crop Peanut Program—National Average Loan Rates and Sales Policy for Loan Stocks," ASCS, 21 April 1981.

"Final Impact Statement: Sale of Commodity Credit Corporation (CCC) Butter Stocks on Competitive Bid Basis for Export," ASCS, 22 May 1981.

Draft Impact Analysis: Support Program for Milo, 1981–82 Marketing Year," ASCS, 8 June 1981.

"Final Impact Statement: National Program Acreage, National Allocation Factor, and Deficiency Payment Rate for 1980 Crop, Upland Cotton," ASCS, 1 June 1981.

"Final Regulatory Impact Analysis: Price Support for 1981 and Subsequent Loans," ASCS, 25 August 1981.

"Final Impact Statement: 1981 Crop, Upland and Extra-Long Staple Cotton Loan Program Differentials," ASCS, 16 June 1981.

"Preliminary Regulatory Impact Analysis: Amendment to Forestry Incentives Program Regulations," ASCS, 29 September 1981.

"Final Regulatory Impact Analysis: Farmer-Owned Feed Grain Reserve Program for 1981," ASCS, 8 October 1981.

"Preliminary Regulatory Impact Analysis: 1982 Crop Flue-Cured Tobacco Marketing Quota," ASCS, 16 October 1981.

"Final Regulatory Impact Analysis: Amendment to Water Bank Program," ASCS, 23 October 1981.

NOTES

1. Some of the early influential documents include reports of the President's Water Resources Policy Commission (1950); reports of the Commission on Organization of the Executive Branch of the Government (Second Hoover Commission) (1955); U.S. Bureau of the Budget, *Circular A-47* (1952); and Senate Resolution 148, 85th Cong., 1st sess. (1958).

2. U.S. Federal Interagency River Basin Committee, Subcommittee on Benefits and Costs, *Proposed Practices for Economic Analysis of River Basin Projects*, p. 4.

3. Major, *Multiobjective Water Resources Planning*; Cohon, *Multiobjective Programming and Planning*; and Zeleny, *Multiple Criteria Decisionmaking*.

4. U.S. Council on Environmental Quality, "Regulations on Implementing National Environmental Quality Act Procedures."

5. Viscusi, "Presidential Oversight."

6. Executive Order 12291 was published in the *Federal Register* 46 (1981): 13191–98. This and various other materials were included in "Materials on President Reagan's Program of Regulatory Relief," distributed by the White House for release on 6 June 1981.

7. For a recent and articulate statement of the point being made here, see Wolfe, "A Theory of Non-Market Failure," *Public Interest* 55 (Spring 1979): 114–33.

8. Earlier drafts of the OMB guidance memorandum reflect even more clearly the jargon of professional economists, e.g.: "The aim is to achieve a global, not local, maximum of net benefits" (April 1981).

9. For corroboration of the point that OMB has failed to use its authority to ensure consistency, see U.S. General Accounting Office, "Improved Quality, Adequate Resources, and Consistent Oversight Needed if Regulatory Analysis Is to Help Control Costs of Regulations," pp. 51–52.

10. The OMB guidance memorandum refers to OMB *Circular A-94*, 27 March 1972, which advocates the use of the 10 percent real rate of discount. The 10 percent rate seems to reflect roughly the average pretax real rate of return on capital on the economy, though other methods of calculating the discount rate produce lower results. For example, the real long-run interest rate and the social rate of time preference (estimated as the product of the real rate of growth in the economy and the elasticity of marginal utility with respect to consumption) both suggest discount rates in the range of 3 to 6 percent.

11. The appendix of EPA's "Guidelines for Performing Regulatory Impact Analyses" (Draft, 22 June 1982) on the choice of a discount rate is a notable exception. The EPA delegates the choice of an appropriate discount rate to individual program offices and analysts, on the assumption that different programs and regulations face different financing and budgetary constraints and thus different opportunity costs of capital.

12. The count of regulations and their disposition comes from U.S. Office of Management and Budget, "Executive Order 12291 on Federal Regulation," Tables 1 and 5. These counts are not entirely accurate. For example, some of the rules which OMB designates as having RIAs (such as price support regulations for the wheat reserve program) were exempted as emergency measures, and others (the proposed marine sanctuary for the Channel Islands and Point Reyes, California) had an RIA performed.

13. One exception is the Environmental Protection Agency, which has defined a "major" increase in costs or prices as 50 percent.
14. U.S. Office of Management and Budget, "Executive Order 12291 on Federal Regulation," p. 36.
15. See, for example, the Office of Surface Mining Reclamation and Enforcement's final rule, "Permanent and Interim Regulatory Program Modifications, Extraction of Coal: With Regard to Two Acre Exemptions," OMB Press Release, 23 April 1982.
16. These exemptions are listed in Table 7 of U.S. Office of Management and Budget, "Executive Order 12291 on Federal Regulation," pp. 37–39.
17. Materials Transportation Bureau, Department of Transportation, "Transportation of Liquids by Pipeline: Addition of Water to Pipelines Transporting Anhydrous Ammonia," *Federal Register* 46 (1981): 39–44.
18. For this analysis we have read the RIAs for the rules listed in Table 5 of U.S. Office of Management and Budget, "Executive Order 12291 on Regulation." In addition, we obtained several other RIAs written for the "midnight rules" subjected to special scrutiny by the Bush Task Force on Regulatory Relief, as described in "Statement by the Vice-President on Regulatory Relief," Press Release, 25 March 1981.
19. See, for example, "Materials on Regulatory Relief," pp. 5–7; Presidential Task Force on Regulatory Relief, "Reagan Administration Achievements in Regulatory Relief," August 1982.
20. U.S. Department of Labor, "Preliminary Regulatory Impact Analysis on Proposed Office of Federal Contract Compliance Regulations," undated.
21. U.S. General Accounting Office, "Improved Quality," p. 12.
22. U.S. Regulatory Council, *A Survey of Ten Agencies' Experience with Regulatory Analysis*, May 1981, p. 23.
23. The manual lives up to expectations: it concludes with a picture of a pencil (a regulator's?) in a casket, after full-page illustrations of a hammer, saw, and other tools.
24. The Council on Wage and Price Stability consistently found agencies doing an inadequate job of quantifying or even describing the benefits expected from regulations. See Hopkins, Lenard, Morrall, and Pinkston, "A Review of the Regulatory Interventions of the Council on Wage and Price Stability, 1974–1980," pp. 26–27.
25. For example, during the 1970s the federal government invested in a series of negative income tax and housing experiments in order to reduce the uncertainty associated with various changes in welfare programs. The early stages of OTEC plant licensing can be interpreted as an experiment because the first plants will generate new information about costs and benefits, which the Department of Commerce can then use in subsequent licensing procedures. A possible alternative source of information in some cases may be laboratory experiments, particularly to establish valuations of intangible benefits; on experiments in economics, see Charles Plott, "Industrial Organization Theory and Experimental Economics," *Journal of Economic Literature* 20 (December 1982): 1485–1527.
26. Another reason would be for OMB to have a consistent measure of the effectiveness of each of the projects being examined in order to set budgetary or regulatory priorities.
27. U.S. Environmental Protection Agency, "Regulatory Impact Analysis of the

Effluent Limitation Guidelines Regulations for the Iron and Steel Industry,"
Office of Water Regulations and Standards, 17 March 1982.

28. On the potential conflict between legislation and EO 12291, see Cass Sunstein, "Cost Benefit Analysis and the Separation of Powers," *Arizona Law Review* 23 (1981): 1267–82.

29. U.S. Environmental Protection Agency, "Regulatory Impact Analysis of the Revisions to the National Oil and Hazardous Substances Pollution Contingency Plan," Draft report, ICF, Inc., 16 February 1982, p. 4-3.

30. Ibid., p. ES-2.

31. Ibid., pp. 6-1, 6-4, 6-7.

32. Ibid., p. 6-7.

33. U.S. Environmental Protection Agency, "Regulatory Impact Analysis: Data Requirements for Registering Pesticides under the Federal Insecticide, Fungicide, and Rodenticide Act," Office of Pesticide Program, August 1982. EPA 540/9-82-013.

34. Ibid.

35. For corroboration of this point, see U.S. Regulatory Council, *A Survey of Ten Agencies' Experience with Regulatory Analysis*, May 1981, pp. 45–47.

36. *Federal Register* 46 (30 September 1981).

37. The DOT's handbook for preparing RIAs suggests that $340,000 be used as a value of life (Appendix 3, PA-7, Table A-1). Nevertheless, the body of the RIA prepared for seat belt standards fails to put a value on a life saved, arguing that such a procedure is inappropriate and the range of estimates is too wide. The RIA estimates possible automobile fatalities of 35,990 for 1984. Assuming that 22 percent of passengers would use seat belts because of the automatic seat belt regulation and the belts are 50 percent effective, the regulation would save almost 4,000 lives. Using the figure suggested by DOT's handbook (which is lower than most estimates), the dollar value assigned to the lives saved is $1.35 billion, far in excess of the estimated costs.

38. *Federal Register* 26 (29 October 1981).

39. *United States Law Week* 50 (15 June 1982): 2726–27.

40. See, for example, Marguerita Connerton and Mark MacCarthy, "Cost-Benefit Analysis and Regulation: Expressway to Reform or Blind Alley," National Policy Exchange Paper No. 4, October 1981; U.S. House of Representatives, Subcommittee on Oversight Investigations of the Committee on Interstate and Foreign Commerce, "Cost-Benefit Analysis: Wonder Tool or Mirage?" December 1980.

Part III

CONCEPTUAL PROBLEMS IN
MEETING THE BENEFIT-COST
MANDATE OF EXECUTIVE
ORDER 12291

6

A. MYRICK FREEMAN III*

ON THE TACTICS OF BENEFIT
ESTIMATION UNDER
EXECUTIVE ORDER 12291

THE term "tactics" refers to how to employ a given set of weapons and tools to implement some larger strategic design. I assume that the strategic design embodied in Executive Order 12291 is to introduce economic rationality into regulatory decision making by requiring the quantification and measurement of the benefits and costs of proposed regulations. The available weapons are the concepts, analytical techniques, and models that have been developed for the definition and measurement of benefits and costs. Achieving the strategic objective of economically rational regulatory decision making will require that benefit-cost analyses be done for a large number of proposed regulations in the realm of air and water pollution control, toxic substances, solid wastes, hazardous materials, and so forth. The agency in many cases will face time constraints in the form of deadlines for decisions imposed by Congress and the courts or by political considerations. And there will not be enough staff or budget to do first-class, original research on the benefits and costs of all of these regulations in the required time span. The tactical question for the agency is how best to employ the available weapons to achieve the specified objective (defensible estimates of benefits) in a particular set of circumstances while economizing on scarce agency resources.

This chapter focuses on the tactics of benefit estimation for regulatory analyses, not because cost estimation is simple and easy but because my assignment was limited to benefits. It sometimes seems to be assumed that estimating the cost of a regulation is a straightforward problem and that the

*Professor, Bowdoin College. I would like to acknowledge the helpful comments of Wesley Magat, Ernest Manuel, and especially V. Kerry Smith on an earlier draft. Of course, I am solely responsible for any remaining errors.

really serious problems of data, measurements, and so forth arise only when one is trying to fill in the benefit side of the benefit-cost ledger. But of course this is not the case. Either because the technology of control is poorly understood or because of the wide range of choice of control techniques faced by different sources, it may be very difficult to estimate the cost of complying with a regulation. Competently done cost estimates may often have ranges of uncertainty comparable to those of benefit estimates. The tactical questions considered here in the context of benefit estimation are also likely to arise in the estimation of the costs of regulation. Some of the suggestions offered here may also be helpful to those responsible for cost analyses.

I have several times expressed the view that when faced with the assignment of providing an estimate of the benefits of some proposed environmental change, a competent benefit-cost analyst will know what models should be used, what data should be obtained, and what empirical techniques are appropriate.[1] There are two qualifications to this generally optimistic assessment. First, there are conceptual problems in estimating benefits of certain types, for example, the value of reduced risk of death or the valuation of ecological changes with no direct identifiable impact on human welfare.[2] Second, the required data to implement some components of the models may not be readily available or may require the resolution of scientific questions on which there is presently much uncertainty. One important example is the effect on human health and especially mortality of chronic exposures to suspected carcinogens and to some forms of air pollution. It is easy to recommend that more resources be devoted to basic research on these economic and scientific questions. But this will not be of much immediate help to the benefit-cost analyst charged with the responsibility of implementing Executive Order 12291.

The problem faced by EPA benefit-cost analysts is not so much one of sharpening and refining the existing tools of benefit estimation or developing new methods. Their problem is more immediate and serious. It is that they have neither the time, the staff resources, nor the research funds that would be required to execute the conceptually correct research plan *de novo* for each and every proposed environmental regulation. The problem for me to deal with here is that, given that EPA analysts with limited resources are not able to carry out a first-class research plan for every proposed regulation, what can be done to use existing studies and to carry out "shortcut" estimation techniques that will be true to the spirit of the executive order, will be defensible on scientific and analytical grounds, and yet will be within the existing resource constraints binding the agency?

The EPA draft "Guidelines for Performing Regulatory Impact Analyses" at one point show a recognition of this set of problems. But the "Guidelines" provide almost no specific advice on how to deal with the problem. In the introduction, the "Guidelines" state, "In some cases, off-the-shelf methodologies and studies can serve as the basis for benefit and cost analyses. In other cases, more analysis is necessary to fill conceptual and empirical gaps."[3] The first alternative economizes on the use of the agency's analytical resources. But the use of models and analyses developed for one purpose to estimate the benefits of another form of environmental change may result in biased and erroneous estimates. The second alternative may be technically feasible and within the state of the art, but it may take more time than is allowed by the schedule of regulatory decision making or it may require more resources than the agency has at hand.

In this chapter I take up two sets of questions. The first is under what conditions is it reasonable to use off-the-shelf studies and models developed for other purposes as a basis for deriving estimates of the benefits of specific regulations. The second question is under what circumstances will it be desirable on tactical grounds for the agency to devote significant analytical resources to undertaking new studies and developing new models for benefit estimation of particular regulations. I should note that there is too large a variety of regulatory proposals and of studies for me to provide a detailed set of answers to these questions which can be applied in all circumstances. In this chapter I have the more limited objective of discussing a couple of examples that may have wider applicability and attempting to develop a way of looking at these questions and identifying some general considerations that should be taken into account by EPA analysts as they make their tactical decisions in implementing Executive Order 12291.

USING MODELS FOR BENEFIT ESTIMATION

A number of benefit estimation models have been developed for various air and water pollutants in the United States. Some have focused on the estimation of benefits to particular regions; others have been national in scope.[4] In this section I take up the question of using such off-the-shelf benefit models for estimating the benefits of additional controls of particular substances at the national or regional level or both. If existing benefit estimation models could be taken off the shelf and manipulated to obtain estimates of new proposed regulations, compliance with Executive Order 12291 would be relatively easy. The suitability of an existing model depends on the extent to which the geographic scope, substances considered, and range of change in pollution analyzed in the existing model conform to the geographic scope, substances, and range of control in the regulation under consideration. And of course, the existing model must be based upon adequate data, sound economic method, and correct empirical technique.

Assuming that the existing model was valid for its original purpose, what conditions must be satisfied in order to use such a model to estimate the benefits of other regulations? The answer to this question depends in part on how the model is to be used. If a benefit model has been properly specified and its parameters have been estimated, the model can be repeatedly solved for different configurations of its independent variables to provide estimates of the benefits of alternative levels and patterns of control of the pollutants covered in the model. Of course, one must be cautious in extrapolating beyond the range of the data used to estimate the model.

A more interesting question for analysts faced with obtaining usable benefit estimates with a minimum of effort is whether, and if so under what circumstances, a benefit estimation model developed for one purpose can be used to generate benefit estimates for a different problem in a different setting. For example, can a national benefits model be used to estimate the benefits of controlling a pollutant in a single region? Or can a regional benefits model be used to estimate the national benefits of controlling that substance?

In order to provide a basis for considering these questions in more detail, I will first lay out the structure of a conceptually correct model for benefit estimation and discuss some of its implications. I will then discuss three ways in which such a model might be taken off the shelf to be used for generating benefit estimates in a different setting: (1) using a national aggregate model to estimate the benefits of controlling pollution in a particular region or industry; (2) using a regional or industry model to estimate the national or aggregate benefits of pollution control; and (3) using a model developed for one region to estimate the benefits of pollution control for a different region.

The first step is to define the scope of the model. Does it apply to the nation as a whole or to a specific regional entity, for example, a Standard Metropolitan Statistical Area (SMSA), a river basin, or an air shed? The scope of the model should be broad enough to capture all of the important physical, environmental, and economic relationships affected by the regulation being analyzed. Assume that there is only one polluting substance discharged into the environment. Let D represent the quantity of this substance which is discharged per year. Suppose that environmental quality can be measured by a single parameter, Q. Let X represent the level of an activity that is adversely affected by pollution. Finally, let W represent the level of economic welfare associated with X, measured in money. It might be helpful to think of the following example: D is biochemical oxygen demand (BOD); Q is dissolved oxygen (DO); X is recreation days per year. The model can be expressed as:

(1) $Q = Q(D)$, $\quad (\dfrac{dQ}{dD} < 0)$

(2) $X = X(Q)$, $\quad (\dfrac{dX}{dQ} > 0)$

(3) $W = W(X)$, $\quad (\dfrac{dW}{dX} > 0)$

By substitution we have:

(4) $W = f(D)$, $\quad (\dfrac{dW}{dD} < 0)$

The benefit of a pollution control regulation that reduces D from D_1 to D_2 ($= \Delta D$) is

(5) $B = \Delta W = f(D_2) - f(D_1)$

$\qquad\qquad = B(\Delta D)$

where B is an aggregate of the compensating or equivalent variations of all people affected by the change in D. Estimating the benefit of a proposed regulation entails first predicting the responses of affected discharges, that is, ΔD, and then tracing the effects of ΔD through the links described by equations (1)–(3) to calculate the resulting welfare change in monetary terms.

Of course, this simple representation of the problem obscures a number of details and complications that have to be reckoned with. First, most environmental problems have an important spatial component. Discharges may come from several (or many) sources at different locations; and Q may vary across space according to the spatial pattern of discharges, dispersion, and so forth. These spatial characteristics must be reflected in the benefits model. Similarly, there may be an important temporal dimension to discharges and measures of environmental quality. Some activities may be sensitive primarily to changes in long-term averages of pollution levels whereas others are affected primarily by peaks of pollution causing acute effects.

With many people within the affected area (region or nation), it may be necessary to take account of differences in preferences and incomes that might affect the values people place on environmental changes. And people at different locations may experience different levels of environmental quality. Ideally, a benefit estimate would treat each individual separately and sum the estimated welfare changes across all affected parties. But some degree of aggregation into groups based on income, location, and other factors is frequently a practical necessity.

Each individual may engage in several activities, so that changes in Q affect him or her through several pathways. Each of the major pathways, for example, recreation or health, must be analyzed separately.

Changes in Q can affect people directly as consumers by altering their activities; or the effects can be indirect as when pollution raises producers' costs and causes changes in prices and quantities in output and factor markets. And finally, both producers and individuals can engage in averting behavior or mitigating activities. For example, people can move away from polluted neighborhoods or filter their drinking water. And farmers can shift away from pollution-sensitive crops and cultivars. Measures of benefits must reflect the effect of the major averting and mitigating activities available to people.

Suppose that a model has been built to calculate the benefits of a nationwide pollution-control regulation and that its parameters have been estimated. Further suppose that the model has the basic structure described here and has adequately dealt with the complications mentioned above. Under what conditions and in what ways, if any, can this model be used to estimate the benefits of a regulation affecting only one sector or one region of the economy? If the objective is to estimate the benefits of controlling pollution in one region, and if the boundaries of the region of concern are consistent with the regional disaggregations underlying the national model, then regional benefits can be calculated by recomputing the national model on the basis of changes in discharges and environmental quality only in the region of concern. For example, if an estimate of the national health benefits of air pollution control had been calculated from a macro-epidemiological analysis using SMSAs as the unit of observation, this model could be used to calculate the health benefits for any SMSA on the basis of the air quality, population, socioeconomic characteristics, and so forth, for that SMSA. This is true because the national benefit, if calculated explicitly on the basis of the model, is simply the sum of the benefits calculated for each of the regional components of the model. Several national benefit models with the potential for being used in this manner have been devised.[5]

Can a national model of benefits be used to estimate the benefits of a regulation imposed on a specific industry? As above, the answer is "yes" provided that it is possible to calculate the reduction in discharges from this industry for each regional unit. For example, Lewis J. Perl and Frederick C. Dunbar used a national model of the benefits of controlling SO_2 emissions to estimate the benefits of alternative control requirements on the electric utility industry. And EPA used the national fishing participation model devised by William J. Vaughan and Clifford S. Russell to estimate the recreation fishing benefits of best available treatment effluent limitations on steel industry facilities on three rivers in eastern Ohio and western Pennsylvania.[6]

Are there any reasonable shortcuts to this procedure of calculating new solutions to these models for alternative sets of conditions? Specifically, is it possible to use some proportionality factor such as benefits per unit of discharge controlled to calculate the benefits of region- or industry-specific regulations? Suppose that we have an estimate of the national benefits of a policy that results in an aggregate decrease of discharges of $\Delta\overline{D}$. Let $\overline{B}$ be our estimate of national benefits. We now wish to evaluate an additional regulation on industry i that will result in a further decrease in discharges equal to ΔD_i. Under what conditions can the benefits of this regulation, B_i, be computed as in equation (6)?[7]

$$(6) \quad B_i = \frac{\overline{B}}{\Delta\overline{D}} \cdot \Delta D_i$$

$$= d_i \cdot \overline{B}$$

where

$$d_i = \frac{\Delta D_i}{\Delta\overline{D}}$$

This requires that the term

$$\frac{dB}{dD}$$

derived from equation (4) be a constant, which in turn requires that the underlying model of (1)–(3) be linear; the coefficients relating activities to quality and benefits to activities be the same across regions; and either there be only one activity affected by pollution or all activities be carried out in the same proportions in all regions. Given these conditions, a one-hundred-ton reduction in discharges at a given location has the same effect on the

national average ambient environmental quality as a one-hundred-ton reduction spread equally over all sources in the nation. And similarly all
spatial distributions of changes in Q which result in the same change in the
average Q will yield the same aggregate change in uses of the environment
and in benefits. But if any of these conditions is not met, the term

$$\frac{dB}{dD}$$

will depend on the particular pattern of the changes in D, Q, and X produced by each regulation. And the full model must be solved for each
alternative regulation.

The linearity assumption may be a reasonable first approximation for
some forms of air pollution. Rollback models have frequently been used to
estimate changes in ambient air quality as a proportion of changes in total
emissions. And at least for some effects of air pollution (for example,
human health), there is some empirical evidence for linear dose-effect
functions. It is my impression that the assumption of linearity in a national
water pollution benefits model is much less plausible. The relationships
between primary pollutants such as organic matter (BOD) and primary
indicators of water quality such as dissolved oxygen involve substantial
nonlinearities. Also, the effects of changes in water quality on activities
such as water-based recreation may involve threshold effects and other
forms of nonlinearities. In any event, if national models of air and water
pollution control benefits are to be used in the simple fashion described
here, then some consideration of the question of nonlinearities and the way
in which they might bias simple calculations would have to be investigated.

Consider the case when one substance affects several activities, for
example, as particulate matter may affect human health, household cleaning, and materials. The linearity of the model combined with identical
spatial distributions of all of the affected activities is sufficient to permit the
simple extrapolation of benefits as a proportion of changes in discharges.
But if, for example, a pollutant affects both agricultural crop yields and the
health of urban populations, the benefits of further control of this pollutant
will depend upon whether additional controls affect primarily urban or rural
air quality. Then simple extrapolations will not be correct unless the coefficients relating benefits to ambient quality are the same for all affected
activities.

The second question to be considered is under what conditions can a
benefits model estimated for a particular region be used to calculate the
national benefits of a pollution-control policy. The answer involves issues
that are analogous to those just discussed. The effects of a pollutant on

activities and welfare depend on a number of factors, which may vary both within and across regions. If the empirical model of individual behavior on which the regional estimate is based is sufficiently detailed to capture the effects of within-region variation in these factors, if the range of variation is comparable to the range in other regions, and if it is reasonable to assume that the coefficients are the same across regions, then the model can be applied to other regions and the results summed to obtain a national benefits estimate. But simple extrapolations to national benefits from known B_i and ΔD_i such as

$$\overline{B} = \frac{B_i}{\Delta D_i} \cdot \Delta \overline{D}$$

or

$$\overline{B} = \frac{1}{d_i} \cdot B_i$$

will be satisfactory only if the conditions outlined in the preceding section are satisfied.[8]

Using a benefits model estimated for one region to calculate benefits for another region involves essentially the same considerations as outlined above. The key question is the extent to which differences in environmental characteristics and the populations' socioeconomic characteristics in the two regions can be taken account of. For example, EPA used a willingness-to-pay survey of households in the Charles River basin near Boston as the basis for estimating the benefits of BAT controls on the steel industry in three river basins in eastern Ohio and western Pennsylvania.[9] Gramlich had estimated regression equations to explain households' willingness to pay as a function of income, age, education, and so forth. These equations were used by EPA to predict households' willingness to pay in the three river basins under study on the assumption that the only relevant differences between the two regions were in the variables used in the regression equation. But to the extent that the rivers in the two regions represent different recreational resources, and to the extent that there are differences in the availability of substitute sites in the two regions, then EPA's extrapolation is subject to error.

THE VALUE OF ADDITIONAL RESEARCH

A major question faced by benefit-cost analysts in the real world is when to commit additional scarce analytical resources to the task of producing more accurate or scientifically defensible estimates of the benefits or costs of a proposed regulation. Conceptually, the answer to the question is to commit the additional resources if the value of the information to be produced, in an expected value sense, is greater than the cost of producing the information. In this section I examine this question in the context of a simple model of decision making under uncertainty, and I consider some implications of this model for tactical decison making about research to support benefit-cost analysis.[10]

Suppose that a regulation to control the discharge of a pollutant into a river basin has been proposed. To focus attention on the problem at hand, assume that the costs of meeting the regulation are known. At any point in time it must be true that there is some information on the likely value of the benefits of the regulation. Even without further analysis, it should be possible to say that the probability is approximately equal to one that the benefits are no less than zero and no more than the total personal income of the region. With some reasonable expenditure of effort, for example by employing very crude and simple models and assumptions, it should be possible to develop a range of possible values of benefits and to attach a probability to each alternative value within the range. Suppose that this has been done and that the decision on the regulation must be made now, without obtaining additional information through research. The decision maker who is an expected value maximizer would use the probabilities to calculate the expected value of benefits and compare this with the known costs, adopting the regulation if expected net benefits were greater than zero.[11]

Now suppose instead that a research project has been identified which, if undertaken, would resolve the uncertainty about benefits. Should the research project be undertaken? This is a meaningful question because, at least in the context of regulatory decision making, not all research is worth doing. The answer to the question is "yes" only if the value of the information produced by the research exceeds the cost of the research project. The value of the research information arises from the fact that it allows the decision maker to postpone a commitment to incur the cost of the regulation until after it is known whether the benefits will exceed the cost. The value of the information is the difference between the expected net benefits with the research and without it.

Consider the following simple example. The cost of the proposed regulation is $10 million per year. Suppose that the application of three different models and sets of assumptions suggests that benefits could be as high as $20 million per year, $11 million per year, or as low as $2 million per year with probabilities of .3, .4, and .3 attached to the alternative possible outcomes. The risk-neutral decision maker who must make a choice on the basis of the information at hand will calculate the expected net benefits of regulation as follows:

$$E[NB]_{NS} = \sum_{i=1}^{3} P_i(B_i - C_i)$$

$$= .3(\$20-\$10) + .4(\$11-\$10) + .3(\$2-\$10)$$
$$= \$1 \text{ million}$$

where the subscript NS stands for "no study." Because expected net benefits are positive, the regulation should be approved. This is shown as the upper branch labeled "No Study" in the decision tree of Figure 6.1.

Let us assume that if the research project is undertaken, it will completely eliminate the uncertainty about the magnitude of benefits. That is, it will reveal which of the three possible values of benefits is the true value. A more realistic example in which the research only reduces but does not eliminate uncertainty will be considered below.

The lower branch of the decision tree in Figure 6.1 shows the possible outcomes. Because before the study a probability of .3 was assigned to the case in which benefits were $20 million, we must assign a probability of .3 to the outcome that research will show the true value of benefits to be $20 million. The outcomes and probabilities must be the same in both branches of the decision tree.

If the research reveals that benefits are only $2 million, the regulation would not be adopted. But there is a .7 probability that the research will reveal net benefits in excess of costs and that the regulation will be adopted. Ignoring for the moment the cost of the research itself, the expected value of net benefits when the research is undertaken and the decision is postponed until the information is available can be calculated as follows:

$$E[NB]_S = \sum_{i=1}^{3} P_i(B_i - C_i)$$

$$= .3(\$20-\$10) + .4(\$11-\$10) + .3(0-0)$$
$$= \$3.4 \text{ million}$$

where the subscript S stands for "study."

The value of the information produced by the research study, V, is the increase in the expected value of benefits:

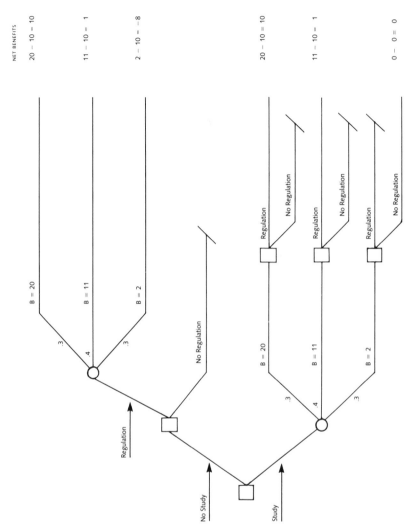

NET BENEFITS

$20 - 10 = 10$

$11 - 10 = 1$

$2 - 10 = -8$

$20 - 10 = 10$

$11 - 10 = 1$

$0 - 0 = 0$

Figure 6.1. Decision tree for research outcomes with benefit uncertainty

$$V = E[NB]_S - E[NB]_{NS}$$
$$= \$3.4 \text{ million} - \$1 \text{ million}$$
$$= \$2.4 \text{ million}$$

Undertaking the research increases the expected value of net benefits by $2.4 million. As long as the research costs less than $2.4 million, it is worthwhile to undertake it.

The value of this simple model of the decision-making problem is the insight it gives concerning what aspects of the problem are most important and what facets of the problem one should look at when faced with more complex decisions. The most important implications of this view of the decision process are as follows.

1. No research should be undertaken unless it has the potential for changing the decision. The value of the information produced by the research is zero if what will be learned would not lead to a different decision concerning the regulation. For example, if all of the possible benefit outcomes are greater than the cost of the regulation, the expected value of net benefits is positive and the regulation should be undertaken. But more important, even if the lowest possible benefit turned out to be true value, the regulation still would have been worthwhile. Alternatively, if all of the possible benefit outcomes are less than the cost of the regulation, there is no possibility that undertaking the research would lead one to change the initial decision not to impose the regulation.[12]

2. If before the research is undertaken the expected value of benefits is greater than the cost of the regulation, the value of information depends only on the probabilities attached to those outcomes where benefits are less than costs and the magnitude of the negative net benefits of those outcomes. In other words, to determine the value of information, one must focus only on those possible outcomes that would cause one to regret the decision that would be made in the absence of the research. The value of information is greater the larger are the negative benefits associated with adverse outcomes and the higher are the probabilities of their occurrence.[13]

3. The value of information may be positive even if the expected net benfits of the regulation are negative. Suppose that the possible outcomes for benefits are the same as the preceding numerical example and Figure 6.1. But assume that costs are known with certainty to be $12 million. Then in the absence of research the expected net benefits are $-\$1$ million $[.3(20-12) + .4(11-12) + .3(2-12)]$. Because the regulation would not be approved, $E[NB]_{NS} = 0$. If the research were undertaken, there is a .3 probability that benefits will be found to be greater than costs and that the

regulation will be approved; the probability is .7 that benefits will be found to be less than costs leading to no regulation. Thus

$$V = \quad .3(\$20-\$12) + .4(0-0) + .3(0-0) - 0$$
$$= \quad \$2.4$$

As before, only research outcomes that would alter the decision enter into the calculation of the value of information. And the value of carrying out the research is higher the higher are the probabilities attached to those outcomes and the larger are those outcomes.

4. I have said that the analyst should undertake studies whenever the value of the information exceeds the cost of the study. For the agency with no effective budget constraint, the cost of a study is its monetary or budgetary cost. The decision maker should buy all studies that show a value of information greater than their budgetary cost. But if the agency has a binding research budget constraint, the value of information from any one study must be compared with the shadow price or opportunity cost of carrying out that study. The opportunity cost is the value of information foregone by diverting resources from the next most valuable study. In an agency faced with a requirement to analyze many proposed regulations with a severely constrained analytical budget, the shadow price of information could be several times higher than the budget cost. This makes it all the more important to determine the value of information to be gained from alternative studies under consideration.

5. It is a relatively straightforward matter to expand the model outlined here to consider a larger number of alternative research strategies with different costs and potentially different values of information. The model can also be expanded to take cost uncertainty explicitly into account. Then the model can be used to estimate the values of research strategies aimed only at better estimates of benefits, at better estimates of costs, or at better estimates of both benefits and costs.

6. It is possible to make the model more realistic by recognizing that a research project may only reduce the magnitude of uncertainty about benefits rather than eliminate it or that there may be uncertainty about the success of a research project. To examine the latter possibility, suppose that there is only a .1 probability that the proposed research will provide information that will distinguish between the three possible benefit outcomes of the numerical example of Figure 6.1. The expected net benefits of the regulation with no study are the same as before ($1 million). But the lower branch of the decision tree must be modified. See Figure 6.2. There is a .9

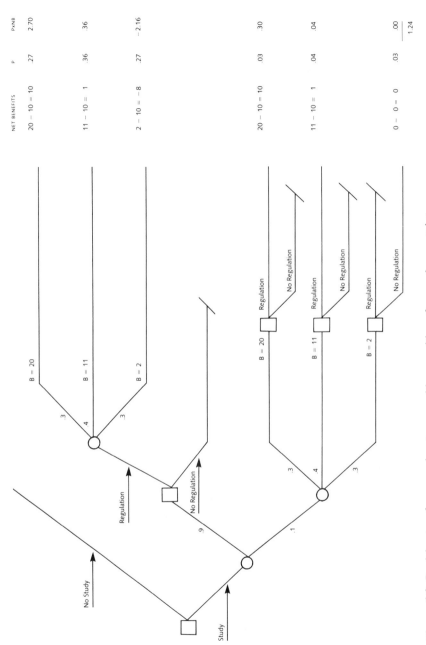

NET BENEFITS	P	P×NB
20 − 10 = 10	.27	2.70
11 − 10 = 1	.36	.36
2 − 10 = −8	.27	−2.16
20 − 10 = 10	.03	.30
11 − 10 = 1	.04	.04
0 − 0 = 0	.03	.00
		1.24

Figure 6.2. Decision tree for research outcomes with recognition of research uncertainty

probability that the experiment will be unsuccessful and that nothing new will be learned. Then the decision will have to be made on the basis of expected net benefits as before. But there is a .1 probability that a successful experiment will eliminate the uncertainty. The probability that benefits will be shown to outweigh costs is .07(.1 × .7). Figure 6.2 shows all of the possible outcomes and payoffs. The expected net benefits with the study, $E[NB]_S$, are $1.24 million and the value of information is $.24 million, or 10 percent of the value of information from an experiment certain to be successful.

7. This model of the value of information captures only the value of information in improving the decision being analyzed. A research study might produce a benefit model that can later be used at relatively low incremental cost to generate benefit estimates for other decision problems. Thus some consideration should be given to developing benefit models that can be applied to a range of regulatory decision-making problems. For example, a national recreation participation model that predicts changes in recreation activities as a function of changes in water quality levels in each river basin or watershed can be used to estimate recreation benefits for a wide range of water pollution control regulations. The value of such a model is the sum of the values of its information for each of the regulatory decisions to which it contributes.

This discussion has focused on the benefits of the value of information model; and the simple numerical example may have created the impression that the model will be easy to implement (that is, that it has low costs). But, of course, there may be reasons why the model might be difficult to implement in practice and why it might be useful to compare the benefits of using the model with its costs. But in defense of the model, it should be pointed out that any effort to think systematically about the allocation of scarce research resources or to establish research priorities must entail an application of the principles underlying the model if not the formal apparatus of the model itself. Less formal analysis may not yield precise estimates of the value of information for comparison with costs; but it may still be very helpful in ordering research alternatives so that scarce resources can be allocated to activities that are likely to have the highest payoff.

CONCLUSIONS

The tactics for benefit estimation under Executive Order 12291 involve two primary considerations. The first is a search for a simplified approach to estimating the benefits of specific regulations through the extension of or extrapolation from existing models of benefits. There are many circumstances in which properly specified benefit models can be used to calculate benefits under different conditions and for different regional configurations. The conditions under which simple proportionate extrapolations from existing national and regional benefit models can be made are fairly restrictive. But these conditions may be met, at least as a first approximation, in some cases.

The second consideration is how to deploy the agency's scarce analytical resources among alternative benefit research projects so as to maximize the net value of the information obtained (value minus its opportunity cost). I have argued that the formal model of the value of information based on decision analysis provides a useful perspective for thinking about this problem and a framework for organizing available information. I recognize that it may not be either feasible or desirable to write out the model in formal terms on the public record when making choices. This is especially true inasmuch as the model with its subjective probabilities and aura of "guesstimation" may be misunderstood if not ridiculed by those with no training in statistical decision theory. But even if the model is not used in any formal way, it provides a way of organizing the analysis and leads to insights into the problem that I think will be very important to decision makers.

APPENDIX: EXTRAPOLATING THE BENEFITS OF
CONTROLLING STEEL INDUSTRY EFFLUENTS: A REVIEW
AND CRITIQUE

In early 1981, EPA proposed a set of best available technology effluent guidelines for the steel industry. The American Iron and Steel Institute (AISI) suggested that an estimate of the national benefits of achieving the 1985 water pollution control objectives that I had prepared for the Council on Environmental Quality in 1979 be the basis for estimating the benefits of the regulation. I had estimated the national benefits to be $12.3 billion per year in 1978 dollars.[14] AISI used the following calculations to estimate the benefits of the proposed BAT regulations:

Pollution loading:	Steel industry discharges by weight as a percentage of total U.S. discharges of all substances (tons per year) in 1968	=	6.5%
Reduction in discharges because of BAT:	Reduction in steel industry discharges as a percentage of total steel industry discharges	=	2%
Benefits of proposed regulation:	.065 × .02 × $12.3 billion	=	$16 million per year[15]

Because this estimate of benefits was an order of magnitude smaller than the EPA estimates of annual costs available at that time, the industry understandably argued that the proposed regulations were too stringent on economic grounds.

Was this approach to estimating the benefits of the BAT regulation a proper use of the underlying national benefit model? I think that the answer is "no" for three reasons: a flaw in the logic of their extrapolation, the likely nonlinearity of the national benefits model, and the fact that the national benefits model covered a different range of substances and effects than the proposed BAT regulation on the steel industry.

In the notation of the text, the AISI extrapolation was

$$B_S = \frac{D_S}{\overline{D}} \cdot \frac{\Delta D_S}{D_S} \cdot \overline{B}$$

$$= \frac{\Delta D_S}{\overline{D}} \; \overline{B}$$

where the subscript S refers to the steel industry and $\overline{D}$ is total national discharges before the control policy is implemented. This corresponds to the extrapolation proposed in the text at equation (6) only if the national policy results in the total elimination of discharges, that is, only if $\overline{D} = \Delta \overline{D}$. If an estimate of $\Delta \overline{D}$ were to be substituted in the above calculation, the extrapolated benefit estimate would be larger.

As for the linearity assumption, the major component of the national benefit estimate was improved water-based recreation. Most of the studies on which the national estimate was based assumed some threshold of water quality (usually dissolved oxygen) below which a water body would not be used for recreation. The nonlinearity of the relationship between discharges and dissolved oxygen for a river combined with the presumed threshold in the relationship between water quality and recreation activity mean that the spatial pattern of the reduction in discharges of the steel industry would be a very important factor in estimating the recreation benefits of the BAT regulation.

Finally, because of differences in the substances controlled one must question whether the national benefits model has any relevance to the estimation of the benefits of BAT limits on steel effluents. According to the *Federal Register* notice of 7 January 1981 (pp. 1858–1907), the BPT standards for the iron and steel industry controlled primarily total suspended solids (TSS), pH, and oil and grease. The BAT standards would control discharges of ammonia-N, fluoride, phenols, cyanide, benzene, napthalene, benzo-(a) pyrene, trichlorethane, nitro-phenol, anthracine, tetrachlorethylene, cadmium, chromium, copper, lead, nickel, and zinc. Most of the activities represented in the national benefit estimate were modeled as functions of either dissolved oxygen levels (a function primarily of BOD discharges) or bacterial contamination. The AISI extrapolation is based on the implicit assumption that the damages per pound of discharge are the same for BOD, TSS, heavy metals, and organic compounds. Also about 30 percent of the total national benefit represents benefits to marine sports and commercial fishing. Yet the proposed regulation would affect primarily discharges into inland freshwater streams. Thus whatever the possible virtues and other flaws of the implicit model underlying my estimate of national water pollution control benefits, it does not seem reasonable to use it in the simple way proposed by AISI for extrapolating the benefits of BAT regulations on the steel industry.

Subsequent to the AISI analysis, EPA also prepared a benefit estimate for its Regulatory Impact Analysis by using an extrapolation from its revision of my national benefits model.[16] The EPA's extrapolation differed from that of AISI in three important respects. First, it used estimates of 1972 discharges for the nation and for the steel industry for the baseline. Because 1972 was the baseline for the national benefit estimate, that extrapolation conforms to equation (6). Second, EPA made an effort to distinguish between the effects of controlling toxic organics and metals and controlling conventional pollutants. And third, it included in the national model an estimate of the human health benefits of controlling toxic discharges. Thus the extrapolation is not vulnerable to the first and third criticisms made of the AISI extrapolation above. EPA's extrapolation is based on the assumption of linearity, however, a point the agency acknowledges in discussing the limitations of the estimate.[17]

NOTES

1. For a description and evaluation of most of the available techniques and models for estimating the benefits of environmental improvement, see Freeman, *The Benefits of Environmental Improvement*. For a critical review and evaluation of recent empirical estimates of the benefits of air and water pollution control, see Freeman, *Air and Water Pollution Control*.

2. For discussion of these points, see Freeman, "The Health Implications of Residuals Discharges," pp. 156–62, and Freeman, *Benefits of Environmental Improvement*, p. 257.

3. See U.S. Environmental Protection Agency, "Guidelines for Performing Regulatory Impact Analyses," p. 1.

4. See Freeman, *Air and Water Pollution Control*. In this book, I also developed synthesis or best-judgment estimates of the aggregate national benefits of controlling air and water pollution.

5. Lave and Seskin, *Air Pollution and Human Health*; Mendelsohn and Orcutt, "An Empirical Analysis of Air Pollution Dose-Response Curves"; Ryan et al., "An Estimate of the Nonhealth Benefits of Meeting the Secondary National Ambient Air Quality Standards"; Bell and Canterbery, *An Assessment of the Economic Benefits Which Will Accrue to Commercial and Recreational Fisheries from Incremental Improvements in the Water Quality of Coastal Waters*; and Vaughan and Russell, *Freshwater Recreational Fishing*. Actually Lave and Seskin's estimate of national health benefits was not based on a formal calculation from their model. But their model could easily be used to calculate national benefits as an aggregate of benefits across SMSA's. See National Economic Research Associates, Inc., *Cost-Effectiveness and Cost-Benefit Analysis of Air Quality Regulation*, for an example of such a calculation.

6. Perl and Dunbar, "Cost Effectiveness and Cost-Benefit Analysis of Air Quality Regulation"; Vaughan and Russell, *Freshwater Recreational Fishing*; U.S. Environmental Protection Agency, "Guidelines for Performing Regulatory Impact Analyses," December 1983.

7. For a discussion of two efforts to use this approach to estimate the benefits of

proposed EPA regulations on effluents from the steel industry, see the appendix to this chapter.

8. For examples of national benefit estimates calculated from regional-based models, see Watson and Jaksch, "Air Pollution"; Feenberg and Mills, *Measuring the Benefits of Water Pollution Abatement*, chap. 9; National Academy of Sciences, *Air Quality and Automobile Emissions Control*, chap. 4; Polinsky and Rubinfeld, "Property Values and Benefits of Environmental Improvement"; and Heintz, Hershaft, and Horak, "National Damages of Air and Water Pollution." These studies are discussed in Freeman, *Air and Water Pollution Control*.

9. Gramlich, "Demand for Clean Water"; U.S. Environmental Protection Agency, *An Economic Assessment of the Benefits of the Final Effluent Limitations Guidelines for Iron and Steel Manufacturing*.

10. For a simple introduction to the value of information model, see Stokey and Zeckhauser, *A Primer for Policy Analysis*, pp. 201–54. For a more rigorous development, see Raiffa, *Decision Analysis*.

11. A more complete analysis would involve a comparison of alternative levels of the regulation in an effort to find the level that maximized expected net benefits, that is, at which expected marginal benefits equaled expected marginal costs.

12. This can be shown algebraically as follows. In the case where the study is undertaken, the regulation is imposed only if $B_i > C_i$; otherwise $NB_i = 0$. Consider the case where $B_i > C_i$ for all i. Then:

$$V = E[NB]_S - E[NB]_{NS}$$
$$= \sum_i P_i (B_i - C_i) - \sum P_i(B_i - C_i)$$
$$= 0$$

Alternatively, if $B_i > C_i$ for all i, even without the study the regulation would not be undertaken. $E[NB]_{NS} = 0$, and since $NB_i = 0$ for all i, $V = 0$.

13. This can be illustrated with the numerical example above.

$$V = E[NB]_S - E[NB]_{NS}$$
$$.3(20-10) + .4(11-10) + .3(0-0)$$
$$- .3(20-10) - .4(11-10) - .3(2-10)$$
$$= -.3(2-10)$$
$$= 2.4$$

The first five elements of V sum to zero, and V is determined only by the last term.

14. The 1979 work is Freeman, *Benefits of Environmental Improvement*. This estimate is higher than the one given in Freeman, *Air and Water Pollution Control*. The downward revision in my estimate reflects the availability of additional studies, which influenced my synthesis or best-judgement estimates.

15. Rice and Stuart, "Cost Benefit Analysis of the Proposed BPT/BAT for the Steel Industry."

16. U.S. Environmental Protection Agency, *Economic Assessment*.

17. See, for example, U.S. Environmental Protection Agency, *Economic Assessment*. 1:20 and 2:22–23, 40–41.

7

CARLISLE FORD RUNGE*

ECONOMIC CRITERIA AND "NET SOCIAL RISK" IN THE ANALYSIS OF ENVIRONMENTAL REGULATION

EXECUTIVE Order 12291 results from regulatory reforms in which environmental regulations are to be subjected to benefit-cost analysis. Its impact is felt in increased demand for benefits estimates for regulatory alternatives. These estimates can be used to evaluate as well as to gain control over the regulatory process.[1] The order calls on federal agencies to prepare regulatory analyses of the impact of regulations in terms of net social benefits. As part of the development of these benefits estimates, it also requires an assessment of health risks associated with these alternatives and the valuation of risk reductions associated with these regulations.[2] A significant and unresolved barrier to its implementation is the absence of a clear analytical relationship between net benefits and net risks of regulation. Current approaches to the problem are often at odds, creating considerable confusion. One approach is to treat risks as an issue entirely separate from benefits, explicitly disavowing the possibility of comparison. For example, the Clean Air Act as amended in 1977 precludes benefit-cost analysis for the purpose of setting primary standards for criteria pollutants—these standards must be set to avoid risks to human health. Yet

*Assistant Professor, Department of Agricultural and Applied Economics, University of Minnesota. Thanks are due to Don Waldman, V. Kerry Smith, and Tom Feagans for suggestions and comments. This chapter was revised during a visiting fellowship in the Food and Agricultural Policy Program of Resources for the Future. This chapter is based, in part, on a paper by the author entitled "Risk Assessment and Environmental Benefits Analysis" in the *Natural Resources Journal*, vol. 13, July 1983. Thanks are due the editors for permission to use the material in this chapter.

in other cases, risks and benefits are treated as comparable. More than ten federal statutes require or propose the use of "risk-benefit analysis" as if an accepted basis for comparative analysis exists. Unfortunately, it does not.[3] This chapter proposes a framework for comparison based on a simple constrained maximization exercise in which uncertainty gives rise to risks that constrain benefits. The major regulations treated are air quality standards, although the analysis may be generalized to other areas of environmental regulation.

The first section focuses on the need for careful elaboration of the types of uncertainty involved in air quality regulation and the consequent risks posed to human life and health. Comparing (a) uncertainty in regulatory benefits analysis with (b) uncertainty in assessing health risks, it is argued that setting air quality standards involves both. Together, the interaction of Type (a) and Type (b) uncertainty defines net social risk, the subject of the second section. The properties of net social risk are explored, and it is shown that increased certainty respecting either (a) or (b) can substitute for stricter regulations in reducing this risk. Because the appropriate level of net social risk is a valuative question, this level is modeled in the third section as a constraint on net social benefits of regulation, analogous to questions of social welfare such as income distribution. Whether the risk constraint is binding is thus a welfare judgment over the trade-off between net benefits and net risks, captured by the shadow value of the constraint. Determining this value would allow regulatory dilemmas involving risk-benefit decisions to be resolved with more clarity.

The chapter concludes with some implications of this analysis for environmental policy. In particular, it can be shown that current approaches to regulatory reform could be more efficient, in the economic sense of the term, if efforts were made to reduce the uncertainty resulting from lax enforcement and lower levels of research associated with Reagan administration policy. This result holds whether or not regulations raise the targeted level of air quality. Less risk and more efficiency, in other words, can be seen as complementary rather than competing policy objectives.

REGULATORY AND SCIENTIFIC UNCERTAINTY

Regulatory Uncertainty

Benefits analysis for a good such as air quality involves estimation of willingness to pay by the area under a demand curve derived from direct or indirect expressions of individual preferences. Assuming such a demand curve can be estimated, alternative supply levels of clean air can then be described as a function of different regulatory policies. An increase in EPA's primary SO_2 standard, for example, can be expected to lead to a shift in the supply of air quality measured for this criteria pollutant. In principle, estimates of increases in consumer surplus are then calculable.[4]

Uncertainty arises in at least two areas in this calculation. First, on the demand side, exact estimates of willingness to pay are difficult to achieve. Especially in cases of public goods such as air quality, demand estimates are subject to bias, although recent research suggests the degree of bias is sensitive to the estimation method.[5] These errors can in principle be overcome with increasingly sophisticated methods.[6] A second source of uncertainty is on the supply side. Increases in the supply of clean air are inherently difficult to measure. The ability of federal regulation to achieve targeted state and regional air quality levels is also uncertain because of the lack of knowledge concerning the way a change in standards affects the complicated transmission mechanism linking emissions from point sources to air quality. Furthermore, simply choosing a particular primary air quality standard does not mean that the standard will be implemented and enforced through state implementation programs and secondary standards.[7]

Together, these problems can be described as *regulatory uncertainty*, reflecting the difficulty of estimating benefits resulting from air quality standards when regulated levels are not achieved with certainty. Even when they are, preferences for the result may be inaccurately represented by estimates of demand. Regulatory or Type (a) uncertainty is thus subdivided into uncertainties resulting from inaccurate estimates of demand for regulation (a-d) and uncertainties resulting from inaccurate estimates of supply (a-s). Because both result in difficulties in estimating consumer surplus, the net benefits of regulation are impossible to forecast with certainty. Both Type (a-d) and Type (a-s) uncertainty are related to health risk but are essentially distinct from the type of uncertainty most important in current risk-assessment studies.

Scientific Uncertainty

Under the Clean Air Act as amended in 1977, the federal government is responsible for primary air quality standards stringent enough to protect the public health with an "adequate margin of safety." Assessment of environmental risk inside the Environmental Protection Agency has focused on the health effects of primary National Ambient Air Quality Standards. When a particular pollutant "may reasonably be anticipated to endanger the public health or welfare," the administrator of EPA must publish an air quality criteria document, which forms the scientific basis for the standard.

NAAQSs define the degree of protection from adverse health effects to be achieved, stated as time-averaged pollutant concentrations and the expected number of cases in which these concentrations will be exceeded per unit of time. Health risks associated with a standard are risks of adverse health effects for a given population in a given time period during which the standard is being met. They are essentially estimates grounded in scientific data. The uncertainty associated with these estimates is meant to be distinct from the regulatory uncertainty raised by the possibility of noncompliance or nonenforcement.[8]

Primary standards accompanying the criteria document also are theoretically distinct from attainment costs. Neither cost estimates nor the uncertainty surrounding them is a germane consideration, entering only at the level of state implementation and the development of secondary standards to protect the public welfare.[9] This separation of costs from health risks has motivated a careful inquiry into the definition of such risks but has heightened the sense that some basis for comparing net benefits with health risks must be found.

Scientific analysis of health risks associated with NAAQSs is based on two presumptions. The first is that it is possible to identify some level of air quality that functions as a scientific threshold so that a margin of safety can be determined. Below this threshold there are unacceptable risks of health impairment to the population. Second, it is presumed possible to model the relationship between human health and air quality, so that this scientific threshold can be determined and primary standards set to avoid it. Both presumptions are questionable given existing knowledge. The level of air quality identified as a threshold is uncertain because of an absence of complete information concerning pollutants and their health effects. Even such scientific information on health effects as exists is subject to false associations between pollutants and morbidity and mortality.[10]

This scientific or Type (b) uncertainty is the main focus of environmental risk assessment. If hard scientific information cannot be found, recent EPA research has extended its efforts to reduce risk by encoding more subjective, "transcientific" judgments by experts on chemical and biological processes.[11]

In summary, regulatory or Type (a) uncertainty involves absence of information concerning the supply of and demand for regulated air quality. This lack occurs because of errors in estimating consumer preferences, ignorance about the transmission mechanism from point-source abatement to air quality, and uncertainties in implementing and enforcing primary standards. Reducing this uncertainty would improve policy makers' ability to estimate the impacts and thus the net benefits of regulation. Scientific or

Type (b) uncertainty results from lack of information on the relationship between human health and air quality and resulting errors in determining threshold levels at which unacceptable risks are posed to certain populations. Reducing this uncertainty would improve policy makers' ability to set primary standards in such a way that health thresholds for these groups are not crossed.

NET SOCIAL RISK

In the formulation of environmental policy, regulatory uncertainty and scientific uncertainty are not separable. Their interaction is one cause of current regulatory dilemmas. Regulatory uncertainty may be defined with respect to the choice of a primary standard and an accompanying set of secondary standards and state implementation plans. Restricting attention to a single criteria pollutant such as SO_2, the standard in period i is simply A_i. The regulatory dilemma is as follows. If the impact measured for SO_2 resulting from a NAAQS on sulfur oxides is Type (a) uncertain, there is some probability that realized air quality after implementation and enforcement will fall below the threshold level deemed an unacceptable risk to human health. But because this threshold is itself Type (b) uncertain, even a NAAQS with known impacts on air quality may have uncertain effects on health risks to well-defined populations. Therefore, the interaction of the two types of uncertainty becomes the relevant concern.

The interaction of regulatory and scientific uncertainty produces a composite measure of the impact of a particular standard on human health, which may be defined as net social risk. To see this more clearly, let

$Q(A_i)$ = a random variable defining the level of air quality associated with a particular standard, in this case for SO_2

T_i = a random variable defining the threshold level of air quality deemed an unacceptable risk to the health of a well-defined population.

These variables are assumed to be continuously distributed with nonzero mean and variance:

$$E(Q) = \mu_Q; V(Q) = \sigma_Q^2$$
$$E(T) = \mu_T; V(T) = \sigma_T^2$$

Note that σ_Q^2 and σ_T^2 represent regulatory and scientific uncertainty, respectively.

In more formal terms the regulatory dilemma described above is that for any well-defined group, the level of air quality Q associated with a standard A_i may be less than the threshold level deemed an unacceptable health risk T_i. The probability of this event is the net social risk associated with the standard. Net social risk R exists when there is some positive probability that the level of air quality associated with the implementation and enforcement of the NAAQS is less than that prescribed by the threshold.[12] The positive probability of this event is given as

$$R \quad = \quad Pr\,(Q < T) > 0$$
$$= \quad Pr[(Q - T) < 0] > 0$$

The difference $(Q - T)$ defines a third random variable $\Delta(A_i)$, the convolution of Q and $(-T)$, distributed with its own mean and variance. This variable captures the difference between the air quality achieved under the standard and the scientific threshold of acceptable risk. Clearly, net social risk R is a function of this difference. Specifically, it is the case that

$$E(\Delta) \quad = \quad \mu_\Delta = \mu_Q - \mu_T$$
$$V(\Delta) \quad = \quad \sigma_\Delta{}^2 = \sigma_Q{}^2 + \sigma_T{}^2 - 2\sigma_{QT}$$

The expectation μ_Δ is therefore a function of the expected impact of the standard on air quality (μ_Q) as well as the expected threshold of health risk (μ_T). Because uncertainty surrounds both of these air quality levels, the variance of Δ is a measure of uncertainty from both regulatory and scientific sources because $\sigma_\Delta{}^2$ is an additive function of $\sigma_Q{}^2$, $\sigma_T{}^2$, and σ_{QT}. Because regulatory standards must be set once a threshold is determined, lags associated with this process imply that the contemporaneous correlation between Q and T, σ_{QT}, is zero.[13]

This formulation allows a more precise description of the interaction of Type (a) regulatory and Type (b) scientific uncertainty resulting in net social risk. If R is judged to be unacceptably high, there are two major ways to reduce it. First, policy makers can attempt to raise the expected effect of the standard on air quality. Given a fixed level of uncertainty around μ_Q caused by problems of translating the standard into actual air quality, one obvious way to raise μ_Q is by upping the primary standard. This assumes that the expected threshold defining an acceptable health hazard to the population (μ_T) is fixed on the basis of scientific data. If this threshold is considered more subjectively, different interpretations may lead to different thresholds. If we assume that μ_T is fixed, however, then setting μ_Q low raises the net social risk that a threshold of unacceptable health risk will be crossed. Setting it higher lowers net social risk but is likely to involve greater regulatory costs. This trade-off will become more explicit in a constrained maximization framework below.

Turning to the variance term σ_Δ^2, it is clearly possible to reduce the uncertainty that the standard is too low by reductions in either σ_Q^2 or σ_T^2 or both. Regulatory uncertainty can presumably be reduced by increased information on the linkages between primary standards and air quality. In addition to better measurement, information on the transmissions of SO_2 from point sources to general air quality will reduce σ_Q^2, together with assurance that the standard will be implemented and enforced. Scientific uncertainty, the focus of EPA's risk-assessment efforts, can be reduced by better information on links from SO_2 to morbidity and mortality. This will allow more well-defined thresholds for particular criteria pollutants. [14]

In summary, net social risk may be considered the probability that standards are too low to avoid a threshold of hazard. This probability will be greater the fewer cases are accepted of adverse health affects per unit of time and the lower primary standards are set in relation to this threshold. The more uncertainty that surrounds both standard and threshold, the more uncertainty exists over whether the standard is sufficient to avoid such hazards.

NET SOCIAL RISK AS A CONSTRAINT ON REGULATORY BENEFITS

Choosing an acceptable level of net social risk is fundamentally an ethical question because standards and thresholds involve normative judgments. "Acceptable" health hazards defining a threshold may result in damage or even death if the standard chosen is low. Willingness to accept these hazards must result from an explicit or implicit trade-off between net social benefits and human life and health. The assessment of risk is thus linked to the value attached to morbidity and mortality. [15] If net benefits are measured as efficiency gains, the normative character of net social risk suggests that it is part of a social welfare function constraining efficient economic choices.

Treating net social risk in this way acknowledges its relationship to other issues of social welfare, including equity. Indeed, the distinction between equity and acceptable net social risk is blurred. To decide how high the probability should be that a standard is within range of an unacceptable threshold is to put a value on adverse effects to some individuals. A decision to accept high rather than low net social risks is therefore a decision to treat different persons differently. Such distinctions are at the heart of equity judgments, making them a question of social welfare. [16]

One response minimizing the importance of such questions is that if net social risks are borne collectively, they impose comparatively little private burden as the numbers in the population at risk increase.[17] But as Anthony Fisher noted, the nonexcludable public good characteristics of risky regulations may lead to the opposite conclusion: risks may rise with increasing numbers if each person bears the same amount.[18] Furthermore, if the population at risk varies over time, the assumption of collective risk-bearing does not hold either. For a variety of reasons, individuals will not be identically susceptible to health effects from air pollution or other sources over time, making collective risk-bearing implausible.

In addition to equity, net social risk is conceptually linked to what Talbot Page terms the fallacy of regulatory "false negatives."[19] Most risks subject to government regulation proceed on the assumption that pollutants must be proved hazardous to be considered risky. If evidence of hazard is scanty, regulatory decisions setting high standards are viewed as costly and wasteful. Such over-regulation is considered analogous to a "false positive" or Type I statistical error, in which the null hypothesis of no effect is true and is erroneously rejected by overzealous regulation. This view is advanced in a variety of recent EPA documents and policy pronouncements, an approach known as giving pollutants the benefit of the doubt.[20]

In contrast, false negatives occur when failure to find evidence of adverse health effects leads to the fallacious conclusion that no such effects can occur. Acceptance of the null hypothesis of no effect may prove false when more is known about the structure of the problem. In the case of air quality, minimizing the probability of false negatives requires reduced uncertainty regarding both regulatory impacts and scientific links from pollution to human health. As Page notes, "The less uncertain the structure (i.e., the more information available), the more likely it is that a negative finding will lead to a valid conclusion."[21] Reducing both regulatory and scientific uncertainty, and therefore net social risk, makes this structure more clear.

This is true because decreases in either Type (a) or Type (b) uncertainty provide information that increases our understanding of regulatory impacts in relation to health thresholds. To see this, let the null hypothesis be that the air quality associated with a NAAQS is sufficiently high that the threshold of hazard is not crossed and no adverse health effects result, so that $\Delta = (Q - T) > 0$. The alternative hypothesis is that it is crossed, leading to unacceptable hazards, so that $\Delta = (Q - T) < 0$. Hence:

$$H_o \quad : \quad (Q - T) \geqslant 0$$

$$H_a \quad : \quad (Q - T) < 0$$

The relationship between acceptance, rejection, and the truth value of these hypotheses is shown below, together with designation of false positive (Type I) and false negative (Type II) error.

	Decision	
State of the World	*Accept H_o*	*Reject H_o*
H_o true:	correct decision	incorrect decision
$(Q - T) \geqslant 0$		(false positive—
		Type I error)
H_a true:	incorrect decision	correct decision
$(Q - T) < 0$	(false negative—	
	Type II error)	

Because net social risk is given as $R = Pr[(Q - T) < 0] > 0$, a positive value of R can result only if there is some probability that the alternative hypothesis $H_a : (Q - T) < 0$ is true. A false negative finding is possible only if H_a is possible, in which case $R > 0$. Hence attention to false negatives requires a determination of the acceptable level of net social risk.

Modeled as a social welfare constraint on economically efficient outcomes, net social risk can be related directly to benefits analysis. Let an objective function for net social benefits of regulation be defined in terms of expected air quality levels associated with a particular set of national ambient standards. An objective function (G) expresses the expected sum of measurable economic costs $C(A_i)$ and benefits $B(A_i)$ from air quality regulation over a time horizon of n periods. These are maximized when the expected sum of net benefits associated with standards $(A_0, A_1, \ldots A_i \ldots A_n)$ in periods 0 to n is greatest. Benefits are thus expressed as a function of air quality standards in each period.

Air quality standards are the choice variable leading to expected levels of air quality. When net social benefits are discounted at some rate r_i in each period, the expression for the expected sum of net benefits from regulation is as follows:

$$E[G(A_i)] = E \left[\sum_{i=0}^{n} \frac{B(A_i) - C(A_i)}{\prod_{j=0}^{i} (1 + r_j)} \right]$$

These net benefits are subject to regulatory uncertainty associated with the impact of the standards as described above.

In particular, both Type (a) and Type (b) uncertainty may affect overall estimates of benefits resulting from regulation. Type (a) uncertainties contribute to but do not define net social risk. Even if these uncertainties could be eliminated, as long as Type (b) scientific uncertainty continued there would be some level of net risk. This makes clear that resolving problems of demand and supply uncertainty is not sufficient to solve the problem of net social risk, although it is clearly necessary and may result in substantial reductions.

Because choosing an acceptable level of net social risk involves questions of welfare, it is also questionable whether it is appropriate to collapse these issues to a risk-adjusted discount rate. As Wilson argues, methods that deduct a risk premium in the form of an adjusted rate are biased against long-lived investments. Environmental regulations are generally considered to survive changes in best practicable technical methods and the purchase of new plant and equipment, and so they must be considered a long-term public investment.[22]

Now, let a social welfare function denote an acceptable level of net social risk R^* in each period, such that the actual level $R(\overline{A})$ is less than or equal to R^*. The social welfare function implies the constraint $R(\overline{A}) \le R^*$ on the maximization of net benefits. The problem is to maximize the expected level of discounted net benefits subject to the constraint posed by acceptable net social risk.

$$\text{Max } E[G(A_i)] = E\left[\sum_{i=0}^{n} \frac{B(A_i) - C(A_i)}{\prod_{j=0}^{i} (1 + r_j)} \right]$$

$$\text{s.t.}$$
$$R^* - R(\overline{A}) \ge 0,$$
$$A_i \ge 0$$
$$\text{where } \overline{A} = (A_1, A_2, A_3, \ldots A_n)$$

The Lagrangean expression follows, where λ is the shadow value or Lagrangean multiplier associated with the constraint.

$$L = E\left[\sum_{i=0}^{n} \frac{B(A_i) - C(A_i)}{\prod_{j=0}^{i} (1 + r_j)} \right] + \lambda[R^* - R(\overline{A})]$$

Kuhn-Tucker conditions for a maximum are

(1) $\qquad \dfrac{\partial L}{\partial A_i} \le 0 \qquad\qquad A_i \dfrac{\partial L}{\partial A_i} = 0$

(2) $\dfrac{\partial L}{\partial \lambda} \geqslant 0$ $\lambda \dfrac{\partial L}{\partial \lambda} = 0$

                    $A_i \geqslant 0 \quad \lambda \geqslant 0$

These conditions can be useful in measuring the trade-offs between net economic efficiency benefits and net social risks. The first pair represents conditions for a maximum level of net benefits from regulated air quality. Where

$$\frac{\partial L}{\partial A_i} = 0,$$

if it is the case that $A_i > 0$, an interior maximum is achieved by setting expected discounted marginal benefits of regulation (MB) equal to expected discounted marginal costs (MC). If, however, the shadow value of net social risk is positive (the risk constraint is binding), first-order conditions for a maximum require that

$$\frac{\partial L}{\partial A_i} = MB - MC - \frac{\lambda \partial R}{\partial A_i} = 0$$

so that

$$MB - \frac{\lambda \partial R}{\partial A_i} = MC$$

In other words, optimality requires that expected discounted marginal benefits of regulation, minus λ times the marginal value of risk, be set equal to marginal costs. A risk factor equal to

$$\frac{\lambda \partial R}{\partial A_i}$$

has entered the efficiency conditions for a maximum. If $\lambda = 0$, however, the risk constraint is not binding, so first-order conditions for a maximum are

$$\frac{\partial L}{\partial A_i} = MB - MC = 0$$

so that

$$MB = MC$$

Here the risk factor does not affect the marginal efficiency conditions. Hence whether economic efficiency is contrained by a risk factor depends entirely on whether R^* is set so that the risk constraint is binding. A similar story may be told if $A_i = 0$ and a corner solution represents a maximum.

The second set of conditions concerns the risk constraint itself. If the risk constraint is binding and the shadow value is positive, then $R^* = R(\overline{A})$. As the shadow value rises, so does the expression

$$\frac{\lambda \partial R}{\partial A_i},$$

so that the risk factor in the marginal conditions increases in magnitude. The value of λ is tantamount to the social value of acceptable risk. If the constraint is binding, estimating this value is a necessary condition for the formulation of policy.

Note, however, that given R^* (a social welfare judgment) and a particular value of λ associated with a binding risk constraint $R^* = R(\overline{A})$, it is possible to make the constraint nonbinding by reducing $R(\overline{A})$ below R^*. As discussed above, this can result either from raising the expected impact of the standard on air quality (upping μ_Q) or from reducing regulatory and scientific uncertainty (lowering σ_Q^2 or σ_T^2). Increases in the expected impact of the standard will be likely to raise the costs of regulation so that risks are traded off directly for regulatory costs. Reductions in both Type (a) regulatory and Type (b) scientific uncertainty, however, may involve a more favorable trade-off. Because knowledge of the structure of regulation and health hazards has general social utility, it may cost less to trade risk for information than for regulatory stringency. Increasing regulatory and scientific certainty, in short, can slacken the risk constraint at the same time that it improves the general store of knowledge, allowing unconstrained pursuit of net social benefits without increases in the stringency of regulation.

An additional point of analytical interest concerns the solution to the dual formulation of the problem presented here: the minimization of risk subject to a constraint posed by some expected sum of net benefits associated with a particular set of standards. In principle, the solution to this problem should yield a level of acceptable risk consistent with the first exercise. Whether this is so is an interesting empirical question.

POLICY IMPLICATIONS

To summarize, the above analysis is predicated on a distinction between Type (a) regulatory and Type (b) scientific uncertainty. Regulatory uncertainty confronts the ability of benefits analysis to estimate demand for regulations affecting air quality and the impact of these regulations on the quantity of clean air supplied. Health risks, in contrast, are subject to scientific uncertainty about the relationship between pollutants and acceptable thresholds of human morbidity and mortality. Regulatory decisions respecting national ambient air quality standards involve both types of uncertainty. Taken together, these uncertainties define the net social risk that standards may be too low to maintain the thresholds called for under law. Once social welfare judgments establish an acceptable level of net social risk, this risk can be considered a constraint on the net benefits of regulation, which can be slackened only by increasingly stringent standards or reductions in regulatory or scientific uncertainty.

These results have a number of implications for environmental policy. First, they suggest the inescapable interplay between regulation and human health associated with environmental hazards. Because this interplay has social welfare implications, such regulations can never be reduced to pure questions of economic efficiency as long as the constraint of net social risk is binding. Hence there is a need explicitly to identify and estimate the shadow value of acceptable net social risk. Policy makers can then make social welfare judgments that, though still normative, are at least non-arbitrary. Estimating the shadow value of net social risk is therefore an important task of policy research. If this shadow value is positive, it may be appropriate to orient policy so that it reflects the implied trade-off between regulatory benefits and net social risk.[23]

A second implication is the attractiveness of policies that promote greater regulatory and scientific certainty. The above analysis demonstrates that reductions in net social risk can result either from increasing the stringency of environmental regulations or from reducing Type (a) and Type (b) uncertainties. Close attention is therefore required to the comparative costs of these strategies. If, as seems likely, reductions in net social risk may be had without increases in the stringency of regulation, this opens up an important new area of policy emphasis. The agenda is shifted toward reductions in both regulatory and scientific uncertainty.

Regulatory certainty can be increased through research in the entire range of questions linking benefits to the supply of and demand for environmental regulation.[24] Scientific certainty can be increased through efforts inside EPA and elsewhere to monitor and estimate the hazards posed by environmental pollution.[25] These increases in information can make the net social risk constraint nonbinding, freeing regulators to pursue efficiency goals. If such information is useful in other contexts, its acquisition is likely to be less costly than increasingly stringent standards. If information is unavailable, especially in the short run, increasing standards may be a second-best response to unacceptable risk. But a first-best response, especially in the long run, may be increased certainty resulting from expanded research programs in policy and environmental science. Because the two types of uncertainty may be interrelated, research on regulation and scientific hazards must be closely tied in conduct and performance. As Robert Crandall and Lester Lave demonstrate, the scientific basis of regulation is an increasingly important field of interdisciplinary inquiry.[26]

A final set of points questions the wisdom of current policy. It is ironic that administration advocates of regulatory efficiency, who champion the estimation of net regulatory benefits under Executive Order 12291, have reduced support for research activities that might provide insight into the structure of regulation and its impact on health. Both regulatory and scientific uncertainty are likely to increase in the future because of reductions in enforcement of environmental standards as well as declining numbers of scientific staff at EPA and elsewhere. If the foregoing analysis is correct, these increases will reduce the flexibility of policy makers to substitute information for regulation. This leaves a more difficult policy choice between costly increases in environmental standards or admitted increases in net social risk as both regulatory impacts and health effects become more uncertain.

Current policy, opposed to increased stringency of standards, appears to be to tolerate increased risks and even to loosen the definition of acceptable health hazard thresholds. Following a strategy focusing on regulatory false positives, Reagan administration policy makers seem bent on giving a variety of pollutants the benefit of the doubt. The EPA has refused to give priority status to regulation of a variety of substances. Although small amounts of money have been directed to special studies, the large research programs necessary to reduce both regulatory and scientific uncertainty are likely to fall victim to general reductions in EPA programs.[27]

A far more attractive option would be to reduce both regulatory and scientific uncertainty, freeing government to pursue efficiency in regulation without increasing either standards or levels of net social risk. Because different types of uncertainty require different responses, applied policy research must continue to refine the definition of uncertainty so that policies can be constructed to suit specific needs. When high risks are faced and the probability of crossing health thresholds implies serious and widespread consequences, increasing stringency of regulation may be required. In other cases, improved information may be a sufficient response.[28]

Increasing alarm over environmental health hazards resulting from failure to achieve regulatory standards suggests that the public views the risk constraint as binding. Current efforts aimed at reducing the importance of net social risks including policies that give potentially hazardous substances the benefit of the doubt may not reflect the shadow value of net social risk held by society as a whole. Estimates of this value will require further discussion in both academic and policy circles.

NOTES

1. See Baram, "Cost-Benefit Analysis"; Field, "Patterns in the Laws on Health Risks"; and Willey, "Economic Criteria in Environmental Regulation."
2. See U.S. Environmental Protection Agency, "Guidelines for Performing Regulatory Impact Analyses."
3. See Moreau, "Quantitative Assessments of Health Risks by Selected Federal Agencies"; Moreau, Hyman, Stiftel, and Nichols, "Elicitation of Environmental Values in Multiple Objective Water Resource Decision Making"; and Ricci and Molton, "Risks and Benefits in Environmental Law."
4. See Just, Hueth, and Schmitz, *Applied Welfare Economics and Public Policy*.
5. See Bishop and Heberlein, "Measuring Values of Extramarket Goods"; Brookshire, Thayer, Schulze, and d'Arge, "Valuing Public Goods"; and Desvousges, Smith, and McGivney, *Alternative Approaches*.
6. See Fisher and Smith, "Economic Evaluation of Energy's Environmental Costs with Special Reference to Air Pollution."
7. See McKean, "Enforcement Costs in Environmental and Safety Regulation," and for an excellent summary of the problems of estimating the benefits of improvements in environmental quality see Freeman, *Benefits of Environmental Improvement*.
8. See Feagans and Biller, "A General Method for Assessing Health Risks Associated with Primary National Standards."
9. See O'Connor, "Overview of the Criteria Review and Standard Setting Process."
10. See Crandall and Lave, eds., *The Scientific Basis of Health and Safety Regulation*.
11. See Feagans and Biller, "Assessing the Health Risks Associated with Air Quality Standards," n. 8; Feagans and Biller, "General Method"; Richmond, "Risk Assessment and Smog"; "A Framework for Assessing Health Risks Associated with National Ambient Air Quality Standards"; and Richmond, McCurdy, and Jordan, "Risk Analysis in the Context of National Ambient Air Quality Standards."
12. This requires that the densities for Q and T overlap for some interval, which seems plausible if standards are set so as just to meet the threshold level of health risk, as currently mandated. This definition of risk is distinct from those concerned only with the variance of a random variable and is compatible with recent treatments of risk in terms of similar thresholds involving stochastic dominance.
13. If standards were set without a lag, then σ_{QT} could arguably be large and positive. This would offset σ_Q^2 and σ_T^2 in the expression for σ_Δ^2 to a degree

determined by the relative magnitude of these terms. A plausible interpretation is that if regulations could respond contemporaneously to health risks, such quick responses could mitigate scientific and regulatory uncertainty.

14. See Feagans and Biller, "Assessing Health," n. 8.

15. See Richmond, McCurdy, and Jordan, "Risk Analysis," n. 11; and Rowe, "Government Regulation of Societal Risks."

16. See Macrae, *The Social Function of Social Science*. The trade-off between income distribution objectives and efficiency is essentially the same as the trade-off between net social risks and efficiency of regulation adopted here. Both involve the determination of this trade-off by the political process, making social welfare judgments unavoidable. See Maass, "Benefit-Cost Analysis," for more details.

17. See Arrow and Lind, "Uncertainty and the Evaluation of Public Investment Decisions."

18. See Fisher, "Environmental Externalities and the Arrow-Lind Public Investment Theorem."

19. See Page, "A Generic View of Toxic Chemicals and Similar Risks."

20. See EPA, "Guidelines," n. 2; and "EPA's High Risk Carcinogen Policy."

21. Page, "Generic View," p. 232.

22. See Wilson, "Risk Measurement of Public Projects." Wilson and the other contributors to Lind, ed., *Discounting for Time and Risk in Energy Policy*, provide considerable insight into the complexities of long-lived public investment decisions.

23. See Gallagher and Smith, "Measuring Values for Environmental Resources under Uncertainty"; and Viscusi, "Labor Market Valuations."

24. See Bailey, "Risks, Costs and Benefits of Fluorocarbon Regulation"; Jordan, Richmond, and McCurdy, "Regulatory Perspectives on the Use of Scientific Information in Air Quality Standard Setting"; Lave, *Strategy of Social Regulation*; and Regans, Dietz, and Rycroft, "Risk Assessment in the Policy-Making Process."

25. Feagans and Biller, "General Method," n. 11.

26. Ibid., n. 10.

27. See "EPA's High Risk Carcinogen Policy."

28. Latin, "The 'Significance' of Toxic Health Risks."

Part IV

WILL EXECUTIVE ORDER
12291 IMPROVE
ENVIRONMENTAL POLICY
MAKING?

8

ROBERT W. CRANDALL*

THE POLITICAL ECONOMY
OF CLEAN AIR: PRACTICAL
CONSTRAINTS ON WHITE
HOUSE REVIEW

 THE Reagan regulatory relief program represents, in part, a continuation of the trend toward greater White House review of federal regulatory programs that began in the Nixon administration. The "Quality of Life" reviews in the Nixon administration were perhaps the first steps in this direction, but the first broad use of White House review began in 1974 with President Ford's executive order establishing the inflation impact statement for all major regulatory initiatives. This review process was extended by the Carter administration through its Regulatory Analysis and Review Group.

When President Reagan assumed office, he established a new Office of Information and Regulatory Affairs within the Office of Management and Budget. This office was given the responsibility for implementing a new regulatory relief program and more specifically Executive Order 12291, requiring a form of benefit-cost analysis for new major regulatory initiatives. The Reagan program represented a strengthening of the White House review processes initiated by the previous two administrations, for OMB could now reject a regulatory analysis and thus frustrate the attempt to propose new regulations. But the stress was upon regulatory "relief" rather than "reform"; therefore, success was to be measured by the reduction in the rate of flow of new regulations to burden industry.

White House review has grown and developed as a mechanism to assure that regulatory decisions reflect a balancing of costs and benefits rather than simply reflecting the parochial interests of constituent groups that cluster

*Senior Fellow, Economics Studies Program, Brookings Institution.

around individual agencies. For instance, tighter plant safety standards might placate organized labor and even some employers with political influence at the Occupational Safety and Health Administration but fail to deliver much improvement in worker health despite considerable social costs. New investment in nonunion plants might be slowed to the benefit of both existing workers and employers but to the detriment of national economic growth. A full regulatory analysis might uncover the limited benefits relative to the costs to the entire country and thus place pressure upon OSHA to resist the lobbying pressures from favored constituent groups.

Unfortunately, the complexity of most environmental-health-safety regulation makes the application of regulatory review extremely difficult. The review process might serve a major function if each regulatory program consisted of a few rules establishing the institutional framework for controlling externality problems. Alternatively, if the major problem with this form of regulation was the tendency of bureaucrats to initiate successively more extreme regulations, the review process might be used as a moderating influence. Unfortunately, neither of these conditions obtains for most of the newer regulatory programs and certainly not for air pollution policy. As a result, I shall argue, the review process can have only a marginal impact upon a program that needs more radical surgery.

In this chapter I review the structure of air pollution policy to convey a sense of its complexity to the uninitiated reader. I then proceed to an analysis of the deficiencies and inefficiencies in the program. A subsequent section examines the apparent congressional intent in designing environmental policy in general and air pollution policy in particular. Finally, I provide some assessment of how the regulatory review–relief process is likely to work in influencing air pollution policy.

A CAPSULE SUMMARY OF THE AIR POLLUTION PROGRAM

It is difficult to summarize the current federal air pollution policy in a few paragraphs.[1] However detailed the description, it will miss some point that occupies scores of lawyers in Washington and countless others throughout the country because the policy has become extremely complex and requires federal and state government cooperation for implementation. Without this cooperation, the policy cannot be enforced.

Air pollution originates from both stationary and mobile sources. Some pollutants such as hydrocarbons and oxides of nitrogen are emitted by both; others, such as sulfur oxides, are emitted primarily by stationary sources.[2] Carbon monoxide is largely a mobile-source problem, and particulates are emitted mostly by stationary sources although they also come from diesel-powered motor vehicles and various natural sources such as volcanoes and forest fires. Lead emissions come from the burning of leaded gasoline as well as from the processing of lead in stationary sources. Finally, photo-chemical smog is a product of two major pollutants—hydrocarbons and nitrogen oxides—in the presence of sunlight.

The Environmental Protection Agency is entrusted with the responsibility for setting uniform National Ambient Air Quality Standards for each of the above pollutants. These standards are based largely upon health considerations. The language of the Clean Air Act virtually assumes a sharp threshold in these health effects, suggesting that a safe concentration exists. Nonhealth values are important in setting secondary ambient air quality standards, but these standards have had little practical significance in the execution of policy.

Ambient air quality cannot be controlled directly from Washington, nor even from the states. The Congress sets new car emission standards, but it does not set standards for used cars (except for requiring that new cars have pollution controls with limited deterioration over fifty thousand miles of use). Nor does EPA set standards for most stationary sources. The Clean Air Act established air quality control regions (AQCRs) that EPA must delineate. Each of the 247 AQCRs must meet the ambient air quality standards by 1982 or 1987, depending upon the pollutant. The states submit state implementation plans describing how various sources are to be regulated within each AQCR within their jurisdiction.

EPA has the responsibility for setting New Source Performance Standards for all new stationary sources of pollution. These standards are supposed to be set for each industrial category, but in implementation new source standards are to be set tighter for areas with dirty air (nonattainment areas) than in areas with clean air (nondeterioration or PSD areas). In practice, these new source standards are generally the same for a given facility in both areas, but the permitting procedures differ somewhat.

These industrial source and automobile standards, if enforced, provide an upward limit upon total emissions of the major criteria pollutants for a given growth rate of mobile and industrial sources. The effect of this limitation upon air quality is difficult to predict because the interaction between meteorological or topographical conditions and total emissions to determine air quality in any given location is imperfectly understood. The Clean Air Act requires that all monitoring sites in an AQCR meet the ambient standards; therefore, EPA and the states must attempt to regulate air quality, not simply limit emissions.

In addition to the above responsibilities, EPA must set emission standards for hazardous pollutants and regulate visibility to the more pristine areas of the country. It must also assure that the cleaner areas of the country do not suffer a deterioration of air quality. This latter responsibility is part of the prevention of significant deterioration program that limits growth in emissions of particulates and sulfur oxides to maximum increments per year.

The mechanism for coordinating these diverse tasks and assuring timely compliance with ambient air quality standards is the SIP. These plans are extremely lengthy and detailed, often taking several years to develop and promulgate. Each change in a SIP must run through the administrative procedures maze at EPA and the state. EPA cannot require a state to formulate a sensible plan, but it can reject a plan that appears inconsistent with the federal law. If the plan is insufficient to bring about attainment, it may be rejected. If the state does not formulate a plan consistent with meeting the air quality standards by the statutory date, EPA may formulate its own SIP for the state.

Mobile source standards are set by the Congress, but EPA has the responsibility for certifying and testing new automobiles. In addition, EPA must establish rules for the lead content of gasoline, and it must require an inspection and maintenance program for all cars in an AQCR that does not meet the ambient air quality standards for CO or oxidants.

Monitoring and enforcement remain two of the weakest links in the air pollution control chain.[3] Monitoring is required to determine compliance with ambient standards and to enforce emissions standards against all stationary sources. Both monitoring systems have been criticized as inadequate over the past decade. Ambient monitors are not consistently maintained, and they are placed predominantly near the core of urban areas, thereby giving a misleading impression of average air quality.

Monitoring for compliance with emissions limitations is notoriously weak. Continuous stack monitors are very expensive. Few sources are ever monitored on even a sporadic basis. Most reports of compliance with the emissions limitation specified in the SIP are effected through voluntary certification—an unaudited letter from the polluter.

Enforcement responsibilities rest with the states and with EPA, but in practice EPA cannot force compliance in a recalcitrant state. It may deny the state federal transportation and sewer construction money if the state refuses to formulate and enforce a plan designed to achieve eventual compliance with the ambient air quality standards. It may levy civil penalties directly on noncomplying sources of pollution. In practice, however, practical politics interferes with both forms of sanctions. EPA has collected a minuscule amount of civil penalties, and even the denial of federal money has been used sparingly. If a state chooses to proceed slowly with the enforcement of standards against existing sources, EPA finds it very difficult to force compliance from Washington.

PROBLEMS WITH THE CURRENT POLICY

There are no comprehensive studies of the air pollution program that demonstrate its effectiveness in reducing air pollution.[4] In fact, because of delays, poor enforcement, and imperfectly understood dispersion and transport characteristics, it is possible that the entire program has generated little reduction in air pollution despite expenditures of more than $25 billion per year in this pursuit.[5] The data on air quality are so poor that one cannot confidently assert that air quality has improved because of the 1970 Clean Air Act Amendments.[6] It is probable that carbon monoxide and sulfur dioxide concentrations have been reduced, but the reductions in SO_2 may result as much from economic factors as from environmental policy. Surprisingly, some data for the 1960s demonstrate a more rapid improvement in air quality (other than photochemical smog) than occurred in the 1970s.[7]

Static Efficiency

Although the effectiveness of the policy in reducing air pollution is in doubt, its efficiency is not. There can be little doubt that the reliance upon individual point-source standards, the political deals crafted to secure support for the policy, the distinction between new and old sources, and the haphazard enforcement program have combined to give us an extremely inefficient overall policy. EPA data show enormous ranges in the incremental cost of control across sources of the same pollutant. Numerous studies confirm the possibilities for substantial cost savings, and EPA and census data confirm the substantial bias against new sources.

Measuring the incremental cost of air quality improvement is extremely difficult for a number of reasons. First, the relationship between emissions and air quality varies temporally and spatially. Weather conditions and terrain may have an important effect upon air quality for a given distribution of emissions of certain pollutants. Therefore, one may not assume that equalizing the incremental cost of emissions abatement is equivalent to equalizing the incremental cost of air quality improvement in a given air quality region at each monitoring location at all times.

Second, measures of the incremental cost of emissions control are typically engineering estimates based upon the assumption of fixed coefficients in production and consumption. If a given emissions standard causes a firm to substitute against the process in question, the full incremental cost of the standard will not be measured by the additional control costs at that source.

Third, the estimates developed by EPA and its contractors begin with the assumption of no controls and move by increments of control from that required by the weakest extant standard to that required by the tightest standard. As a result, the incremental cost is actually the additional engineering costs for an often fairly sizable increment in abatement. Given different sizes of these incremental abatements across sources, the estimates are at best rough comparisons of the cost of tightening controls at the margin. These limitations in the data must be borne in mind when scrutinizing any tabulation of published incremental control costs.

The range of incremental costs of control is best summarized by a bar graph produced by EPA staff for an internal study on incremental cost-effectiveness that was eventually leaked to the Senate[8] (Figure 8.1). Even though this study is unofficial and controversial even within EPA, it is probably the best source of comprehensive cost data for the major criteria pollutants. The ranges for particulates and sulfur oxides control are very large, reflecting a sizable potential misallocation of resources. There is a difference of at least a factor of four for SO_2 removal costs between utilities and nonferrous smelters. The incremental cost differences for particulates within the steel industry are astronomical although the recent policy changes and lax enforcement may reduce this variance substantially. Ranges of incremental particulate control costs from $22 to as much as $1,030 per ton for the cement and concrete industries or from $31 to $2,577 per ton for utilities speak for themselves.

Numerous studies of the costs of sulfur oxides, particulates, and nitrogen oxide control demonstrate similar inefficiencies in EPA-state standards. These studies suggest that costs could be reduced by as much as 70 percent if the control strategies were efficient.[9] And recent studies undertaken for the steel and chemical industries to demonstrate the cost reductions possible under plantwide standards—the so-called "bubble" concept—reveal large prospective savings.[10] The estimated savings are 4 to 21 percent for steel and 63 to 86 percent for chemicals.

These studies all demonstrate that emissions standards may be very inefficient, but they cannot prove that the result is inefficient without data on actual enforcement. The most outrageously high control costs are probably avoided by lack of compliance, so the actual static inefficiency may be much smaller.

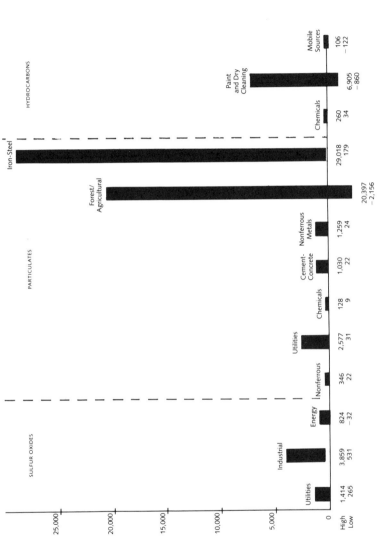

Figure 8.1. Incremental control costs for existing and new source standards in various industries (1980$/metric ton removed)

Source: See Table 8.1.

Nor do the above data prove that the incremental cost of improvements in air quality differs across sources. The relationship between emissions and air quality depends upon a number of meteorological and topographical conditions and even upon the rate of emission of other pollutants. It may be possible that some of the apparent differences in the incremental cost of emissions abatement are efficient when these other conditions are considered. Unfortunately, given the imperfect knowledge about these effects and the problems with the existing monitoring system, it would be difficult to reach a definite judgment on the actual efficiency of the control program. It seems unlikely, however, that requiring very different incremental control costs for emissions of, say, SO_2 in the same area can be conducive to economic efficiency.

New Source Bias

It is perhaps understandable that most pollution-control programs focus special attention upon new sources. It is easier to design and operate these facilities with low rates of discharge than to clean up older facilities. Retrofitting to get a given discharge rate is likely to be much more expensive than designing the plant and equipment to meet the same standard. This does not mean, however, that the new source standards should be pressed so tightly that the incremental cost of control (per unit of pollution abated) is even higher than incremental costs at existing plants.

There are at least two sources of evidence on the bias against new sources: the EPA cost-effectiveness study and evidence on control costs in growing and declining regions of the country. The EPA cost-effectiveness study is far from conclusive because it does not provide estimates for new and old sources of hydrocarbons, and its coverage for the other pollutants is spotty. Nevertheless, the data for particulates and SO_2 in Table 8.1 demonstrate a tendency for standards on new sources to have more onerous incremental abatement costs than those for existing sources. A recent Congressional Budget Office (CBO) study suggests that EPA has underestimated new source costs for SO_2 removal at electric utilities.[11] The CBO study estimates the incremental cost of the current EPA NSPS standards at $2,411 (1980 dollars) per ton removed. This cost is double that estimated in Table 8.1 for western coal. More research on this matter should be done, with cost comparisons made across new and old sources in several states. SIPs vary across the states, and certain states may evidence less bias against new sources than others.

A more dispositive source of evidence is the distribution of abatement costs across states. The states in which industries are growing most rapidly should have the largest share of new facilities. If new sources are given standards that simply reflect their lower control costs per unit of pollution abated, their total control costs per dollar of income generated should be no higher than total control costs at existing sources. On the other hand, if there is a new source bias, total control costs are likely to be higher per dollar of income generated in new sources than in old sources. Aggregating over all sources within a given industry in a state should thus give us some idea of the presence or absence of the new source bias. If there is a new source bias, we should expect control costs to be higher per dollar of value added in the states where an industry is growing than in states where it is declining.

The evidence shown in Table 8.2 is conclusive. For the industries in which air pollution control costs loom large, the cost of air pollution controls per dollar of value added is generally higher in the growing areas of the country than in the declining Frostbelt states of the East and Midwest. The differences are most noticeable in refining, paper, and chemicals, but substantial differences exist for stone, clay, and glass and for metals. The only exceptions are transportation and food processing, but in these industries control costs do not loom large and growth rates are not substantially greater in the Sunbelt. In fact, transportation equipment had been growing more rapidly in the Frostbelt states than in the Sunbelt in the period preceding the year in which these data were generated.

It is possible, of course, for incremental control costs to be equal across new and old sources but for total costs per dollar of value added to be greater in new sources. If the cost of any control at existing sources is very high and if costs initially increase gradually for new sources, the total costs for new sources could be greater than total costs at existing sources with the same value added. This is demonstrated in the top panel of Figure 8.2 in which incremental costs are equated at MC^* for old and new sources (producing the same output). With the incremental cost schedules so disparate, total control costs, the area under the curves, are greater for the new source than for the old source. In the lower panel, there is a new source bias and the new sources' total costs are greater than those for existing sources. In this case, percentage reduction in the actual standards is much closer than in the upper panel. In fact, given the differences between new and existing source standards in emissions reduction, the lower panel seems the more reasonable. Nevertheless, we cannot rule out the possibility that the results in Table 8.2 may reflect some examples of the situation depicted in the top panel of Figure 8.2.

Table 8.1. Estimates of the Incremental Costs of Removing Pollutants from Existing Sources and New Sources
(1980 $ per metric ton removed)

Industry	Existing Sources	New Sources
PARTICULATES		
Electric utilities:		
Eastern coal	252	2,577
Western coal	–	66
Coal cleaning	–	29
Petroleum refining	1	0.50
Chemicals:		
Phosphate fertilizer	9–128	–
Phosphorous	–	–
Defluorinated phosphate rock	–	–
Dicalcium phosphate	–	–
Iron and steel:		
Raw materials	982	1,759–2,872
Sintering	260–670	470–21,459
Coke ovens	181–6,285	1,356–27,387
Blast furnaces	308–10,429	2,130–16,600
BOF	353–3,110	2,461
Electric arc furnace	1,291–2,448	15,589
Automatic scarfing	25,473	–
Continuous casting	–	–
Secondary aluminum	–	–
Secondary brass and bronze	24–569	–
Ferroalloys	–	602–1,259
Secondary lead	34–124	–
Asphalt and concrete	22	343–1,030
Lime	27–132	–
Feed mills	1,745–20,397*	1,525
Grain handling	96–2,388	176
Pulp and paper	0†	92–7,206†
SULFUR DIOXIDE		
Electric utilities:		
Eastern coal	412	265–298
Western coal	–	1,167–1,414
Natural gas processing	340–824	–
Petroleum refining	409	0‡
Iron and steel coking	513	184–579
Sulfuric acid	210	–
Primary copper	24–28	22
Primary lead	64–356	315

Table 8.1. continued

Primary zinc	38	222
Structural clay products	530–841	–
Paper (total reduced sulfur)	0–324‡	92–12,437‡

SOURCE: Environmental Protection Agency, Office of Planning and Management, "The Incremental Cost Effectiveness of Selective EPA Regulations," January 1981.
*Feed mills.
†Existing plants are said to have negative control costs; new plants remove particulates and sulfur as joint products.
‡Some estimates are negative, others are joint with particulate removal.

A Regional Bias

If there is a bias against new sources in clean air policy, it may not derive simply from the standard-setting process. Enforcement against existing sources of pollution is so weak and haphazard in many states that it may be the major cause of the differences in control costs across new and old sources. New sources must generally pass through a permitting process involving EPA. This process is likely to be effective in requiring major new sources to install the required abatement equipment. Of course, these facilities may not be maintained over time, and the facility may drift out of compliance. But the costs of installing the new equipment, even if it is not maintained, may succeed in slowing down investment in a number of heavy industries.

A bias against new sources is consistent with congressional voting records on environmental issues. Congressmen from high-income, slow-growth states in the East and Midwest are the most ardent environmentalists. In a forthcoming study, I show that those votes are not a function of local air quality but are related to low growth rates in per capita income. These votes, in the period 1973–81, came at a time when industry had been shifting rapidly to the South and West.[12]

Table 8.3 arrays the average congressional votes on key environmental issues as measured by the League of Conservation Voters. It is obvious that the proenvironment vote declined monotonically from the Northeast to the Southwest. Western congressmen demonstrated a somewhat stronger environmental voting record than those from the South or Southwest but a decidedly less environmental posture than those from the industrial Northeast. Upon closer analysis, I find that a slow rate of growth in per capita income, a large share of income from manufacturing, Frostbelt location, and a slow rate of growth of new establishments in polluting industries are

Table 8.2. Air Pollution Control Costs in Thousand Dollars of Value Added in Eight Industries, 1979*

Industry	New England	Middle Atlantic	East North Central	West North Central	Frost Belt Costs 1972–77	Percent Growth in Value Added 1972–77
SIC 20 Food Processing	0.042	0.090	1.27	1.80	1.25	53.0
SIC 26 Paper	3.32	1.89	2.81	2.63	2.58	10.3
SIC 28 Chemicals	1.80	3.85	4.07	4.60	3.90	58.2
SIC 29 Refining	–	36.70	23.80	12.70	26.97	200.3
SIC 32 Stone and clay products	4.05	7.49	5.76	8.92	6.95	47.6
SIC 33 Metals	2.93	19.36	15.70	13.90	16.20	54.6
SIC 34 Machinery	1.52	1.16	0.69	0.99	0.90	63.6
SIC 37 Transportation equipment	0.46	1.96	1.07	0.57	1.09	66.8

SOURCE: Bureau of the Census.
*The data represent total outlays and value added in each industry in the states for which census reports the requisite information. Coverage ranges from 66 percent of value added in

conducive to congressional votes for strong environmental policy. These votes are not generally associated with low levels of air or water quality, but the environmental quality data are so poor that this finding remains to be confirmed by further research. I conclude from this analysis that congressmen from the more polluted (particularly in photochemical oxidants) Northeast may well be voting for an environmental policy that includes PSD, percentage reduction of SO_2 emissions, and other impediments to growth so as to forestall the shift of industrial activity to the Sunbelt.

B. Peter Pashigian has also shown that nondeterioration or PSD policy is supported primarily by northern congressmen from urban areas.[13] This policy limits the growth in new sources in areas with air quality that exceeds the national standards. It also requires a lengthy new source review process and case-by-case determination of the best available control technology.

The result of air pollution policy is to make it more difficult for busi-

South Atlantic	East South Central	West South Central	Mountain	Pacific	Sun Belt Costs Value Added	Percent Growth in Value Added 1972–77
0.072	0.093	0.070	0.084	0.069	0.74	63.4
13.60	11.99	8.67	1.95	7.85	10.81	78.3
5.59	10.30	8.73	6.72	3.96	7.44	94.0
22.50	–	37.10	16.10	57.80	42.52	238.0
7.27	8.97	8.76	8.71	10.30	8.78	60.5
21.10	18.80	21.40	136.00	19.40	24.52	72.6
0.48	1.59	0.64	5.35	1.56	1.09	91.0
0.38	0.19	0.39	–	0.81	0.65	50.1

Frostbelt states in SIC 29 to 99 percent of value added in Frostbelt states in SIC 37. In all but three of the sixteen average entries, more than 90 percent of value added is included.

nesses to migrate from the Frostbelt to the Sunbelt. The congressional voting records on environmental policy in general and PSD policy in particular are consistent with the view that there is a bias against new sources by legislative design, for new sources are most likely to be built in the Sunbelt states.

Choice of Priorities

There is accumulating evidence that fine particles and certain sulfate compounds are the most damaging air pollutants.[14] Sulfates and oxides of nitrogen are the precursors of acid rain. Yet despite the evidence, EPA has developed no standards for fine particulates or sulfates. It continues to regulate SO_2 as if the health threat is from local exposure to SO_2 rather than to SO_4 compounds. The 1977 Clean Air Act Amendments require EPA to reexamine the ambient air quality standards. Thus far, it has succeeded only

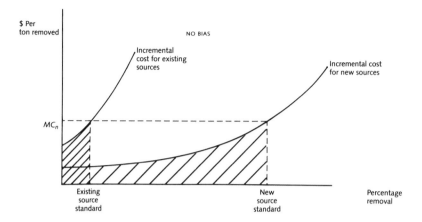

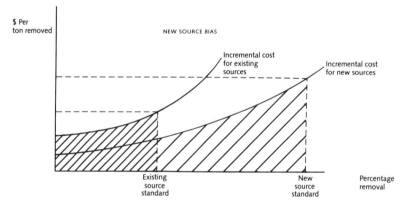

Figure 8.2. The effect of differing control technologies between new and old sources

Table 8.3. Congressional Voting on Key Environmental Issues, 1979–1980

| | Proportion of "Proenvironment" Votes | | |
| | House of Representatives | | Senate |
Census Region	1979	1980	1979–80
New England	73.5	71.7	73.6
Mid-Atlantic	61.7	59.8	67.3
East North Central	50.4	51.0	71.6
West North Central	42.5	49.5	49.4
South Atlantic	37.0	41.0	40.5
East South Central	23.6	28.2	21.3
West South Central	27.6	27.0	20.0
Mountain	28.3	35.3	31.9
Pacific	52.9	52.2	42.6
Pacific (excluding Alaska and Hawaii)	53.6	53.3	51.5

SOURCE: League of Conservation Voters, *How Congress Voted on Energy and the Environment*, annual issues, 1979–80.

in revising the standard for photochemical oxidants, one of the least damaging to human health. It has struggled with the CO standard, another pollutant with relatively minor health effects, but it has been unsuccessful in dealing with the fine particulate–sulfate problem. Had EPA sought to address the most serious problems first, it would have chosen its targets in the opposite order.

Nor has EPA done anything about the long-distance transport problem involving SO_2. If there is a case for a national air pollution policy, it must surely be strongest for these interstate problems. EPA spends enormous resources trying to decide how stringent the air quality standards should be for Cleveland and Boise alike, but it is seemingly impotent in dealing with the dangerous export of sulfates from midwestern states to the East. Obviously, the reason for this neglect is political: it is easier to set a goal for national air quality than to force Ohio or Idaho to reduce the amount of emissions it blows upon its neighbors.

Regulatory Complexity and Monitoring

The problems of standard-setting and monitoring are intertwined. The number of point-source standards and the legislated constraints upon them are truly bewildering. Existing sources in nonattainment areas are to use reasonably available control technology (RACT). Sources in Class I PSD areas may be required to install the best available retrofit technology

(BART). All new sources must meet New Source Performance Standards, but these may be lowest achievable emissions rate (LAER) in nonattainment areas and case-by-case best available control technology (BACT) in clean areas.

These detailed, complex requirements occupy most of the air program's resources and energies. Disputes over major rulemakings, supervision of SIP revisions, and court challenges are more pressing than attention to monitoring and enforcement policies. Congress appears disinterested in the latter problems, ignoring repeated General Accounting Office studies of the inadequacy of monitoring.

GAO has repeatedly questioned the quality of the monitoring system erected by EPA and the states to measure air quality. In 1979, the GAO reported that as many as 81 percent of all monitoring sites had one or more problems that could affect data reliability. In response, EPA developed a plan to assure that a total of more than five thousand monitors be sited and operated in a reliable fashion by federal, state, and local authorities. By the end of 1981, GAO reported that only about one-half of all monitors met EPA specifications.

The poor quality of the monitoring network is in part the result of the limited funding provided for it. In the four fiscal years 1978–81, the total federal, state, and local expenditures on monitoring were only $44 million (current dollars) per year, or about 0.2 percent of the estimated costs of air pollution control. EPA has claimed that even these costs are high because of some nonrecurring costs required to implement the new air-monitoring network. But if the current effort requires substantially less than $44 million per year in recurring costs and does not achieve the goal of a high-quality network, surely additional funding is justified to determine the success of the extremely expensive regulatory program now in place.

To its credit, EPA has attempted to reduce the need for detailed point-source standard-setting and the administrative complexity it involves. Beginning in 1976, it began to seek methods for allowing polluters to trade pollution reduction responsibilities and choosing their own mix of abatement across sources. These "offset" and "bubble" policies have developed steadily despite a few court reversals, the initial hostility of the new Reagan EPA leadership to them, and the foot-dragging by environmental purists in the last administration.[15]

There are still unresolved issues in the definition of a source for applying new source standards, but it seems clear that EPA will continue to move in the direction of allowing firms to trade pollution-reduction responsibilities, thereby eliminating the worst examples of cost inefficiencies in existing sources. Unfortunately, it may be difficult to eliminate the new source bias in this fashion because the Clean Air Act requires new sources to meet technology-based LAER or BACT standards. Otherwise, the barriers to trading pollution abatement responsibilities appear to be crumbling.

THE PROSPECTIVE IMPACT OF THE EXECUTIVE ORDER

Earliest Efforts

The Ford and Carter regulatory reform programs had some minor impact upon EPA's air policy. In the Ford administration, the Council on Wage and Price Stability actively encouraged EPA to develop its "offset" policy—the first example of emissions trading.[16] In the Carter administration, RARG put pressure on EPA to limit the inefficiencies in the new source performance standards for coal-fired utility boilers, and it played an active role in getting EPA to raise its photochemical oxidant standard from 0.08 to 0.12 parts per million.[17]

In the Reagan administration, OMB has had little impact upon the air pollution program for at least two reasons. First, there have not been any new proposed major rules to examine. Second, most of the issues involving air pollution policy have been of a broad, general policy perspective, requiring the development of approaches to new sources, emissions trading, or pending legislation. In none of these areas is the review process useful.[18]

The review process devised under Executive Order 12291 is best applied to specific rulemakings in which regulatory standards are being proposed. These standards generally specify the technology or performance levels for the workplace, for a product, or for a pollution discharge. The issues in such rulemakings are generally of the form, Is the cost of the given standard greater or less than the prospective benefit? Alternatively, it may be, Is there a better way to achieve the same result? If the only problems in regulation were how tight to set individual standards, current regulatory review methods might be helpful. For more complex problems, however, this process is not only ineffective but irrelevant.

The Prospects in 1983

Recall my catalog of the major problems with the air pollution program: inefficiency in the setting of a complex maze of point-source standards, new source bias, ineffective monitoring and enforcement, and poor choice of regulatory priorities. Of these problems, only the first—inefficient point-source standards—is readily amenable to pressure from White House review. But such review is irrelevant to the problems in this case because existing source standards are set by the states in their SIPs. Moreover, the enormous number of individual standards militates against any centralized review. It is far better to seek alternative methods for assuring cost-effectiveness such as EPA's controlled emissions trading policy ("bubbles" and "offsets"). The continued progress in developing the trading policy has not been discernibly affected by the executive order.

The new source bias, I have argued, is a direct product of the regional politics in Congress. In its new source and PSD policies, Congress has wanted to saddle growing sections of the country with tighter standards in part as a means of slowing the migration of industry from the Frostbelt to the Sunbelt.

RARG's largely ineffective assault on the new source standards for coal-burning utility plants illustrates the constraints Congress has placed upon EPA. In formulating the NSPS for electric utilities, EPA could not consider implementing a rational policy of simply allowing trades with existing sources in the area because of the congressional instruction that the new source must install the best technological system of continuous emission reduction. It could not resort to a performance standard for the same reason. It could not impose a tight ceiling upon emissions because Senator Robert Byrd forced EPA to retrench at last-minute White House meetings in order to increase the size of the market for Appalachian high-sulfur coal. It could not allow a mixture of low-sulfur coal and coal washing because it feared a court reversal on the grounds that that was not the best available technological method of continuous emissions reduction available. In the end, RARG was left to criticize the folly of the final NSPS ruling; EPA was left to promulgate the folly.[19]

The ineffective monitoring and compliance systems used by EPA cannot be addressed in a single proposed rulemaking. OMB cannot force EPA to enforce the regulations implicit in the SIP even if it could somehow reconcile such an action with the goals of regulatory relief. Monitoring and enforcement are complex issues that involve state-federal relationships. Monitoring cannot be accomplished without appropriate funds, but OMB cannot use regulatory review to force the Congress or state legislatures to appropriate funds. Nor can EPA force state governments to enforce the letter of their SIPs, and OMB is obviously even more powerless in this situation. Without improved enforcement and monitoring, however, standards will continue to be poorly enforced against existing sources, forcing ever greater restraints on new sources or new automobiles if we are to continue a policy of uniform ambient air quality goals.

If White House review is useful for detailing costly, inefficient, or ineffective new regulations, its most likely uses in constraining air pollution policy would be in promulgating major New Source Performance Standards or National Ambient Air Quality Standards. As I have argued, RARG did not meet with much success in fighting the wasteful NSPS for fossil-fired electric utility boilers, but its impact upon the ozone ambient air quality standard was somewhat greater.

As EPA moves to complete its review of the remaining ambient air quality standards, OMB review could play a substantial role—albeit one that may not be consistent with the language of the Clean Air Act. The Clean Air Act requires that the primary ambient air quality standards be uniform nationally and that they be calibrated so as to protect the health of the most sensitive groups in the population. Neither instruction is consistent with a rational allocation of resources. Surely, not all areas of the country should strive for the same air quality standards. The cost of achieving acceptable air quality and the value of different levels of air quality are likely to vary substantially across the country. Residents in Pittsburgh are undoubtedly forced to spend more per capita to achieve a given particulates standard than residents of, say, Jackson Hole, Wyoming. The value of enhanced visibility to the average resident of Pittsburgh is probably substantially less than to the average resident of Jackson Hole. To suggest that both should strive for the same air quality is absurd.

The health criterion in the Clean Air Act is also difficult to defend. In practice, it is likely that the health evidence available to the administrator does not allow him to conclude that any concentration of any pollutant (for which there are any adverse health effects) above the "background" level is absolutely protective of the health of the most sensitive groups in the population. Some persons with acute respiratory problems are likely to be adversely affected by any increase in these pollutant concentrations. Where does the administrator draw the line? A review of the procedure used in setting the ozone standard would not be reassuring to most readers. The final standard of 0.12 parts per million during the second worst hour of the year was nothing more than a political compromise, not the result of an inquiry that resulted in dispositive evidence that 0.12 was sufficiently below a threshold level to be deemed protective with an adequate margin of safety, as required by the act. In fact, one cannot conclude from the evidence that there is a threshold.

The OMB review process under Executive Order 12291 can, therefore, be of some use in constraining the choices of National Ambient Air Quality Standards by EPA. Given that the Clean Air Act does not provide a practical or rational basis for standard-setting, the actual choice becomes a political matter. Better that such a decision be guided by benefit-cost analysis than by the lobbying strengths of contesting parties. Begun early enough, the regulatory analysis can force the administrator to propose a more sensible range of alternatives than occurred in the ozone case. Having proposed a standard of 0.10 and then asking for comments on standards as "high" as 0.12, Administrator Costle had backed himself into a political corner. His exit was to a level of 0.12, not a higher standard, simply because no higher standard was politically feasible given the initial proposal and President Carter's constituency. One would like to see EPA avoid making such mistakes again. OMB review of proposed ambient standards may be helpful in this regard.

The executive order cannot address the other serious flaws in the current air pollution program because these flaws are either legislated or are the product of federal-state inertia in devising sensible approaches to enforcement and the setting of priorities. Reversing property rights in the fashion required by the standard-setting approach to environmental policy involves enormous political compromises. These compromises are not likely to be affected by OMB oversight.

More important, the considerable strides made by EPA in devising a system of marketable rights or controlled trading have been made without the assistance (or hindrance) of regulatory review. In defining limits on trades, the definition of new sources, or the banking of offsets, EPA simply states that it is not involved in a major rulemaking by OMB standards. The intensive policy-making debates within EPA may be influenced by other agencies including OMB, but the progress of controlled trading from offsets in 1976 to its current dimensions has not been the result of any executive order. The review process is irrelevant to such fundamental policy issues.

NOTES

1. The basic statutory authority is to be found in 42 USC7401 ff.
2. Data on estimated emissions of criteria pollutants—those for which EPA sets ambient air quality standards—may be found in U.S. Environmental Protection Agency, *National Air Pollutant Emissions Estimates, 1980.*
3. There have been numerous studies documenting this weakness. For two recent criticisms, see U.S. General Accounting Office, *Air Quality*; and U.S. General Accounting Office, *Improvements Needed in Controlling Major Air Pollution Sources.* Recently, GAO criticized EPA's current monitoring effort in *Problems in Air Quality Monitoring System Affect Data Reliability.*
4. Most analyses are little more than an attribution of all reductions in estimated emissions or airborne concentrations to regulation, for example, annual reports

of the Council on Environmental Quality or National Commission on Air Quality, *Clearing the Air*.

5. See Rutledge and Trevathan, "Pollution Abatement and Control Expenditures, 1972–1980," p. 51.
6. See the section "Regulatory Complexity and Monitoring" in this chapter.
7. See Crandall, *Controlling Industrial Pollution*, chap. 2.
8. See ibid., chap. 3.
9. See ibid., chap. 3, for more details. A recent study of SO_2 control in Los Angeles suggests much smaller savings (Hahn and Noll, "Tradable Air Pollution Permits in the Overall Regulatory System").
10. See Putnam, Hayes, and Bartlett, "Analysis of the Cost Impact of Plantwide Emissions Control on Four Domestic Steel Plants"; and Maloney and Yandle, "Bubbles and Efficiency."
11. See U.S. Congressional Budget Office, "The Clean Air Act, Electric Utilities, and the Coal Market."
12. See Crandall, *Controlling Industrial Pollution*, chap. 7.
13. See Pashigian, "Environmental Regulation."
14. See Lave and Seskin, *Air Pollution and Human Health*; Chappie and Lave, "The Health Effects of Air Pollution"; and Ostro and Anderson, "Morbidity, Air Pollution, and Health Statistics."
15. For a detailed view from an insider's perspective, see Levin, "Getting There."
16. U.S. Council on Wage and Price Stability, "EPA Air Emission Tradeoff Policy."
17. U.S. Council on Wage and Price Stability, *Environmental Protection Agency's Proposal for the Revision of New Source Performance Standards for Electric Utility Steam Generating Units*; and Regulatory Analysis Review Group, "Environmental Protection Agency's Proposed Revision to the National Ambient Air Quality Standard for Photochemical Oxidants," 16 October 1978.
18. For instance, the singular triumph of those pressing for a rational emissions trading policy was the April 1982 proposal to relax a number of constraints on trading. This was deemed as not a "major" action because it reduces costs and involves voluntary actions by polluters.
19. See Ackerman and Hassler, *Clean Coal/Dirty Air*, for the details of this sorry story. See also Crandall, "The Use of Environmental Policy to Reduce Economic Growth in the Sun Belt."

9

PAUL R. PORTNEY*

THE BENEFITS AND COSTS OF REGULATORY ANALYSIS

"SAUCE for the goose," according to proverb, "is sauce for the gander." In the context of the subject of this book, this can be taken to mean that we should scrutinize proposed reforms of the rulemaking process every bit as carefully as the regulations that process produces. Just as we apply crude benefit-cost tests to environmental, occupational safety and health, or consumer product or highway safety rules, so, too, should we ask what we gain from more analysis of federal regulation and at what cost.

Policy analysis and evaluation seldom seem to be directed at programs that march beneath the banner of "reform" or "reorganization." Thus several recent administrations have promised government reorganization (usually meaning the creation of a new, cabinet-level department or the consolidation or elimination of existing ones) even though seat-of-the-pants *ex ante* analysis suggested that these efforts would either fail altogether (as with the proposed Department of Natural Resources) or would not be worth the effort required even if they were to succeed (the Department of Education being a case in point). Similarly, I will assert without proof that highly publicized programs to eliminate waste, fraud, and abuse in the federal government will inevitably not be worth whatever public (or private) resources are devoted to them. But both types of programs appear to be spared from careful evaluation because they are billed as "reforms."

Will regulatory reform programs meet the same fate? Will the benefits and costs of regulatory analysis be ignored at the same time such analysis is being applied to the outputs of the rulemaking process? Can regulatory analysis withstand such scrutiny? Is sauce for the goose not for the gander?

It is the purpose of this chapter to make a modest start toward analyzing

*Senior Fellow, Quality of the Environment Division, Resources for the Future. Thanks are due Robert Crandall, William Desvousges, and especially V. Kerry Smith for their helpful comments on an earlier version.

the current as well as previous administrations' regulatory reform pro-grams. My attention will be centered exclusively on the requirement in Executive Order 12291 (and the comparable requirement in Executive Order 12044) that all final or proposed "major" rules be accompanied by regulatory impact analyses—analyses that identify the social costs and benefits of the regulatory approach actually selected by the agency, as well as those of the other alternatives considered. I will not consider the regula-tory reforms that increase public participation in rulemaking or that alter in other ways the procedures agencies must follow in issuing rules, although these requirements might benefit from a calculation of benefits and costs.

In the following section, I discuss the likely costs—both direct and indirect—of regulatory oversight and offer some very tentative estimates of the magnitudes of these costs. I then turn to the benefits of regulatory analysis as mandated in EO 12291 and its predecessors. Here, too, I distinguish between more and less quantifiable benefits, in much the same way analysts of many conventional regulatory programs must. Although I make no attempt to estimate the annual benefits of regulatory analysis, I offer an opinion as to how they may compare to costs. In the final section I attempt to draw some tentative conclusions and offer a recommendation.

Before turning to the costs and benefits of regulatory analysis, however, I have two initial observations to make. First, it will no doubt occur to readers that the same asymmetry that afflicts benefit-cost analysis of gov-ernment regulations or large-scale public investment projects also hinders my task here. Specifically, it is much more difficult to identify, much less quantify, the benefits of mandated regulatory analysis than it is the costs. This should bring a smile to the faces of those who have been prodded by interagency regulatory overseers (as I once was) to push ahead and quantify benefits, complaints about the difficulty of doing so notwithstanding.

My second observation is that the calculations of benefits and costs must always be incremental to some baseline. This baseline might be the status quo—if it is expected to continue in the absence of policy change—or it might be a new set of circumstances expected to evolve even in the face of inaction. Benefits and costs are measured as departures from this baseline state of the world. This observation is relevant to my task here for an important reason: there was regulatory analysis before EO 12291 and even before its predecessor, EO 12044. Thus if I were to confine my analysis to the former executive order alone, I would be forced to conclude that, in the case of several important regulatory agencies, there are no benefits or costs associated with it because it has changed very little.

Because this would make for a much less appetizing product, I am taking a slightly different tack here. Specifically, the benefits and costs to which I shall refer will, unless otherwise noted, be the results of regulatory analysis in general, rather than to efforts arising from EO 12291 alone. This assumption will enable me to consider the effects of analyses performed, say, by the Environmental Protection Agency or the Department of Health and Human Services, both of which were conducting important regulatory analyses well before EO 12291. For certain other agencies new to the game, the costs and benefits of regulatory analysis in general would be identical to those arising from EO 12291. With this housekeeping detail behind us, let us turn to a consideration of the costs and benefits of regulatory analysis.

THE COSTS OF REGULATORY ANALYSIS

Like the costs of pollution control or workplace or consumer safety, the costs of regulatory analysis have both direct and indirect components. The direct costs of regulatory analysis and oversight are those arising from the conduct of benefit-cost studies of both proposed and final regulations, the review of these studies by regulatory agency personnel (whether the studies are done intra- or extramurally), and the subsequent review and analysis of these studies by the Office of Information and Regulatory Affairs at the Office of Management and Budget. Finally, these direct costs would include any involvement of an interagency adjudicatory body (such as the Presidential Task Force on Regulatory Relief or one of the present administration's cabinet councils) called in to resolve a dispute between a regulatory agency and the regulatory overseers.

Although far from simple, the direct costs of regulatory analysis may lend themselves more to quantification than either indirect costs or benefits, both to be discussed below. For instance, consider the cost of preparing Regulatory Impact Analyses at either the Environmental Protection Agency or the Occupational Safety and Health Administration at the Department of Labor. At both agencies, these RIAs—or at least the individual cost and benefit analyses upon which the RIAs are eventually based—are generally done by outside contractors. And at both agencies, the cost of the analyses required to support a major proposed regulation under EO 12291 can vary substantially. These costs will depend upon the nature of the industry being regulated (costs may be more difficult to estimate in an industry with many heterogenous firms than in a small oligopolistic industry), the technological complexity of the alternatives being considered, and the nature of the benefits assessment associated with the proposed rule (generally, regulations protecting health are more expensive to analyze because the analysis often involves original epidemiological research).

How large is the variation in costs arising from RIAs? A reasonable estimate is that an intramurally or extramurally conducted RIA will range in cost from about $100,000 to several million dollars, including the cost of any underlying and more basic cost or benefit studies. If this latter figure seems high, keep in mind that under EO 12291 RIAs must accompany both proposed and final rules, with considerable changes between the two sometimes being required. In the case of a regulation like EPA's 1979 rule governing New Source Performance Standards for coal-fired electric utilities, both the preliminary and final cost analyses involved considerable expense modeling the coal market impacts associated with various alternatives being considered, exclusive of the cost of the benefits assessment or, at the very least, the exposure analysis that would be required for such a regulation today.

Thus I believe it is fair to say that we have already witnessed a number of major federal regulations for which all the required analyses have cost in excess of $1 million. In fact, one office within the Environmental Protection Agency has recently entered into a three-year contract with a consortium of consulting companies headed by a large Washington-based firm to analyze the agency's recent final regulations under the Resource Conservation and Recovery Act of 1976. If all the options in this contract are exercised, the total amount spent by this one office alone will come to about $25 million.[1] There would be additional expenditures on analyses, by, say, EPA's Office of Policy and Resource Management or its Office of Research and Development to determine total analytical costs at EPA for this one set of regulations.

Although examples can be found of such multimillion-dollar RIAs, they are presently the exception rather than the rule. Many RIAs (including underlying cost and/or benefit analyses) will cost much less than $1 million, and some may even fall short of the $100,000 mark I arbitrarily establish as a minimum. For present purposes, let us peg at $400,000 the cost of an RIA for a major rule.[2]

This figure would be much larger if I were to amortize each regulatory agency's annual research budget over the total number of regulations forthcoming each year. Such an attribution of costs would have some justification because almost all the basic research undertaken by regulatory agencies should be related in some way either to the evaluation of previous regulatory actions or to the development of information upon which future actions might be based. I have tried to confine my very rough estimates to costs that are directly linked to specific regulatory actions and analyses.

How many such analyses are performed each year? This, of course, depends upon regulatory actions initiated by the agencies, which in turn depends upon the regulatory zeal of the administration and on the authorizing legislation, which often creates deadlines for the issuance of regulations. That the present administration is less zealous than its predecessors should surprise no one. For instance, according to OIRA, the number of final regulations published in the *Federal Register* was 21 percent lower in 1981 than in a comparable period in 1980.[3] During this same period, according to OMB, the number of proposed regulations fell by one-third, from 4,979 to 3,317.[4] These figures refer to all regulations, however, the great majority of which are "minor" and for which RIAs are not required and are generally not performed.

It is possible to get some handle on "major" federal regulatory activity in the recent past. For instance, between mid-February 1981 and the end of the (calendar) year, 43 major proposed or final regulations were published in the *Federal Register*.[5] Of these, only 22 were accompanied by RIAs, the requirement having been waived in the other cases because the regulation was an emergency one or was subject to statutory deadline, because in OMB's view sufficient analysis had already been done, or because it was decided to conduct the analysis following the promulgation of the rule (it is unclear what good Regulatory Impact Analysis does when it follows the finalization of a major rule).

In a more recent and partially overlapping report,[6] OMB has cataloged major rules submitted to it for review under President Reagan's executive order. According to this report, between 17 February 1981 and 6 January 1983, OMB had received for review 104 major rules. Of these, 34 were submitted with no RIA and 70 included such an analysis. Piecing these two reports together, it would appear that about 50 major rules per year have been proposed or finalized by federal regulatory agencies in the nearly two years the Reagan administration has been in office. Of these, regulatory analyses have accompanied about 35 per year. This number is roughly in keeping with RIAs conducted in the Carter administration. For instance, the late Council on Wage and Price Stability reported in January 1981 that it had intervened in 31 proposed rulemakings in calendar year 1978.[7] Because COWPS was at that time the administration's principal regulatory oversight group, its figure can be accepted as an accurate reflection of regulatory activity.

Thus if an average RIA costs on the order of $400,000, we can estimate that this first component of the cost of Regulatory Impact Analysis is very roughly $14 million per year. This figure will obviously be much higher in years when expensive analyses, such as those pertaining to RCRA, are being done, although those will be exceptional cases. Also, RIA contracting expenses will be much higher as EPA and OSHA begin to reconsider such important and controversial standards as those governing exposures to lead in the workplace or those establishing maximum permissible concentrations of the so-called "criteria" air pollutants under section 109 of the Clean Air Act. Even when several such "supramajor" regulations are considered in a single year, total annual contracting expenses attributable to Regulatory Impact Analysis are unlikely to exceed $20 million.

There are other direct costs attributable to regulatory analysis. For instance, each regulatory agency invests many of its own resources in monitoring and managing even those RIAs that are contracted out. Suppose each agency devotes two person-years of staff time for in-house regulatory analysis to each major rule (clearly a generous assumption). With 25 to 40 major rules per year, this cost would amount to $2.5 to $4.0 million annually at $50,000 per person-year. Finally, regulatory analysis and oversight by OMB must be included in direct costs. Within OIRA I will assume that there are fifteen people working full time on the review of agency-prepared RIAs (a number which again I believe to be an upper bound). At $50,000 per person-year, this adds $750,000 to the direct cost of Regulatory Impact Analysis. Including time spent by interagency groups adjudicating disputes between, say, OMB and the line agencies might bring the combined OMB–White House oversight total to $1 million.

Thus combining the work done in-house by regulatory agencies and by their contractors with OMB–White House review and oversight efforts suggests that the direct cost of the regulatory analysis done under EO 12291 is on the order of $17.0–$25 million annually. Having offered up this appealing target, I hasten to add several caveats. First, it should be clear that this estimate is extremely rough. It is sensitive first to the number of RIAs prepared each year. Some regulatory analysis is done on the so-called "minor" regulations for which formal RIAs are not required. These would have to be included in any precise accounting of direct costs. If agencies try to circumvent requirements for regulatory analysis by "breaking up" major rules into several "minor" ones, RIA costs may fall. But because OMB can require RIAs for certain rules with less than a $100 million annual impact on the economy, and is unlikely to be fooled by such "unbundling," it is unlikely that the number of rules being analyzed at any one time will fall too much.

Second, my estimate is sensitive to the number of new regulations being proposed each year. Under a more regulatorily zealous administration, more proposed major rules would be forthcoming, and hence RIA costs would be greater. Next, let me again point out that I have concerned myself only with the impact analyses accompanying proposed and/or final rules. My estimate does not include the cost of paperwork management and reduction at OMB, the costs of preparing regulatory calendars or agendas, or other costs that might be reasonably associated with regulatory reform. Finally, I have ignored any increased expenditures in the private sector designed to influence the Regulatory Impact Analyses. I have done so in part because it would be impossible to determine the magnitude of these expenditures but also because firms will finance a good part of these costs out of money originally allocated to influence the regulatory process in other, more traditional ways. Thus these costs would not be true resource costs associated with the conduct of RIAs, but rather internal redistributions of funds within firms.

What can be said about the indirect costs associated with regulatory analysis? Only that they can take several different forms. Unfortunately, it is not possible to be more quantitative than that. The first of these indirect costs is that associated with the delays introduced by regulatory analysis. This requirement means that the rulemaking process is stretched out longer than it would otherwise be and that prospective regulatees must wait longer to learn of their fate. Of course, they are unlikely to object if they believe that regulatory analysis will tend to result in less onerous regulations.

Regulatory analysis and its oversight may also introduce costs in the form of uncertainty. Because there are more hoops for a rule to pass through, there are more places for changes to be made. Here, too, businesses and other regulatees are probably willing to live with this uncertainty because they view regulatory analysis and oversight as working to their advantage. But this is not always the case. For instance, OSHA and its regulatees had come to a truce on proposed standards governing the labeling of hazardous substances in the workplace when, to the chagrin of business, OMB interceded and attempted to reopen the rulemaking. Also, the virtues of regulatory analysis may not be obvious to the steel industry and other particulate emitters. As a result of EO 12291, they are now confronted with several carefully done benefit-cost studies that suggest that the relaxation of the NAAQS for particulates they sought may not be economically justified.

Indirect costs in two other areas might be associated with regulatory impact or benefit-cost analysis. For instance, Steven Kelman has argued that the attempt to quantify and value the outputs of regulatory actions "devalues" what are actually basic "rights."[8] Thus, Kelman might argue, there is an ethical cost to Regulatory Impact Analysis. This I find most unpersuasive, for at least two reasons. First, although there is certainly room for disagreement about the final mix of goods and services the federal government provides, most would agree with the way in which those decisions are made. Congress establishes overall limits on federal spending for a year, then that total is allocated across competing programs, ostensibly on the basis of the pros and cons (or benefits and costs) of those programs.

This approach is necessary, of course, because the federal budget is not sufficient to provide all the guns and all the butter we want—or, in this case, all the childhood health and nutrition programs and all the national defense. But the same is true of regulatory priorities, even though they are pursued not through the federal budget but by mandating compliance costs on individuals, state and local governments, and business regulatees. Resources directed to regulation are no different from those taxed away from individuals and used for direct federal spending—that is, they are limited. Thus there must be some way to compare regulatory priorities and ensure that resources are being devoted to their most productive uses. This is the raison d'être for Regulatory Impact Analysis. Far from devaluing rights, if conducted honestly Regulatory Impact Analysis may make it possible to maximize the "rights" accorded individuals through regulation, be they safe consumer products, clean air or water, a healthy workplace, or other outputs of the regulatory system. Thus I believe we can safely dismiss the notion of ethical costs to Regulatory Impact Analysis.

A final cost we might consider pertains not so much to Regulatory Impact Analysis itself as to its misuse. For if such analysis is used not to help make decisions on important regulatory matters but rather to justify decisions made on political or other grounds, another sort of cost will be incurred. It will take the form of public cynicism about any and all analytic efforts in government. Although such a cost may not lend itself to quantification, it would nevertheless be real. This is why—to take a purely hypothetical example—we must take benefit-cost analysis as seriously when it points to the tightening of, say, the air quality standard for particulates as we do when it points toward, say, the relaxation of a similar standard for carbon monoxide.

THE BENEFITS OF REGULATORY ANALYSIS

Technically, the benefits associated with regulatory analysis should be measured by individuals' willingness to pay. But because regulatory analysis does not trade in readily observable organized markets, willingness to pay is difficult to observe. In principle, however, it should not be hard to visualize. If, as a result of Regulatory Impact Analysis, dead-weight losses are avoided that would otherwise have been incurred, this is a benefit that can be measured by the size of the forestalled loss. An example would be the scaling back of a proposed environmental standard that had gone beyond the point at which marginal benefits were equal to marginal costs. Similarly, if analysis results in the recognition of even greater net benefits from a regulation than would otherwise have been the case, that, too, could be counted as a benefit of regulatory analysis.

Unfortunately, there have not been many attempts to review the effects of regulatory analysis on final rules. By far the most comprehensive effort has been that of the now defunct Council on Wage and Price Stability. In a 1981 report, COWPS reviewed thirty-one regulatory proceedings in which it had intervened in 1978, divided fairly evenly between the independent agencies typically regulating price and entry and the so-called social regulatory agencies having responsibility for environment, safety, or health.[9] COWPS is careful to point out that it is nearly impossible to determine why a proposed rule has been changed before being made final. Changes occur not only because of COWPS intervention but also because of comments from outside parties, agency personnel, political pressure, and other factors.

Nevertheless, COWPS was at least able to conclude that of the thirty-one rulemakings in which it intervened, there was "significant" improvement in the rule between its proposed and final form in eight cases, "moderate" improvement in nine cases, no improvement in seven cases, and no basis on which to judge in seven other cases for which no final rule had been promulgated at the time the report was written. Thus in seventeen of twenty-four instances some improvement was noted in the rulemaking process, with "improvement" meaning a movement toward a more economically efficient rule. Besides COWPS involvement, the report notes, other factors pointing toward improvements in proposed rules included follow-up White House staff prodding the regulatory agency and media coverage of the proposed rulemaking.[10]

Unfortunately, COWPS made no attempt to measure the efficiency gains between the proposed and final forms of the rules that were improved. Had it done so, we might have some idea of the benefits resulting from regulatory analysis and oversight.[11] Such improvements have been estimated for particular rulemakings, however. For instance, in his recent book on regulation, Lawrence J. White examines in some detail EPA's 1978 revision of the National Ambient Air Quality Standard for ozone and other photochemical oxidants. In that rulemaking, EPA was originally willing to relax the standard from 0.08 parts per million (ppm) to 0.10 ppm. After analyzing the costs and benefits of ozone control, President Carter's Regulatory Analysis Review Group suggested that a standard in the range of 0.14 to 0.16 ppm appeared more easily defensible. Nevertheless, RARG and the White House economists supporting it drew the line at a standard of 0.12 ppm and fought for it. To make a long story short, that is where the standard was finally set. Of this decision White writes, "There was a public perception that the EOP [Executive Office of the President] won a major victory when EPA moved from the 0.10 ppm standard proposed . . . to the 0.12 ppm standard promulgated in the final rule. It is far from clear that the RARG report or the EOP had any effect. . . . But, regardless of the reason for the change, the country will save between $1.0 billion and $3.8 billion per year, in perpetuity, starting in the mid-1980s."[12]

Is this alleged saving of $1–$3.8 billion (the difference in the annual cost of meeting a 0.12 ppm standard as opposed to a 0.10 ppm standard) a measure of the benefits of regulatory analysis in the ozone case? The answer is "no" for at least two reasons. First, as White points out, we cannot be sure that EPA relented and agreed to a standard of 0.12 ppm solely because of the analysis proffered by the RARG staffers. Second, and more important, the cost savings would overestimate the benefits of regulatory analysis, even if the change in the standard was the result entirely of regulatory analysis. From the cost savings would have to be subtracted any adverse health effects that would result from the additional 0.02 ppm exposure to ozone. These would be expected to arise from the 918,000 additional hours of exposure to "unhealthy" levels of ozone which the RARG group estimated would result from the relaxation.

These are not the only effects that would have to be netted out of cost savings before one could determine the benefits of regulatory analysis. Although RARG ignored such effects in its report, ozone and other photochemical oxidant pollution has also been linked to reductions in agricultural output, to impairment of visibility, and to certain materials damages.[13] If these potential health and other effects are not believed serious, one would tend to view the cost savings as an accurate measure of the benefits of regulatory analysis. If one assigned very large values to the health and other impairments likely to arise from the additional 0.02 ppm of atmospheric ozone, one might attribute little or no (or even negative) net benefits to the RARG intervention.

Other specific issues can be examined in an attempt to quantify the benefits of regulatory analysis. EPA's 1979–80 proposed revision of the NAAQS for carbon monoxide comes to mind, as does OSHA's workplace standards for both acrylonitrile and cotton dust. One might also scrutinize the Department of Health, Education, and Welfare's regulation governing access for the handicapped to public transportation systems. But similar problems in identifying benefits will arise in each case. Specifically, it will be impossible to pinpoint the effect of regulatory analysis and oversight on the rules as proposed, as well as on any changes in the rule between proposal and finalization. Moreover, if the final standard is less strict than that proposed originally—even if this change results entirely from regulatory analysis and oversight—one must net out of cost savings any health or other benefits associated with the stricter standard that will not arise with the weaker one. In summary, estimating the direct benefits of regulatory analysis is very difficult to do.[14]

In spite of the difficulties alluded to above, I do believe it is possible to speculate about the probable relationship between direct costs and benefits. Remember that I have estimated the costs of regulatory analysis at $17 to $25 million annually, based on about twenty-five major regulatory proceedings per year. These regulations will, by definition, impose annual compliance costs on the economy of at least $2.5 billion and perhaps as much as $25 billion (if a number of rules are truly major as in the case of ozone, hazardous waste disposal, asbestos standards, and so on). Thus if regulatory analysis and oversight result in no more than a 0.1 to a 1 percent annual cost saving when compared to total incremental compliance costs, it will pay for itself. In fact, it seems possible that $25 million could easily be saved by the careful analysis of a single important regulation.

Savings are particularly likely to result if the regulatory agencies take seriously the requirement in EO 12291 to consider a variety of alternatives to regulation. Consider for a moment the use of economic incentives such as effluent charges or marketable discharge permits in place of source-by-source discharge standards. Countless studies have shown the potential cost savings associated with the former as contrasted with the latter.[15] In one study, an incentives-based approach was shown capable of saving more than 90 percent of control costs while still ensuring that environmental goals were met.[16] Thus if regulatory analysis results in but one 25 percent cost saving on a $100 million major rule—a very distinct possibility, I would argue—it will have proved economically efficient.

I have yet to consider at least one very important indirect benefit of regulatory analysis and oversight. I refer to the improved understanding it fosters of the economic implications of federal regulatory activity. This understanding is shared by regulators themselves, members of the legislative, judicial, and executive branches, and the general public. I would argue that all these groups would know much less about regulation than they know now were it not for the development in the mid-1970s of a tradition of scrutinizing regulatory proposals, a tradition that has extended to the present and is currently embodied in EO 12291.

Consider for a moment the long-term benefits that might result from this heightened knowledge. First, by analyzing the costs and benefits of alternative approaches to regulation, it will be possible to improve resource allocation within the regulatory area. That is, the cost per person-hour of exposure to hazardous substances can be reduced, as can the cost per life saved resulting from safer highways or consumer products.

More important, I believe, is the possibility of improving resource allocation across the whole range of "off-" and "on-budget" government activities. We do not restrict our life-saving or health-enhancing activities to the regulatory sector alone. Some take place through the direct federal expenditures of the Department of Health and Human Services, the Department of Transportation, and other federal agencies. To the extent that analytical methods are employed to evaluate health and safety for these on-budget programs, as well as for regulatory programs, cost-effectiveness analysis can be greatly extended. Ultimately, it might be possible to ensure that the whole range of prenatal maternal health, childhood inoculations and nutrition, adult smoking prevention, and other spending programs are resulting in similar health outputs per dollar as regulatory programs designed to reduce air or water pollution, clean up the workplace, or protect consumers.

CONCLUSION

I have made a very rough attempt to assess the benefits and costs of mandatory Regulatory Impact Analysis, like that required in EO 12291 or its predecessors. Based on ballpark estimates of the numbers of major rules issued each year, the average costs associated with each such rule, and the manpower costs to regulatory agencies and OMB oversight groups, I concluded that between $17 million and $25 million was being spent each year on the conduct and review of Regulatory Impact Analyses. These costs will grow if and when such analyses are done in more detail, or when greater numbers of major regulations are forthcoming, perhaps in a subsequent administration.

It is very difficult to develop even ballpark estimates of benefits. In spite of a careful review of its 1978 regulatory interventions, COWPS was able to point only to instances when its analyses appeared to change proposed rules in the direction of increased economic efficiency. Although more information is available for specific regulations, even here it is hard to determine the benefits flowing from Regulatory Impact Analysis. Nevertheless, in view of the substantial annual economic impact of twenty-five or so major rules (at least $2.5 billion annually), I have suggested the great likelihood that Regulatory Impact Analysis will cover its cost, if not return it several times over. In fact, I argue, the entire annual cost of Regulatory Impact Analysis could easily be recouped on a single major rulemaking. This is especially likely if agency analysis or executive branch oversight suggests ways that economic incentives or other innovative approaches can supplement or supplant more traditional source-by-source regulation.

One final observation is in order. Regulatory analysis and especially oversight will generate direct and indirect benefits much more easily when regulations are published and available for all to see. Not only are published critiques of regulatory agency analyses more likely to influence the sophistication with which those analyses are conducted but much of the educational function of regulatory analysis is lost if citizens are unable to examine both an agency's supporting analysis and a constructive criticism of that analysis by the relevant oversight group.

This is one of the major deficiencies, to my mind, of the present administration's regulatory reform (relief?) program. Whereas in the past COWPS or RARG analyses were filed on the public record during the comment period, no such reviews are now available. This only reinforces the beliefs of some that it is political pressures rather than efficiency concerns that motivate OMB involvement in the regulatory process. Regulatory Impact Analysis is controversial enough as it is. It will not long survive if it comes to be viewed as a front for political shenanigans.

NOTES

1. Apparently, some part of this $25 million may be spent on analysis not directly related to cost or benefit estimates. Nevertheless, a good part of whatever money is eventually spent will go toward the development of information required under EO 12291. If all of the options on this contract are exercised, it would be the largest procurement for economic impact analysis in EPA's history.

2. This figure is higher than but not out of line with other estimates of the cost of regulatory analysis. See, for instance, the testimony of Milton J. Socolar, acting comptroller general of the United States, before the Committee on Governmental Affairs of the United States Senate, 23 June 1981. See also the Congressional Budget Office Cost Estimate of S. 1080, 28 October 1981 in Senate Committee on the Judiciary *Report to Accompany S. 1080*, 30 November 1981, pp. 174–75.

3. U.S. Office of Management and Budget, "Executive Order 12291 on Federal Regulation," p. 6.
4. Ibid.
5. Ibid., pp. 28–32.
6. U.S. Office of Management and Budget, "Major Rules Submitted for Review under E.O. 12291."
7. Hopkins, Lenard, Morrall, and Pinkston, "Review of the Regulatory Interventions," pp. 36–37.
8. Kelman, "Cost Benefit Analysis," pp. 33–40.
9. See U.S. Office of Management and Budget, "Major Rules."
10. Ibid., pp. 38–41.
11. It would be tempting to argue that this would be an "upper-bound" measure of benefits because these gains would be attributable not only to COWPS intervention but also to other factors mentioned above. Such an assumption would be incorrect, however. The fact that proposed rules were subject to COWPS scrutiny may well have influenced their form as originally proposed, as well as changes between proposal and finalization. Thus true benefits of COWPS analysis and intervention are unobservable.
12. White, *Reforming Regulation*, p. 69.
13. For a discussion of these effects, see U.S. Environmental Protection Agency, *Air Quality Criteria for Ozone and Other Photochemical Oxidants*.
14. This discussion raises another interesting point. According to current interpretations, the Clean Air Act, the Occupational Safety and Health Act, and certain other "social" regulatory statutes appear to prohibit benefit-cost comparisons in standard-setting. Rather, air quality and occupational health standards are to be set at levels that provide a margin of safety against adverse health effects. In view of this interpretation, one might ask how benefit-cost or other economic analyses could have any effect on the levels at which standards are set. If they can have no effect, are the benefits associated with RIAs not zero for these standards?

In fact, ambient standard-setting—either outdoors or indoors—is not such a simple matter. The set of studies linking indoor or outdoor pollutants to ill health never identify an agreed-upon threshold concentration. Some studies find adverse health effects appearing at certain levels yet other studies find no effects at considerably higher levels. In addition, regulatory agencies like EPA or OSHA have considerable latitude in determining which groups of individuals ought to be protected.

As a result of these complicating factors, regulatory agencies often set standards above levels at which at least some adverse health effects are believed to occur. For instance, EPA's proposed 1980 revision of the National Ambient Air Quality Standard for carbon monoxide would have left a number of individuals who suffer from hemolytic anemia unprotected against certain carbon monoxide–induced adverse health reactions. (See U.S. Council on Wage and Price Stability, "Environmental Protection Agency Proposed National Ambient Air Quality Standards for Carbon Monoxide," pp. 25–27.) Given the discretion in standard-setting which these uncertainties create, I believe it fair to say that benefit-cost analysis can be taken into account in standard-setting, if only in a sub rosa way. In other words, because a range of standards can be justified on health grounds alone, it is possible to find a health-based justification for a standard that is based on, or at least influenced by, benefit-cost considerations. Thus it is indeed possible for regulatory analyses to affect standard-setting and to generate benefits in the process.

15. For a recent collection of such studies, see Schelling et al., *Incentive Arrangements for Environmental Protection*.

16. Mathtech, Inc., *An Analysis of Alternative Policies for Attaining and Maintaining a Short-term NO_2 Standard*, pp. 5–23.

APPENDIX: TEXT OF
EXECUTIVE ORDER 12291*

By the authority vested in me as President by the Constitution and laws of the United States of America, and in order to reduce the burdens of existing and future regulations, increase agency accountability for regulatory actions, provide for presidential oversight of the regulatory process, minimize duplication and conflict of regulations, and insure well-reasoned regulations, it is hereby ordered as follows:

Section 1. *Definitions.* For the purposes of this Order:

(a) "Regulation" or "rule" means an agency statement of general applicability and future effect designed to implement, interpret, or prescribe law or policy or describing the procedure or practice requirements of an agency, but does not include:

(1) Administrative actions governed by the provisions of Sections 556 and 557 of Title 5 of the United States Code;

(2) Regulations issued with respect to a military or foreign affairs function of the United States; or

(3) Regulations related to agency organization, management, or personnel.

(b) "Major rule" means any regulation that is likely to result in:

(1) An annual effect on the economy of $100 million or more;

(2) A major increase in costs or prices for consumers, individual industries, Federal, State, or local government agencies, or geographic regions; or

(3) Significant adverse effects on competition, employment, investment, productivity, innovation, or on the ability of United States–based enterprises to compete with foreign-based enterprises in domestic or export markets.

(c) "Director" means the Director of the Office of Management and Budget.

(d) "Agency" means any authority of the United States that is an "agency" under 44 U.S.C. 3502(1), excluding those agencies specified in 44 U.S.C. 3502(10).

(e) "Task Force" means the Presidential Task Force on Regulatory Relief.

Sec. 2. *General Requirements.* In promulgating new regulations, reviewing existing regulations, and developing legislative proposals concerning regulation, all agencies, to the extent permitted by law, shall adhere to the following requirements:

(a) Administrative decisions shall be based on adequate information concerning the need for and consequences of proposed government action;

(b) Regulatory action shall not be undertaken unless the potential benefits to society for the regulation outweigh the potential costs to society;

(c) Regulatory objectives shall be chosen to maximize the net benefits to society;

(d) Among alternative approaches to any given regulatory objective, the alternative involving the least net cost to society shall be chosen; and

(e) Agencies shall set regulatory priorities with the aim of maximizing the

Federal Register 46 (19 February 1981): 13193–98.

aggregate net benefits to society, taking into account the condition of the particular industries affected by regulations, the condition of the national economy, and other regulatory actions contemplated for the future.

Sec. 3. *Regulatory Impact Analysis and Review.*

(a) In order to implement Section 2 of this Order, each agency shall, in connection with every major rule, prepare, and to the extent permitted by law consider, a Regulatory Impact Analysis. Such Analyses may be combined with any Regulatory Flexibility Analyses performed under 5 U.S.C. 603 and 604.

(b) Each agency shall initially determine whether a rule it intends to propose or to issue is a major rule, *provided that,* the Director, subject to the direction of the Task Force, shall have authority, in accordance with Sections 1(b) and 2 of this Order, to prescribe criteria for making such determinations, to order a rule to be treated as a major rule, and to require any set of related rules to be considered together as a major rule.

(c) Except as provided in Section 8 of this Order, agencies shall prepare Regulatory Impact Analyses of major rules and transmit them, along with all notices of proposed rulemaking and all final rules, to the Director as follows:

(1) If no notice of proposed rulemaking is to be published for a proposed major rule that is not an emergency rule, the agency shall prepare only a final Regulatory Impact Analysis, which shall be transmitted, along with the proposed rule, to the Director at least 60 days prior to the publication of the major rule as a final rule;

(2) With respect to all other major rules, the agency shall prepare a preliminary Regulatory Impact Analysis, which shall be transmitted, along with a notice of proposed rulemaking, to the Director at least 60 days prior to the publication of a notice of proposed rulemaking, and a final Regulatory Impact Analysis, which shall be transmitted along with the final rule at least 30 days prior to the publication of the major rule as a final rule;

(3) For all rules other than major rules, agencies shall submit to the Director, at least 10 days prior to publication, every notice of proposed rulemaking and final rule.

(d) To permit each proposed major rule to be analyzed in light of the requirements stated in Section 2 of this Order, each preliminary and final Regulatory Impact Analysis shall contain the following information:

(1) A description of the potential benefits of the rule, including any beneficial effects that cannot be quantified in monetary terms, and the identification of those likely to receive the benefits;

(2) A description of the potential costs of the rule, including any adverse effects that cannot be quantified in monetary terms, and the identification of those likely to bear the costs;

(3) A determination of the potential net benefits of the rule, including an evaluation of effects that cannot be quantified in monetary terms;

(4) A description of alternative approaches that could substantially achieve the same regulatory goal at lower cost, together with an analysis of this potential benefit and costs and a brief explanation of the legal reasons why such alternatives, if proposed, could not be adopted; and

(5) Unless covered by the description required under paragraph (4) of this subsection, an explanation of any legal reasons why the rule cannot be based on the requirements set forth in Section 2 of this Order.

(e) (1) The Director, subject to the direction of the Task Force, which shall resolve any issues raised under this Order or ensure that they are presented to the President, is authorized to review any preliminary or final Regulatory Impact Analysis, notice of proposed rulemaking, or final rule based on the requirements of this Order.

(2) The Director shall be deemed to have concluded review unless the Director advises an agency to the contrary under subsection (f) of this Section:

(A) Within 60 days of a submission under subsection (c)(1) or a submission of a preliminary Regulatory Impact Analysis or notice of proposed rulemaking under subsection (c)(2);

(B) Within 30 days of the submission of a final Regulatory Impact Analysis and a final rule under subsection (c)(2); and

(C) Within 10 days of the submission of a notice of proposed rulemaking or final rule under subsection (c)(3).

(f) (1) Upon the request of the Director, an agency shall consult with the Director concerning the review of a preliminary Regulatory Impact Analysis or notice of proposed rulemaking under this Order, and shall, subject to Section 8(a)(2) of this Order, refrain from publishing its preliminary Regulatory Impact Analysis or notice of proposed rulemaking until such review is concluded.

(2) Upon receiving notice that the Director intends to submit views with respect to any final Regulatory Impact Analysis or final rule, the agency shall, subject to Section 8(a)(2) of this Order, refrain from publishing its final Regulatory Impact Analysis or final rule until the agency has responded to the Director's views, and incorporated those views and the agency's response in the rulemaking file.

(3) Nothing in this subsection shall be construed as displacing the agencies' responsibilities delegated by law.

(g) For every rule for which an agency publishes a notice of proposed rule-making, the agency shall include in its notice:

(1) A brief statement setting forth the agency's initial determination whether the proposed rule is a major rule, together with the reasons underlying that determination; and

(2) For each proposed major rule, a brief summary of the agency's preliminary Regulatory Impact Analysis.

(h) Agencies shall make their preliminary and final Regulatory Impact Analyses available to the public.

(i) Agencies shall initiate reviews of currently effective rules in accordance with the purposes of this Order, and perform Regulatory Impact Analyses of currently effective major rules. The Director, subject to the direction of the Task Force, may designate currently effective rules for review in accordance with this Order, and establish schedules for reviews and Analyses under this Order.

Sec. 4. *Regulatory Review.* Before approving any final major rule, each agency shall:

(a) Make a determination that the regulation is clearly within the authority delegated by law and consistent with congressional intent, and include in the Federal Register at the time of promulgation a memorandum of law supporting that determination.

(b) Make a determination that the factual conclusions upon which the rule is based have substantial support in the agency record, viewed as a whole, with full attention to public comments in general and the comments of persons directly affected by the rule in particular.

Sec. 5. *Regulatory Agendas.*

(a) Each agency shall publish, in October and April of each year, an agenda of proposed regulations that the agency has issued or expects to issue, and currently effective rules that are under agency review pursuant to this Order. These agendas may be incorporated with the agendas published under 5 U.S.C. 602, and must contain at the minimum:

(1) A summary of the nature of each major rule being considered, the objectives and legal basis for the issuance of the rule, and an approximate schedule for completing action on any major rule for which the agency has issued a notice of proposed rulemaking;

(2) The name and telephone number of a knowledgeable agency official for each item on the agenda; and

(3) A list of existing regulations to be reviewed under the terms of this Order, and a brief discussion of each such regulation.

(b) The Director, subject to the direction of the Task Force, may, to the extent permitted by law:

(1) Require agencies to provide additional information in an agenda; and

(2) Require publication of the agenda in any form.

Sec. 6. *The Task Force and Office of Management and Budget.*

(a) To the extent permitted by law, the Director shall have authority, subject to the direction of the Task Force, to:

(1) Designate any proposed or existing rule as a major rule in accordance with Section 1(b) of this Order;

(2) Prepare and promulgate uniform standards for the identification of major rules and the development of Regulatory Impact Analyses;

(3) Require an agency to obtain and evaluate, in connection with a regulation, any additional relevant data from any appropriate source;

(4) Waive the requirements of Sections 3, 4, or 7 of this Order with respect to any proposed or existing major rule;

(5) Identify duplicative, overlapping and conflicting rules, existing or proposed, and existing or proposed rules that are inconsistent with the policies underlying statutes governing agencies other than the issuing agency or with the purposes of this Order, and, in each such case, require appropriate interagency consultation to minimize or eliminate such duplication, overlap, or conflict;

(6) Develop procedures for estimating the annual benefits and costs of agency regulations, on both an aggregate and economic or industrial sector basis, for purposes of compiling a regulatory budget;

(7) In consultation with interested agencies, prepare for consideration by the President recommendations for changes in the agencies' statutes; and

(8) Monitor agency compliance with the requirements of this Order and advise the President with respect to such compliance.

(b) The Director, subject to the direction of the Task Force, is authorized to establish procedures for the performance of all functions vested in the Director by this Order. The Director shall take appropriate steps to coordinate the implementation of the analysis, transmittal, review, and clearance provisions of this Order with the authorities and requirements provided for or imposed upon the Director and agencies under the Regulatory Flexibility Act, 5 U.S.C. 601 *et seq.*, and the Paperwork Reduction Plan Act of 1980, 44 U.S.C. 3501 *et seq.*

Sec. 7. *Pending Regulations.*

(a) To the extent necessary to permit reconsideration in accordance with this Order, agencies shall, except as provided in Section 8 of this Order, suspend or postpone the effective dates of all major rules that they have promulgated in final form as of the date of this Order, but that have not yet become effective, excluding:

(1) Major rules that cannot legally be postponed or suspended;

(2) Major rules that, for good cause, ought to become effective as final rules without reconsideration. Agencies shall prepare, in accordance with Section 3 of this Order, a final Regulatory Impact Analysis for each major rule that they suspend or postpone.

(b) Agencies shall report to the Director no later than 15 days prior to the effective date of any rule that the agency has promulgated in final form as of the date of this Order, and that has not yet become effective, and that will not be reconsidered under subsection (a) of this Section:

(1) That the rule is excepted from reconsideration under subsection (a), including a brief statement of the legal or other reasons for that determination; or

(2) That the rule is not a major rule.

(c) The Director, subject to the direction of the Task Force, is authorized, to the extent permitted by law, to:

(1) Require reconsideration, in accordance with this Order, of any major rule that an agency has issued in final form as of the date of this Order and that has not become effective; and

(2) Designate a rule that an agency has issued in final form as of the date of this Order and that has not yet become effective as a major rule in accordance with Section 1(b) of this Order.

(d) Agencies may, in accordance with the Administrative Procedure Act and other applicable statutes, permit major rules that they have issued in final form as of the date of this Order, and that have not yet become effective, to take effect as interim rules while they are being reconsidered in accordance with this Order, *provided that,* agencies shall report to the Director, no later than 15 days before any such rule is proposed to take effect as an interim rule, that the rule should appropriately take effect as an interim rule while the rule is under reconsideration.

(e) Except as provided in Section 8 of this Order, agencies shall, to the extent permitted by law, refrain from promulgating as a final rule any proposed major rule that has been published or issued as of the date of this Order until a final Regulatory Impact Analysis, in accordance with Section 3 of this Order, has been prepared for the proposed major rule.

(f) Agencies shall report to the Director, no later than 30 days prior to promulgating as a final rule any proposed rule that the agency has published or issued as of the date of this Order and that has not been considered under the terms of this Order:

(1) That the rule cannot legally be considered in accordance with this Order, together with a brief explanation of the legal reasons barring such consideration; or

(2) That the rule is not a major rule, in which case the agency shall submit to the Director a copy of the proposed rule.

(g) The Director, subject to the direction of the Task Force, is authorized, to the extent permitted by law, to:

(1) Require consideration, in accordance with this Order, of any proposed major rule that the agency has published or issued as of the date of this Order; and

(2) Designate a proposed rule that an agency has published or issued as of the date of this Order, as a major rule in accordance with Section 1(b) of this Order.

(h) The Director shall be deemed to have determined that an agency's report to the Director under subsections (b), (d), or (f) of this Section is consistent with the purposes of this Order, unless the Director advises the agency to the contrary:

(1) Within 15 days of its report, in the case of any report under subsections (b) or (d); or

(2) Within 30 days of its report, in the case of any report under subsection (f).

(i) This Section does not supersede the President's Memorandum of January 29, 1981, entitled "Postponement of Pending Regulations", which shall remain in effect until March 30, 1981.

(j) In complying with this Section, agencies shall comply with all applicable provisions of the Administrative Procedure Act, and with any other procedural requirements made applicable to the agencies by other statutes.

Sec. 8. *Exemptions.*

(a) The procedures prescribed by this Order shall not apply to:

(1) Any regulation that responds to an emergency situation, *provided that,* any such regulation shall be reported to the Director as soon as is practicable, the agency shall publish in the Federal Register a statement of the reasons why it is impracticable for the agency to follow the procedures of this Order with respect to such a rule, and the agency shall prepare and transmit as soon as is practicable a Regulatory Impact Analysis of any such major rule; and

(2) Any regulation for which consideration or reconsideration under the terms of this Order would conflict with deadlines imposed by statute or by judicial order, *provided that,* any such regulation shall be reported to the Director together with a brief explanation of the conflict, the agency shall publish in the Federal Register a statement of the reasons why it is impracticable for the agency to follow the procedures of this Order with respect to such a rule, and the agency, in consultation with the Director, shall adhere to the requirements of this Order to the extent permitted by statutory or judicial deadlines.

(b) The Director, subject to the direction of the Task Force, may, in accordance with the purposes of this Order, exempt any class or category of regulations from any or all requirements of this Order.

Sec. 9. *Judicial Review.* This Order is intended only to improve the internal management of the Federal government, and is not intended to create any right or benefit, substantive or procedural, enforceable at law by a party against the United States, its agencies, its officers or any person. The determinations made by agencies under Section 4 of this Order, and any Regulatory Impact Analyses for any rule, shall be made part of the whole record of agency action in connection with the rule.

Sec. 10. *Revocations.* Executive Orders No. 12044, as amended, and No. 12174 are revoked.

BIBLIOGRAPHY

Ackerman, Bruce A., and William T. Hassler. *Clean Coal/Dirty Air: Or How the Clean Air Act Became a Multibillion-Dollar Bail-Out for High-Sulfur Coal Producers and What Should Be Done About It.* New Haven: Yale University Press, 1981.

American Enterprise Institute for Public Policy Research. "Major Regulatory Initiatives during 1981." Working paper No. 19. Washington, D.C., 13 May 1982.

————. "Major Regulatory Initiatives during 1981." Washington, D.C., 9 December 1982.

Andrews, Richard N. L. *Environmental Policy and Administrative Change: Implementation of the National Environmental Policy Act.* Lexington, Mass.: Lexington Books, 1976.

————. "NEPA in Practice: Environmental Policy or Administrative Reform?" *Environmental Law Reporter* 6 (March 1976): 50001–9.

Arrow, K. J., and R. C. Lind. "Uncertainty and the Evaluation of Public Investment Decisions." *American Economic Review* 60 (1970): 364–78.

Arthur, W. B. "The Economics of Risk to Life." *American Economic Review* 71 (1981): 54–64.

Ashby, Eric, and Mary Anderson. *The Politics of Clean Air.* Oxford: Clarendon Press, 1981.

Bailey, Martin J. *Reducing Risks to Life: Measurement of the Benefits.* Washington, D.C.: American Enterprise Institute for Public Policy Research, 1980.

————. "Risks, Costs and Benefits of Fluorocarbon Regulation." *American Economic Review* 72 (1982): 247–50.

Baram, Michael S. "Cost-Benefit Analysis: An Inadequate Basis for Health, Safety and Environmental Regulatory Decisionmaking." *Ecology Law Quarterly* 8 (1980): 473–531.

Bardach, Eugene, and R. A. Kagan. *Social Regulation: Strategies for Reform.* San Francisco: Institute for Contemporary Studies, 1982.

Bell, Frederick W., and E. Ray Canterbery. *An Assessment of the Economic Benefits Which Will Accrue to Commercial and Recreational Fisheries from Incremental Improvements in the Water Quality of Coastal Waters.* Tallahassee: Florida State University, Department of Economics, 1975.

Bishop, R. C., and T. A. Heberlein. "Measuring Values of Extramarket Goods: Are Indirect Measures Biased?" *American Journal of Agricultural Economics* 61 (1979): 926–30.

Blomquist, Glenn. "The Value of Human Life: An Empirical Perspective." *Economic Inquiry* 19 (January 1981): 157–64.

Bower, B. T. "Studies of Residuals Management in Industry." In E. S. Mills, ed., *Economic Analysis of Environmental Problems.* University–National Bureau Conference Series 26. New York: Columbia University Press, 1975.

Bradford, David F. "Benefit-Cost Analysis and Demand Curves for Public Goods." *Kyklos* 23 (1970): 1145–59.

Broder, I. E., and J. M. Morrall. "The Economic Basis for OSHA's and EPA's General Carcinogen Regulations." In Richard Zeckhauser, ed., *What Role for Government?* Durham: Duke University Press, 1982.

Brookshire, D. S., M. Thayer, W. D. Schulze, and R. C. d'Arge. "Valuing Public Goods: A Comparison of Survey and Hedonic Approaches." *American Economic Review* 72 (1982): 165–77.

Brown, James, and Harvey Rosen. "On the Estimation of Structural Hedonic Price Models." *Econometrica* 50 (1982): 765–68.

Calvert Cliffs Coordinating Committee v. AEC, 449 F.2d 1109, (D.C. Circuit 1971).

Cannon, Lou. *Reagan.* New York: G. P. Putnam's Sons, 1982.

Chappie, Mike, and Lester B. Lave. "The Health Effects of Air Pollution: A Reanalysis." *Journal of Urban Economics* 12 (1982): 346–76.

Clark, Timothy B., Marvin H. Kosters, and James C. Miller III. *Reforming Regulation.* Washington, D.C.: American Enterprise Institute for Public Policy Research, 1980.

Cohon, Jahred L. *Multiobjective Programming and Planning.* New York: Academic Press, 1978.

Conservation Foundation. *State of the Environment, 1982.* Washington, D.C.: Conservation Foundation, 1982.

Costle, Douglas. "Bright Light in the Wrong Place: The Limits of Benefit-Cost Analysis in Environmental Regulation." Paper presented at the Conference on Benefit-Cost Analysis in Environmental Regulation, Chicago, 15 October 1980.

Crandall, Robert W. *Controlling Industrial Pollution: The Economics and Politics of Clean Air.* Washington, D.C.: Brookings Institution, 1983.

————. "The Use of Environmental Policy to Reduce Economic Growth in the Sun Belt: The Role of Electric Utility Rates." Paper presented at a Conference on Public Utility Regulation, Rutgers University, April 1982, in Michael Crew, ed., *Regulatory Reform and Public Utilities*, pp. 125–40. Lexington, Mass.: D. C. Heath, 1982.

Crandall, Robert W., and Lester Lave, eds. *The Scientific Basis of Health and Safety Regulation.* Washington, D.C.: Brookings Institution, 1981.

Crandall, Robert W., and Paul R. Portney. "The Environmental Protection Agency in the Reagan Administration." In Paul R. Portney, ed., *Natural Resources and the Environment: The Reagan Approach.* Washington, D.C.: Urban Institute, forthcoming.

Dales, J. H. *Pollution, Property and Prices.* Toronto: University of Toronto Press, 1968.

Dasgupta, Partha, Stephen Marglin, and A. K. Sen. *Guidelines for Project Evaluation.* New York: United Nations, 1972.

Davidson, Paul, F. Gerald Adams, and Joseph J. Seneca. "The Social Value of Water Recreational Facilities Resulting from an Improvement in Water Quality: The Delaware Estuary." In A. V. Kneese and S. G. Smith, eds., *Water Research.* Baltimore: Johns Hopkins University Press, 1966.

Davies, J. Clarence III, and Barbara S. Davies. *The Politics of Pollution*. 2d ed. Indianapolis: Pegasus, 1975.

Desvousges, William H., V. Kerry Smith, and Matthew P. McGivney. *A Comparison of Alternative Approaches for Estimating Recreation and Related Benefits of Water Quality Improvements*. Environmental Benefits Analysis Series. Washington, D.C.: U.S. Environmental Protection Agency, 1983.

Dorfman, Robert. "Forty Years of Cost-Benefit Analysis." Discussion Paper No. 498. Harvard Institute of Economic Research, August 1976.

————, ed. *Measuring Benefits of Government Investments*. Washington, D.C.: Brookings Institution, 1965.

Dorfman, Robert, and Nancy S. Dorfman, eds. *Economics of the Environment*. New York: Norton, 1972.

Eads, George. "White House Oversight of Executive Branch Regulation." In Eugene Bardach and R. A. Kagan, *Social Regulation: Strategies for Reform*. San Francisco: Institute for Contemporary Studies, 1982.

Eads, George, and Michael Fix. *Relief, Not Reform: The Reagan Regulatory Strategy*. Washington, D.C.: Urban Institute, 1984.

Eckstein, Otto. *Water-Resource Development: The Economics of Project Evaluation*. Cambridge, Mass.: Harvard University Press, 1958.

Environmental Law Institute. "Cost-Benefit Analysis and Environmental, Health and Safety Regulation: An Overview of the Agencies and Legislation." Washington, D.C., 1980.

"EPA's High Risk Carcinogen Policy." *Science* 218 (1982): 975–78.

Executive Order 12044. "Improving Government Regulations." *Federal Register* 43 (1978): 12661–70.

Executive Order 12291. *Federal Register* 46 (1981): 13193–98.

Feagans, T. B., and W. F. Biller. "A General Method for Assessing Health Risks Associated with Primary National Quality Standards." U.S. Environmental Protection Agency, Research Triangle Park, N.C., 1981.

————. "Assessing the Health Risks Associated with Air Quality Standards." *Environmental Professional* 3 (1981): 235–48.

Feenberg, Daniel, and Edwin S. Mills. *Measuring the Benefits of Water Pollution Abatement*. New York: Academic Press, 1980.

Feiveson, Harold A., Frank W. Sinden, and Robert H. Socolow. *Boundaries of Analysis: An Inquiry into the Tocks Island Controversy*. Cambridge, Mass.: Ballinger, 1976.

Feldstein, Martin S., and Michael Rothschild. "Towards an Economic Theory of Replacement Investment." *Econometrica* 42 (May 1974): 393–423.

Ferland, Kathey A. "Benefit-Cost Analysis in Environmental Decision-Making: A Case Study of the Implementation of E.O. 12291 in the Environmental Protection Agency." Master's thesis, University of North Carolina, 1983.

Field, R. I. "Patterns in the Laws on Health Risks." *Journal of Policy Analysis and Management* 1 (1982): 257–60.

Fischoff, Bernard R., Paul Solvic, and Sarah Lichtenstein. "Weighing the Risks." *Environment* 21 (May 1979): 17–38.

Fisher, Ann. "The Scientific Bases for Relating Health Effects to Exposure Levels." *Environmental Impact Assessment Review* 3 (March 1982): 27–42.

Fisher, Anthony C. "Environmental Externalities and the Arrow-Lind Public Investment Theorem." *American Economic Review* 63 (1973): 722–25.

Fisher, Anthony C., John V. Krutilla, and Charles J. Cicchetti. "The Economics of Environmental Protection." *American Economic Review* 63 (1972): 605–19.

Fisher, Anthony C., and V. Kerry Smith. "Economic Evaluation of Energy's Environmental Costs with Special Reference to Air Pollution." *Annual Review of Energy* 7 (1982): 1–35.

Freeman, A. Myrick III. *Air and Water Pollution Control: A Benefit-Cost Assessment*. New York: John Wiley, 1982.

———. "Air and Water Pollution Policy." In Paul Portney, ed., *Current Issues in U.S. Environmental Policy*. Baltimore: Johns Hopkins University Press, 1978.

———. *The Benefits of Environmental Improvement: Theory and Practice*. Baltimore: Johns Hopkins University Press, 1979.

———. "Equity, Efficiency, and Discounting." *Futures* 9 (October 1977): 28–29.

———. "The Health Implications of Residuals Discharges: A Methodological Overview." In V. Kerry Smith and John V. Krutilla, eds., *Explorations in Natural Resource Economics*. Baltimore: Johns Hopkins University Press, 1982.

Fuller, Dan Alan. "Steam Electric Generation under Residual Emission Constraints: A Cost Function Approach Incorporating Perceptions of State Enforcement Activity." Ph.D. dissertation, University of North Carolina at Chapel Hill, 1983.

Gallagher, David R., and V. Kerry Smith. "Measuring Values for Environmental Resources under Uncertainty." Chapel Hill: University of North Carolina, 1982.

Gerking, Shelby, and William D. Schulze. "What Do We Know about Benefits of Reduced Mortality from Air Pollution Control?" *American Economic Review* 71 (1981): 228–34.

Gollop, Frank M., and Mark J. Roberts. "Environmental Regulations and Productivity Growth: The Case of Fossil-fueled Electric Power Generation." *Journal of Political Economy* 91 (1983): 654–74.

Graham, John D., and James V. Vaupel. "Value of a Life: What Difference Does It Make." *Risk Analysis* 1 (March 1981): 89–95.

Gramlich, Frederick W. "The Demand for Clean Water: The Case of the Charles River." *National Tax Journal* 30 (1977): 183–94.

Hahn, Robert W., and Roger G. Noll. "Tradable Air Pollution Permits in the Overall Regulatory System: Problems of Regulatory Interactions." California Institute of Technology, 1982.

Harrington, Winston, and Alan J. Krupnick. "Stationary Source Pollution Policy and Choices for Reform." In H. M. Peskin, P. R. Portney, and A. V. Kneese, eds., *Environmental Regulation and the U.S. Economy*. Baltimore: Johns Hopkins University Press, 1981.

Haveman, Robert H., and Gregory B. Christiansen. "Environmental Regulations and Productivity Growth." In H. M. Peskin, P. R. Portney, and A. V. Kneese, eds., *Environmental Regulation and the U.S. Economy*. Baltimore: Johns Hopkins University Press, 1981.

Haveman, Robert, and Julius Margolis. *Public Expenditures and Policy Analysis*. Chicago: Markham, 1970.

Heintz, H. T., A. Hershaft, and G. C. Horak. "National Damages of Air and Water

Pollution." Report submitted to the U.S. Environmental Protection Agency, 1976.

Hopkins, Thomas D. "E.O. 12291 and OMB Regulatory Impact Analysis Guidance." Paper presented at U.S. Department of Transportation Seminar, Washington, D.C., 22 April 1982.

Hopkins, Thomas D., Thomas Lenard, John Morrall III, and Elizabeth Pinkston. "A Review of the Regulatory Interventions of the Council on Wage and Price Stability, 1974–1980." January 1981.

Jasonoff, Sheila. "Negotiation or Cost-Benefit Analysis: A Middle Road for U.S. Policy?" *Environmental Forum* 2 (1983): 37–43.

Jones, Charles O. *Clean Air.* Pittsburgh: University of Pittsburgh Press, 1975.

Jones-Lee, Michael W. "The Value of Changes in the Probability of Death or Injury." *Journal of Political Economy* 82 (1974): 835–49.

Jordan, Bruce, Harvey Richmond, and Thomas McCurdy. "Regulatory Perspectives on the Use of Scientific Information in Air Quality Standard Setting." Paper presented at the annual meeting of the American Association for the Advancement of Science, Eugene, Ore., 1981.

Just, Richard, Darrell L. Hueth, and Andrew Schmitz. *Applied Welfare Economics and Public Policy.* Englewood Cliffs, N.J.: Prentice-Hall, 1982.

Kapp, K. W. *Social Costs of Private Enterprise.* Cambridge, Mass.: Harvard University Press, 1950.

Kelman, Steven. "Cost-Benefit Analysis: An Ethical Critique." *Regulation* 5 (January–February 1981): 33–40.

———. "Economists and the Environmental Muddle." *Public Interest* 64 (1981): 12–16.

Kneese, Allen V., Robert Ayres, and Ralph d'Arge. *Economics and the Environment: A Materials Balance Approach.* Baltimore: Johns Hopkins University Press, 1970.

Kneese, Allen V., and Blair T. Bower. *Managing Water Quality: Economics, Technology, and Institutions.* Baltimore: Johns Hopkins University Press, 1968.

Krupnick, Alan J., Wesley Magat, and Winston Harrington. "Understanding Regulatory Decision-Making: An Econometric Approach." *Policy Studies Journal* 11 (1982): 44–54.

Krutilla, John V. "Conservation Reconsidered." *American Economic Review* 46 (1967): 777–86.

———. "Welfare Implications of Benefit Cost Analysis." *Journal of Political Economy* 69 (1961): 226–35.

Krutilla, John V., and Otto Eckstein. *Multiple Purpose River Development: Studies in Applied Economic Analysis.* Baltimore: Johns Hopkins University Press, 1958.

Krutilla, John V., and Anthony C. Fisher. *The Economics of Natural Environments.* Baltimore: Johns Hopkins University Press, 1975.

Latin, H. A. "The 'Significance' of Toxic Health Risks: An Essay on Legal Decision-making under Uncertainty." *Ecology Law Quarterly* 10 (1982): 339–95.

Lave, Lester B. *Strategy of Social Regulation: Decision Framework for Policy.* Washington, D.C.: Brookings Institution, 1981.

Lave, Lester B., and Eugene P. Seskin. *Air Pollution and Human Health.* Baltimore: Johns Hopkins University Press, 1977.

Levin, Michael H. "Getting There: Implementing the Bubble Policy." In Eugene
    Bardach and Robert A. Kagan, eds., *Social Regulation: Strategies for Reform*.
    San Francisco: Institute for Contemporary Studies, 1982.
Lind, Robert C. "A Primer on the Major Issues Relating to the Discount Rate for
    Evaluating National Energy Policy." In Robert C. Lind, ed., *Discounting for
    Time and Risk in Energy Policy*. Baltimore: Johns Hopkins University Press,
    1982.
Linnerooth, Joanne. "The Value of Human Life: A Review of the Models." *Eco-
    nomic Enquiry* 17 (1979): 52–74.
Liroff, Richard A. *Air Pollution Offsets: Trading, Selling and Banking*. Washing-
    ton, D.C.: Conservation Foundation, 1980.
Litai, D., D. C. Lanning, and N. C. Rasmussen. "The Public Perception of Risk."
    Paper presented at the International Workshop on Analysis of Actual vs. Per-
    ceived Risks, National Academy of Science, Washington, D.C., June 1981.
Little, I. M. D. *A Critique of Welfare Economics*. Oxford: Oxford University Press,
    1950.
Little, I. M. D., and J. A. Mirrlees. *Manual of Industrial Project Analysis in
    Developing Countries*. Paris: Organization for Economic Cooperation and De-
    velopment, 1969.
Maass, Arthur. "Benefit-Cost Analysis: Its Relevance to Public Investment Deci-
    sions." *Quarterly Journal of Economics* 80 (1966): 208–26.
_____. "Public Investment Planning in the United States: Analysis and Critique."
    Public Policy 18 (1970): 211–43.
Maass, Arthur, et al., *Design of Water Resource Systems*. Cambridge, Mass.:
    Harvard University Press, 1962.
McKean, Roland. "Enforcement Costs in Environmental and Safety Regulation."
    Policy Analysis 6 (1980): 269–89.
MaCrae, Duncan. *The Social Function of Social Science*. New Haven: Yale Univer-
    sity Press, 1976.
Magat, Wesley A., ed. *Reform of Environmental Regulation*. Cambridge, Mass.:
    Ballinger, 1982.
Major, David. *Multiobjective Water Resources Planning*. Water Resources Mono-
    graph No. 4. Washington, D.C.: American Geophysical Union, 1977.
Maloney, M. T., and Bruce Yandle. "Bubbles and Efficiency: Cleaner Air at Lower
    Cost." *Regulation* 4 (May–June 1980): 49–52.
Manuel, Ernest H., Jr., Robert L. Horst, Jr., Kathleen M. Brennan, William N.
    Lanen, Marcus C. Duff, and Judith K. Tapiero. "Benefits Analysis of the
    Alternative Secondary National Ambient Air Quality Standards for Sulfur Di-
    oxide and Total Suspended Particulates." U.S. EPA Contract No. 68-02-3392.
    Research Triangle Park, N.C., August 1982.
Mathtech, Inc. "An Analysis of Alternative Policies for Attaining and Maintaining a
    Short-term NO_2 Standard." Prepared for EPA, the Council on Environmental
    Quality, and the Council of Economic Advisers, 1979, pp. 5–23.
Meidema, Allen. "Factor Demand and Particulate Emission Control Regulations:
    The Case of Steam Electric Power Plants." Ph.D. dissertation, North Carolina
    State University, 1974.
Mendelsohn, Robert, and Guy Orcutt. "An Empirical Analysis of Air Pollution

Dose-Response Curves." *Journal of Environmental Economics and Management* 6 (1979): 95–106.

Miller, James C. III, and Bruce Yandle. *Benefit-Cost Analysis of Social Regulation.* Washington, D.C.: American Enterprise Institute for Public Policy Research, 1979.

Mishan, Ezra. *Cost-Benefit Analysis.* London: Allen & Unwin, 1975.

————. *Cost-Benefit Analysis of Social Decisions.* New York: Praeger, 1972.

————. *Economics for Social Decisions: Elements of Cost-Benefit Analysis.* New York: Praeger, 1973.

Mishan, Ezra, and Talbot Page. "The Methodology of Cost Benefit Analysis—with Particular Reference to the Ozone Problem." Social Science Working Paper 249. California Institute of Technology, January 1979.

Mitchell, Robert Cameron, and Richard T. Carson. "An Experiment in Determining Willingness to Pay for National Water Quality Improvements." Draft report prepared for U.S. Environmental Protection Agency. Resources for the Future, Washington, D.C., June 1981.

Moreau, David H. "Quantitative Assessments of Health Risks by Selected Federal Agencies: A Review of Present Practices with Special Attention to Non-Carcinogenic Substances." U.S. Environmental Protection Agency, Research Triangle Park, N.C., 1980.

Moreau, David H., Eric Hyman, B. Stiftel, and Robert Nichols. "Elicitation of Environmental Values in Multiple Objective Water Resource Decision Making." Department of City and Regional Planning, University of North Carolina, Chapel Hill, 1980.

Mosher, Lawrence. "Reaganites, with OMB's List in Hand, Take Dead Aim at EPA's Regulations." *National Journal* 13 (1981): 256–59.

Mueller, Dennis C. *Public Choice.* Cambridge: Cambridge University Press, 1979.

Nathan, Richard P. "The Reagan Presidency in Domestic Affairs." Paper presented at the Conference on the Reagan Presidency at Mid-Term, Princeton University, November 1982.

National Academy of Sciences. *Decisionmaking for Regulating Chemicals in the Environment.* Appendix H. Washington, D.C.: National Academy of Sciences, 1975.

————, Coordinating Committee on Air Quality Studies. *Air Quality and Automobile Emissions Control.* Vol. 4, *The Costs and Benefits of Automobile Emissions Control.* Washington, D.C., 1974.

National Commission on Air Quality. *Clearing the Air.* Washington, D.C., 1981.

National Economic Research Associates, Inc. *Cost-Effectiveness and Cost-Benefit Analysis of Air Quality Regulation: The Business Roundtable Air Quality Project.* Vol. 4. New York: Business Roundtable, 1980.

Navarro, Peter. "Clean Air Act Amendment: Energy, Environmental, Economic, and Distributional Impacts." *Public Policy* 29 (1981): 121–46.

O'Connor, John. "Overview of the Criteria Review and Standard Setting Process." U.S. Environmental Protection Agency, Office of Air Quality Planning and Standards, Research Triangle Park, N.C., 1981.

Okun, Arthur M. *Equality and Efficiency: The Big Tradeoff.* Washington, D.C.: Brookings Institution, 1975.

Olson, Craig A. "An Analysis of Wage Differentials Received by Workers on Dangerous Jobs." *Journal of Human Resources* 14 (1981): 168–85.

Ostro, Bart D. "The Effects of Air Pollution on Work Loss and Morbidity." *Journal of Environmental Economics and Management* 10 (1983): 371–82.

Ostro, Bart D., and Robert C. Anderson. "Morbidity, Air Pollution, and Health Statistics." Paper presented at the Joint Statistical Meetings of the American Statistical Association and Biometric Society, Detroit, 12 August 1981.

Padgett, Joseph, and Harvey Richmond. "The Process of Establishing and Revising National Ambient Air Quality Standards." *Journal of the Air Pollution Control Association* 33 (1983): 13–16.

Page, Talbot. "Discounting and Intergenerational Equity." *Futures* 9 (October 1977): 377–82.

———. "A Generic View of Toxic Chemicals and Similar Risks." *Ecology Law Quarterly* 7 (1978): 207–46.

———. "Intergenerational Justice as Opportunity." Mimeo. 1981.

Palmquist, Raymond B. "Estimating the Demand for Air Quality from Property Value Studies." Unpublished paper, North Carolina State University, November 1982.

Pashigian, B. Peter. "Environmental Regulation: Whose Self Interests Are Being Served." Mimeo. University of Chicago Graduate School of Business, October 1981.

———. "How Large and Small Plants Fare under Environmental Regulation." *Regulation* 2 (September–October 1983): 19–23.

Perl, Lewis J., and Frederick C. Dunbar. "Cost Effectiveness and Cost-Benefit Analysis of Air Quality Regulation." *American Economic Review* 72 (1982): 208–13.

Pittman, Russell W. "Issues in Pollution Control: Interplant Cost Differences and Economies of Scale." *Land Economics* 57 (1981): 1–17.

Polinsky, A. Mitchell, and Daniel L. Rubinfeld. "Property Values and Benefits of Environmental Improvement: Theory and Measurement." In Lowdon Wingo and Alan Evans, eds., *Public Economics and the Quality of Life*. Baltimore: Johns Hopkins University Press, 1977.

Portney, Paul R. "How *Not* to Create a Job." *Regulation* 6 (November–December 1982): 35–38.

Putnam, Hayes, and Bartlett. "Analysis of the Cost Impact of Plantwide Emissions Control on Four Domestic Steel Plants." U.S. Environmental Protection Agency, September 1979.

Raiffa, Howard. *Decision Analysis*. Reading, Mass.: Addison-Wesley, 1968.

Regans, J., T. Dietz, and R. Rycroft. "Risk Assessment in the Policy-Making Process: Environmental Health and Safety Protection." Paper presented at the annual meeting of the American Political Science Association, Denver, 1982.

Ricci, P. F., and L. S. Molton. "Risks and Benefits in Environmental Law." *Science* 214 (1981): 1096–1100.

Rice, M. A., and L. M. Stuart. "Cost Benefit Analysis of the Proposed BPT/BAT for the Steel Industry: A Suggested Approach." Unpublished draft, 22 April 1981.

Richmond, Harvey J. "Criteria for Specifying Alternative Primary Standards."

Memorandum, Ambient Standards Branch, U.S. Environmental Protection Agency, 3 May 1983.

——. "A Framework for Assessing Health Risks Associated with National Ambient Air Quality Standards." *Environmental Professional* 3 (1981): 225–34.

——. "Risk Assessment and Smog: An Innovative Approach to the Margin of Safety Issue." MPA thesis, University of North Carolina, 1979.

——, Thomas McCurdy, and Bruce Jordan. "Risk Analysis in the Context of National Ambient Air Quality Standards." Paper presented at the annual meeting of the Air Pollution Control Association, New Orleans, 1982.

Rose-Ackerman, Susan. "Market Models for Pollution Control." *Public Policy* 25 (1977): 383–406.

Rourke, Francis. *Bureaucracy, Politics, and Public Policy.* Boston: Little, Brown, 1969.

Rowe, W. D. "Government Regulation of Societal Risks." *George Washington Law Review* 45 (1977): 944–68.

Ruckelshaus, William D. "Science, Risk, and Public Policy." Address to the National Academy of Sciences, Washington, D.C., 22 June 1983.

Ruff, Larry. "The Economic Common Sense of Pollution." *Public Interest* 19 (1970): 69–85.

Russell, Clifford S., ed. *Collective Decision Making: Applications from Public Choice Theory.* Baltimore: Johns Hopkins University Press, 1979.

Russell, Clifford S., and William J. Vaughan. "Fresh Water Recreational Fishing: The National Benefits of Water Pollution Control." Washington, D.C.: Resources for the Future, November 1982.

——. *Steel Production: Processes, Products and Residuals.* Baltimore: Johns Hopkins University Press, 1976.

Rutledge, Gary L., and Susan L. Trevathan. "Pollution Abatement and Control Expenditures, 1972–1980." *Survey of Current Business* 62 (February 1982): 51.

Ryan, John W., et al. "An Estimate of the Nonhealth Benefits of Meeting the Secondary National Ambient Air Quality Standards." Report to the National Commission on Air Quality, 1981.

Scalia, Antonin. "Regulation—The First Year." *Regulation* 6 (January–February 1982): 19.

Schelling, Thomas C., et al. *Incentive Arrangements for Environmental Protection: A Critical Examination.* Cambridge, Mass.: MIT Press, 1983.

Schulze, William D., Ralph C. d'Arge, and David S. Brookshire. "Valuing Environmental Commodities: Some Recent Experiments." *Land Economics* 57 (1981): 151–73.

Smith, V. Kerry. "Benefit Cost Analysis and Risk Assessment." Unpublished paper, University of North Carolina, 25 April 1983.

——. "The Role of Site and Job Characteristics in Hedonic Wage Models." *Journal of Urban Economics* 13 (1983): 296–321.

Smith, V. Kerry, and Carol C. S. Gilbert. "The Valuation of Environmental Risks Using Hedonic Wage Models." Working Paper No. 83-W23. Vanderbilt University, October 1983.

Smith, V. Kerry, and John V. Krutilla. "Toward Reformulating the Role of Natural Resources in Economic Models." In V. Kerry Smith and John V. Krutilla, eds.,

Explorations in Natural Resource Economics. Baltimore: Johns Hopkins University Press, 1982.

Smith, V. Kerry, and William J. Vaughan. "The Implications of Model Complexity for Environmental Management." *Journal of Environmental Economics and Management* 7 (1980): 184–206.

————. "Strategic Details and Process Analysis Models for Environmental Management: An Econometric Analysis." *Resources and Energy* 3 (1981): 39–54.

Squire, Lyn, and Herman G. van der Tak. *Economic Analysis of Projects.* Baltimore: Johns Hopkins University Press, 1975.

Stokey, Edith, and Richard Zeckhauser. *A Primer for Policy Analysis.* New York: Norton, 1978.

Swaczy, Barbara. "The Visible Paw and the Monkey Wrench: The Uses of Inflation Impact Statements." Unpublished paper, University of Michigan School of Natural Resources, 1976.

Swartzman, Daniel A., Richard A. Liroff, and Kevin G. Croke. *Cost-Benefit Analysis and Environmental Regulations: Politics, Ethics and Methods.* Washington, D.C.: Conservation Foundation, 1982.

Thaler, Richard, and Sherwin Rosen. "The Value of Saving a Life: Evidence from the Labor Market." In Nester Terleckj, ed., *Household Production and Consumption.* New York: National Bureau of Economic Research, 1975.

Tietenberg, Thomas. "The Design of Property Rights for Air Pollution Control." *Public Policy* 22 (1974): 225–92.

Tran, Ngoc-Bich, and V. Kerry Smith. "The Role of Air and Water Residuals for Steam Electric Power Generation." *Journal of Environmental Economics and Management* 10 (1983): 35–49.

U.S. Bureau of the Budget. *Circular A-47.* Washington, D.C., 31 December 1952.

U.S. Congress, House Committee on Energy and Commerce. *Presidential Control of Agency Rulemaking: Hearings.* 97th Cong., 1st sess., 1981.

U.S. Congress, House Committee on Governmental Operations. *Stream Channelization: Hearings before a Subcommittee on Conservation and Natural Resources.* June 1971.

U.S. Congress, House Committee on Interstate and Foreign Commerce. *Use of Cost-Benefit Analysis by Regulatory Agencies: Joint hearings before Subcommittees on Oversight and Investigations and on Consumer Protection and Finance.* 96th Cong., 1st sess., July and October 1979.

U.S. Congress, Joint Economic Committee. *The Analysis and Evaluation of Public Expenditures: The PPB System.* Committee print, 91st Cong., 1st sess., 1969.

U.S. Congress, Joint Economic Committee. *Guidelines for Estimating the Benefits of Public Expenditures: Hearings before a Subcommittee on Economy in Government.* 91st Cong., 1st sess., May 1969.

U.S. Congress, Senate. *Policies, Standards, and Procedures in the Formulation, Evaluation, and Review of Plans for Use and Development of Water and Related Land Resources.* Senate Document No. 97, 87th Cong., 2d sess., 1962.

U.S. Congress, Senate Committee on Governmental Affairs. *Study on Federal Regulation.* 95th Cong., 2d sess., Vol. 6, 1978.

U.S. Congressional Budget Office. "The Clean Air Act, the Electric Utilities, and the Coal Market: Cost Estimate of S. 1080, 28 October 1981." In *Report of the Senate Committee,* pp. 174–75. 30 November 1981.

U.S. Council on Environmental Quality. *Environmental Quality.* Annually since 1970.

————. "Regulations on Implementing National Environmental Policy Act Procedures." *Federal Register* 44 (1979): 873.

U.S. Council on Wage and Price Stability. "Environmental Protection Agency's Proposal for the Revision of New Source Performance Standards for Electric Utility Steam Generating Units." Report of the Regulatory Analysis Review Group, 15 January 1979.

————. "Environmental Protection Agency's Proposed National Ambient Air Quality Standards for Carbon Monoxide." 25 November 1980, pp. 25–27.

————. "Environmental Protection Agency's Proposed Revision to the National Ambient Air Quality Standard for Photochemical Oxidants." Report of the Regulatory Review Group, 16 October 1978.

————. "EPA Air Emission Tradeoff Policy." 7 March 1977.

U.S. Department of Transportation. "Guidance for Regulatory Evaluations." Office of Industry Policy, Office of the Assistant Secretary for Policy and International Affairs, 15 April 1982.

U.S. Environmental Protection Agency. *Air Quality Criteria for Ozone and Other Photochemical Oxidants.* Document No. EPA-600/8-78-004. April 1978.

————. *An Economic Assessment of the Benefits of the Final Effluent Limitations Guidelines for Iron and Steel Manufacturing.* 1982.

————. "Guidelines for Performing Regulatory Impact Analyses." Draft, various dates. Version of 22 June 1982 in *Environment Reporter* 16 (July 1982): 385–92.

————. "Guidelines for Performing Regulatory Impact Analyses." Appendix A: Regulatory Impact Analysis Guidance for Benefits. Draft, 29 July 1982.

————. "Guidelines for Performing Regulatory Impact Analyses." Appendix B: Regulatory Impact Analysis Guidance for Cost Analysis. Draft, 29 July 1982.

————. "Guidelines for Performing Regulatory Impact Analyses." Appendix C: Regulatory Impact Analysis Guidance for the Discount Rate. Draft, 5 April 1982 (under revision).

————. "Guidelines for Performing Regulatory Impact Analyses." Appendix D: Regulatory Impact Analysis Guidance for Economic Impact Analysis. Draft, 30 July 1982.

————. "Guidelines for Performing Regulatory Impact Analyses." Appendix E: Hypothetical Case Studies. N.d.

————. *National Air Pollutant Emissions Estimates, 1980.* Office of Air Quality Planning and Standards, 1982.

————. "Water Quality Criteria Documents: Availability." *Federal Register* 45 (1980): 79318–79.

————, Science Advisory Board, Subcommittee on Economic Analysis. "Economics in EPA." 18 June 1980.

U.S. Federal Interagency River Basin Committee, Subcommittee on Benefits and Costs. *Proposed Practices for Economic Analysis of River Basin Projects.* Washington, D.C., 1950.

U.S. Flood Control Act of June 22, 1936. Section 1, 49 U.S. Statute, 1936.

U.S. General Accounting Office. *Air Quality: Do We Know What It Is?* Washington, D.C., May 1979.

_____. "Improved Quality, Adequate Resources, and Consistent Oversight Needed if Regulatory Analysis Is to Help Control Costs of Regulation." Report to the Chairman, Committee on Governmental Affairs, U.S. Senate. 2 November 1982.

_____. *Improvements Needed in Controlling Major Air Pollution Sources.* Washington, D.C., January 1979.

_____. *Problems in Air Quality Monitoring System Affect Data Reliability.* Washington, D.C., 22 September 1982.

U.S. Office of Management and Budget. *Budget Circular No. A-107.* Washington, D.C., 1975.

_____. "Executive Order 12291 on Federal Regulation: Progress during 1981." Report, 23 April 1982.

_____. "Interim Regulatory Impact Analysis Guidance." 6 June 1981.

_____. "Major Rules Submitted for Review under E.O. 12291." Report, 7 January 1983.

U.S. President, Fact Sheet. "The Administration's Progress on Regulatory Relief." The White House, 4 August 1982.

_____. "Reagan Administration Regulatory Achievements." The White House, 11 August 1983.

_____. "Year-End Summary of the Administration's Regulatory Relief Program." The White House, 30 December 1981.

U.S. Regulatory Council. *Regulatory Reform Highlights: An Inventory of Initiatives, 1978–1980.* Washington, D.C., 1980.

U.S. Water Resources Council. "Economic and Environmental Principles and Guidelines for Water and Related Land Resources Implementation Studies." *Federal Register* 47 (1982): 12297–307.

_____. "Principles and Standards for Planning Water and Related Land Resources." *Federal Register* 38 (1973): 24778–869.

_____. "Principles and Standards for Water and Related Land Resources Planning—Level C." *Federal Register* 45 (1980): 64366–400.

Vaughan, William J., and Clifford S. Russell. *Freshwater Recreational Fishing: The National Benefits of Water Pollution Control.* Baltimore: Johns Hopkins University Press, 1982.

Violette, Daniel M., and Lauraine G. Chestnut. "Valuing Reductions in Risks: A Review of the Empirical Estimates." Environmental Benefits Series. U.S. Environmental Protection Agency, June 1983.

Viscusi, W. Kip. "Labor Market Valuations of Life and Limb: Empirical Evidence and Policy Decisions." *Public Policy* 26 (1978): 359–86.

_____. "Presidential Oversight: Controlling the Regulators." *Journal of Policy Analysis and Management* 2 (Winter 1983): 157–73.

Watson, William D., and John A. Jaksch. "Air Pollution: Household Soiling and Consumer Welfare Loss." *Journal of Environmental Economics and Management* 9 (1982): 248–62.

Watt, James, and Jeane Kirkpatrick. Interview. *Public Opinion*, February–March 1981.

Weidenbaum, M. L. *The Future of Business Regulation.* New York: AMACOM Books, 1980.

Weinstein, Milton. "Decision Theoretic Approaches to Evaluating Health Risks:

Insights from Descriptive vs. Normative Analysis." Paper presented at the Allied Social Science Association meetings, New York, 30 December 1982.

Weinstein, Milton C., Donald S. Shepard, and Joseph S. Pliskin. "The Economic Value of Changing Mortality Probabilities: A Decision-Theoretic Approach." *Quarterly Journal of Economics* 94 (March 1980): 373–96.

Weisbrod, Burton A. *Public Interest Law.* Berkeley and Los Angeles: University of California Press, 1978.

White, Lawrence J. *Reforming Regulation: Processes and Problems.* Englewood Cliffs, N.J.: Prentice-Hall, 1981.

Willey, Zach. "Economic Criteria in Environmental Regulation: Prospects for the 1980s." *American Journal of Agricultural Economics* 64 (1982): 935–41.

Wilson, Robert. "Risk Measurement of Public Projects." In Robert C. Lind, *Discounting for Time and Risk in Energy Policy.* Baltimore: Johns Hopkins University Press, 1982.

Wolf, Charles, Jr. "A Theory of Non-Market Failure: Framework for Implementation Analysis." *Journal of Law and Economics* (April 1979), reprinted in abbreviated form as "A Theory of Non-Market Failure," *Public Interest* 55 (1979): 114–33; and in Robert H. Haveman and Julius Margolis, eds., *Public Expenditure and Policy Analysis.* Boston: Houghton Mifflin Company, 1983.

Zeckhauser, Richard. "Preferred Policies When There Is a Concern for Probability of Adoption." *Journal of Environmental Economics and Management* 8 (September 1981): 215–37.

Zeckhauser, Richard, and Donald S. Shepard. "Principles for Saving and Valuing Lives." In A. R. Ferguson and E. P. LeVeen, eds., *The Benefits of Health and Safety Regulation.* Cambridge, Mass.: Ballinger, 1980.

Zeleny, Milan. *Multiple Criteria Decisionmaking.* New York: John Wiley, 1982.

INDEX